Understanding
social security

Also available in the series

Understanding the cost of welfare (Third edition)
Howard Glennerster

"Understanding the costs and financing of welfare has rarely been so lively, engaging and real. Howard Glennerster has produced a text of outstanding scholarship, essential for undergraduate and postgraduate courses right across the social sciences."
Chris Deeming, Reviews Editor for the *Journal of Social Policy* and Chancellor's Fellow and Senior Lecturer, University of Strathclyde

PB £26.99 (US$45.95) **ISBN** 978-1-4473-3404-0 **HB** £70.00 (US$110.00) **ISBN** 978-1-4473-3403-3
288 pages May 2017
INSPECTION COPY AVAILABLE

Understanding health and social care (Third edition)
Jon Glasby

"This welcome third edition updates a most useful textbook for UK social science and social policy students. Its policy analysis is also particularly relevant to professional readers seeking to know how we arrived at the state we're in." Jill Manthorpe, Director of the Social Care Workforce Research Unit, King's College London

PB £21.99 (US$36.95) **ISBN** 978-1-4473-3121-6 **HB** £75.00 (US$110.00) **ISBN** 978-1-4473-3120-9
232 pages January 2017
INSPECTION COPY AVAILABLE

Understanding community (Second edition)
Politics, policy and practice
Peter Somerville

"In developing his conception of beloved community, Peter Somerville brings a fresh and radical perspective to communitarian theory and practice. This book will inspire and provoke readers in equal measure." Jonathan Davies, University of Warwick

PB £23.99 (US$39.95) **ISBN** 978-1-4473-1608-4 **HB** £70.00 (US$110.00) **ISBN** 978-1-4473-1607-7
272 pages April 2016
INSPECTION COPY AVAILABLE

Understanding health policy (Second edition)
Rob Baggott

"Enables students to think critically and innovatively about the highly political nature of health, and the practice of local and national decision making in health care."
Dr Jan Quallington, Head of the Institute of Health and Society, University of Worcester

PB £22.99 (US$38.95) **ISBN** 978-1-4473-0011-3 **HB** £65.00 (US$85.00) **ISBN** 978-1-4473-0012-0
352 pages October 2015
INSPECTION COPY AVAILABLE

For a full listing of all titles in the series visit www.policypress.co.uk

www.policypress.co.uk

INSPECTION COPIES AND ORDERS AVAILABLE FROM

Marston Book Services • PO BOX 269 • Abingdon • Oxon OX14 4YN UK
INSPECTION COPIES
Tel: +44 (0) 1235 465500 • Fax: +44 (0) 1235 465556 • Email: inspections@marston.co.uk
ORDERS
Tel: +44 (0) 1235 465500 • Fax: +44 (0) 1235 465556 • Email: direct.orders@marston.co.uk

Understanding
social security

Third edition

Edited by Jane Millar and Roy Sainsbury

First edition published in 2003, Second edition published in 2009, Third edition published in Great Britain in 2018 by

Policy Press
University of Bristol
1-9 Old Park Hill
Bristol
BS2 8BB
UK
t: +44 (0)117 954 5940
pp-info@bristol.ac.uk
www.policypress.co.uk

North America office:
Policy Press
c/o The University of Chicago Press
1427 East 60th Street
Chicago, IL 60637, USA
t: +1 773 702 7700
f: +1 773-702-9756
sales@press.uchicago.edu
www.press.uchicago.edu

© Policy Press and the Social Policy Association 2018

British Library Cataloguing in Publication Data
A catalogue record for this book is available from the British Library

Library of Congress Cataloging-in-Publication Data
A catalog record for this book has been requested

ISBN 978-1-4473-3947-2 paperback
ISBN 978-1-4473-3949-6 ePub
ISBN 978-1-4473-3950-2 Mobi
ISBN 978-1-4473-3948-9 ePdf

The right of Jane Millar and Roy Sainsbury to be identified as editors of this work has been asserted by them in accordance with the Copyright, Designs and Patents Act 1988.

Cover design by Qube Design Associates, Bristol
Front cover image: www.alamy.com
Printed and bound in Great Britain by CMP, Poole
Policy Press uses environmentally responsible print partners

Contents

Detailed contents

List of tables, figures and boxes

Tables

Figures

Boxes

Acknowledgements

An edited collection is very much a work of collaboration. We would like to thank our contributors for their excellent chapters, their engagement with the book as a whole, and their speedy responses to our comments and queries. Several of the authors in this third edition have been part of the book since the first edition in 2003, some have joined for this round – all have been stimulating and thoughtful partners. On that note, we would also like to thank those authors who contributed to previous editions. Their contributions made the book such a valuable collection, and we refer readers to previous editions, where they will find much material to help them understand how UK social security got to where we find it today.

The team at Policy Press – Catherine Gray, Shannon Kneis, Rebecca Megson, Dawn Rushen and Phylicia Ulibarri-Eglite – have been, as ever, supportive and efficient, guiding the development and production with clarity and purpose.

Finally, we do not forget the origins of the book in the Department of Social Security and then Department for Work and Pensions Summer Schools from the late 1980s to the early 2000s. These provided a forum for communication and enhanced understanding between academic researchers, those responsible for designing policy, and those responsible for delivery on the ground. The origin of the book in the Summer School gave a particular flavour to the approach taken and to the selection of topics in the first and second editions. Sadly, the Summer School in that format no longer exists, but the focus on both policy and practice, on key policy goals and the measures intended to achieve those goals, has remained central to the contents of this volume.

Jane Millar and Roy Sainsbury
January 2018

List of abbreviations

BME	Black and minority ethnic
CPAG	Child Poverty Action Group
DLA	Disability Living Allowance
DSS	Department of Social Security
DWP	Department for Work and Pensions
EEA	European Economic Area
EU	European Union
GDP	Gross Domestic Product
GEW	Genuine and effective work
GPoW	Genuine Prospect of Work Test
HMRC	Her Majesty's Revenue & Customs
HRT	Habitual Residence Test
ISA	Individual Savings Account
ILO	International Labour Office Organization
IMF	International Monetary Fund
LISA	Lifetime Individual Savings Account
MIS	Minimum Income Standard
NHS	National Health Service
NICs	National Insurance contributions
NINo	National Insurance number
OECD	Organisation for Economic Co-operation and Development
ONS	Office for National Statistics
OPCS	Office of Population Censuses and Surveys
PIP	Personal Independence Payment
PPS	Public Service Agreement
PSIC	Person Subject to Immigration Control
SERPS	State Earnings-Related Pension Scheme
TCNs	Third country nationals
UN	United Nations
VAT	Value Added Tax
WHO	World Health Organization

Notes on contributors

Fran Bennett is Senior Research and Teaching Fellow in the Department of Social Policy and Intervention, University of Oxford, UK. Her research interests include social security and poverty, in particular from a gender perspective. She is one of a team of independent experts on UK social policy for the European Commission. She chairs the editorial board of the *Journal of Poverty and Social Justice* and the policy advisory group for Oxfam's poverty programme in the UK, and is an active member of the Women's Budget Group. See www.spi.ox.ac.uk/people/fran-bennett

Emma Carmel is Senior Lecturer in Social Policy at the University of Bath, UK. Her theoretical interests are in understanding the social and political dynamics of public policy governance, working at the intersection of sociology, politics and political economy. Empirically, her work has explored the governance of public policy in the European Union, particularly in migration, welfare and labour market policies. She has published widely on these themes, and is co-editor of *Migration and welfare in the new Europe* (2011). She is the UK principal investigator on a large comparative project, TRANSWEL, investigating the social rights of EU migrants. See www.bath.ac.uk/sps/staff/emma-carmel/

Kevin Farnsworth is a Reader in Comparative and International Social Policy at the University of York, UK. He has published widely on the power and influence of business on social and public policy, economic crisis and austerity, and the relationship between corporate and social welfare. He is the co-editor of the *Journal of International and Comparative Social Policy* (with Zoë Irving) and author of several books including *Corporate power and social policy* (2004), *Corporate versus social welfare* (2012) and, with Zoë Irving, *Social policy in challenging times* (2011) and *Social policy in times of austerity* (2015). See www.york.ac.uk/spsw/staff/kevin-farnsworth/

Dan Finn is Professor Emeritus at the University of Portsmouth, UK. He has been a special adviser for parliamentary inquires and a consultant for The World Bank, European Commission and OECD. His recent work has comprised comparative studies of the Public Employment Service; the devolution and contracting out of employment services; benefit take-up; and the design and impacts of conditional benefit systems and related employment programmes and sanctions. Copies of many of his publications and research reports are available on the University of Portsmouth Research Portal. See www.port.ac.uk/school-of-social-historical-and-literary-studies/staff/professor-dan-finn.html

John Hudson is Professor of Social Policy and Head of the Department of Social Policy and Social Work at the University of York, UK. His research and teaching interests include comparative social policy analysis, the politics of social policy and the impact of culture, societal values and public attitudes on welfare politics. See www.york.ac.uk/spsw/staff/john-hudson

Zoë Irving is Senior Lecturer in Comparative and Global Social Policy at the University of York, UK. Her research interests include the relationship between population size and social policy development, and the social policy of small island states. Her research with Kevin Farnsworth explores economic crisis, austerity and social policy, and includes the edited collections *Social policy in challenging times* (2011) and *Social policy in times of austerity* (2015). She is co-editor of the *Journal of International and Comparative Social Policy* and a former co-editor of *Social Policy Review*. See www.york.ac.uk/spsw/staff/zoe-irving/

Luke Martinelli is a Research Associate at the Institute for Policy Research, University of Bath, UK. His main research interests include social protection and welfare policy, development economics and policy evaluation methods. He is currently working on a project assessing the case for universal basic income in the context of emerging labour market challenges, using techniques including tax/benefit microsimulation and multilevel modelling of the determinants of public attitudes to welfare state reform. See https://researchportal.bath.ac.uk/en/persons/luke-martinelli

Margaret Mbaikaize is a member of the Dole Animators group. She is a single parent who combines her care work for her teenage daughter with a full-time job as a teaching assistant at a primary school in Leeds. Margaret believes that welfare reform is not working, and is committed to speaking out about her own experiences as a single parent trying to secure employment and get by.

Stephen McKay is a Distinguished Professor in Social Research at the University of Lincoln, UK. He has conducted research on the measurement and extent of poverty and the role of social security, as well as analysis of family change. His research interests, in addition to these topics, include the application of quantitative methods to large and complex social science datasets. He was previously editor of the *Journal of Poverty & Social Justice*. For further details, see http://staff.lincoln.ac.uk/smckay

Jane Millar OBE, FBA, FAcSS is Professor of Social Policy in the Institute for Policy Research at the University of Bath, UK. Her research interests include the design, implementation and impact of social policy and comparative research on family policy, social security and employment policy, with particular reference to gender and changing family patterns. She is Chair of the Social Policy Association. See www.bath.ac.uk/sps/staff/jane-millar/

Ruth Patrick is a Postdoctoral Researcher in the School of Law and Social Justice at the University of Liverpool, UK. Her research interests include poverty, welfare reform, social citizenship and participatory research methodologies. She facilitates and supports the Dole Animators, a group of benefit claimants who made an animated film about their experiences of welfare reform, and who continue to be active in challenging popular narratives on 'welfare'. See www.liverpool.ac.uk/law/staff/ruth-patrick

Tess Ridge is an Honorary Professor of Social Policy at the University of Bath, UK. Her research interests include childhood poverty and social exclusion, and policies for children and their families. In particular, her research examines how children fare within the policy process and how best to formulate policies that truly benefit them, including social security policy and child maintenance. See www.bath.ac.uk/sps/staff/tess-ridge

Roy Sainsbury is Professor of Social Policy at the University of York, UK, having held the previous posts at York of Director of the Social Policy Research Unit and of the Centre for Housing Policy. His research interests include social security, welfare reform, disability and employment. He currently serves on the Editorial Boards of the *Journal of Poverty and Social Justice* and the *Journal of Social Security Law* and is a Governor of the Foundation for International Studies on Social Security. See www.york.ac.uk/spsw/staff/roy-sainsbury

Bożena Sojka has an MA in Human Geography (Jan Kochanowski University [JKU], Poland), an MRes in Social Research Methods (Aberdeen), and her PhD (Swansea) examined immigrants' experiences of new racism, using the Republic of Cyprus as an empirical case study. She is Research Associate at the Department of Social and Policy Sciences at the University of Bath, UK. Her research interests are in social identities and belonging, geographies of international migration and different forms of stratification and inequality. This includes an interest in racism and the implications of diversity and nationality for social rights. Empirically, she focuses on the linkages between migration and broader processes of social transformation, and the role of institutions of states in shaping migration policies and processes. See www.bath.ac.uk/sps/staff/bozena-sojka/index.html

Sue Watson is a member of the Dole Animators group. Before becoming disabled, she worked in corporate legal in a variety of roles. Today, she combines her activism for the Dole Animators with voluntary work facilitating a craft group in her local GP surgery, and supporting NHS research and good patient services.

She is interested in social security policy and in trying to create opportunities for conversations between policy-makers and those with the expertise that comes with experience.

Nicola Yeates is Professor of Social Policy in the Department of Social Policy and Criminology at The Open University, UK. She has published widely on international agreements on social protection, and on migration, health and care in a global perspective. Her books include *Understanding global social policy* (2nd edn, 2014), *The global social policy reader* (with C. Holden, 2009), *Globalising care economies and migrant workers* (2009) and *World-regional social policy and global governance* (with B. Deacon et al, 2010). Full details of her research publications are available at http://oro.open.ac.uk/view/person/ny265.html

1

Social security: the landscape

Jane Millar and Roy Sainsbury

The provision of social security – cash transfers to individuals and families – is one of the most important functions of government in modern economies. In the UK about half of the population, over 30 million people, receive financial support through the benefit and tax credit system at any time (Hood and Oakley, 2014). Many more will do so during their lives, as children, as old people, or because they are sick, have a disability, are unemployed, low paid, caring for others or facing one of the many other circumstances that social security helps to cover (Hills, 2017). Social security is the largest single area of government expenditure in the UK, at almost £220 billion in 2015/16, accounting for about 28 per cent of total expenditure and 11.5 per cent of GDP (DWP, 2016a, UK summary). This is a system that is deeply embedded in our society, central to the pursuit of both social and economic goals.

But the extent, range and complexity of social security – the various aims and purposes, the different groups included, the contribution conditions, the means tests, the levels of support and the outcomes – creates a system that is often misunderstood, sometimes maligned and frequently challenged. *Understanding social security* is therefore a topic that concerns us all, and the aim of this book is to critically examine social security policy and provision in the UK, covering issues of aims and purpose, design and implementation, outcomes and impact.

This is the third edition of *Understanding social security*. Previous editions appeared in 2003 and 2009 during the Labour governments of Tony Blair and Gordon Brown respectively, when changes to social security could be seen to have a coherent rationale – to reduce poverty, especially child poverty, and to promote paid employment. This was encapsulated in what was a familiar phrase at the time: 'work for those who can, security for those who can't'. In that context, Chapter 1 of the 2003 edition started by stating that 'Reform of the social security and tax systems is at the heart of the Labour government's aspirations to combat social exclusion, to eradicate child poverty, to increase employment rates among all people of working age, and to modernise the welfare state' (p 1). This agenda was still current while we were writing the 2009 edition, which was before the full extent of the 2008 banking and financial crisis, and the economic recession that followed. The policy agenda was thoroughly shaken as a result, when the coalition government of 2010–15 made the reduction of the budget deficit (the gap between government spending and income) their overarching objective. This led to a programme of 'austerity', in which the social security system was a key target for restrictions to eligibility and cuts in the level of support. Thus, as we prepare the third edition, the policy environment and the key policy goals are very different from 10 years ago. This book is not an assessment of austerity policy and welfare reform (see Bochel and Powell, 2016; Lupton et al, 2016; Cooper and Whyte, 2017; Royston, 2017), but this changed environment and agenda is certainly reflected in the contents.

We return to this discussion later in this chapter, but first, we reflect more generally on social security policy goals and instruments. We pose a number of fundamental questions about the UK system, and then consider the modern context of social security since 2010, a period that could be characterised as one of austerity and 'welfare reform'.

What are the aims of social security?

This question might seem an obvious and simple one to ask in a book called *Understanding social security*, but trying to answer it reveals it as more complex. The question itself seems to carry an assumption, for example, that there is a set of aims that are in some way self-evident, waiting to be revealed. On reflection, this assumption turns out to be entirely unjustified. The 'aims' of social security are highly contentious and contestable. One person's (or political party's) aims will be different to the next person's (or party's). And aims can change over time. Sainsbury sums this up as follows: '... the aims of social security (are) constantly contested, defined and redefined, invented and reinvented, taken up and abandoned' (Sainsbury, 1999, p 35). We can only really answer the question with reference to *whose* aims we are talking about.

But even this doesn't necessarily make answering the question any easier. Walker (2005) makes some useful analytical distinctions in his discussion of social security aims and objectives. First he distinguishes between social security systems (the whole set of measures) and social security schemes (specific benefits or sets of benefits). He further distinguishes between the aims (the purposes ascribed to the system as a whole) and objectives (attached to specific benefits or programmes). Thus the purposes for the overall system 'establish the paradigm within which policy development takes place and that, in turn, provides the *raison d'être* for benefit and tax credit schemes and shapes their objectives' (2005, p 24).

The purposes for the overall system reflect different underlying ideologies – different views about the role of the state, about the responsibilities of citizens and about the causes of poverty. These vary across countries as well as over time. Esping-Andersen (1990), in his influential work on the 'three worlds of welfare capitalism', focuses on the 'de-commodifying' role of welfare states, referring to the extent to which people can maintain a livelihood outside the market. His 'three worlds' contrasts the liberal welfare state (small state, private markets, means-tested) with the conservative (preservation of family and class, insurance-based) and social democratic (solidarity, egalitarian, universal). And in their discussion in Chapter 9 here, Kevin Farnsworth and Zoë Irving emphasise both the economic and the social functions: the social security system helps countries weather economic downturns, and reduces the risk of social unrest.

The objectives for specific benefits and programmes include the desired outcomes (for example, lower rates of child poverty, more people in work, and so on) and also the way in which these outcomes are to be reached. Thus, for example, goals such as accuracy, efficiency and reducing fraud are often included as specific elements in the design of benefits. This is well encapsulated in the phrase that was used to underpin the working of the Benefits Agency (the forerunner of Jobcentre Plus): 'the right amount of benefit to the right person, at the right time, every time' (Harris, 2013, p 133). Simplification is often put forward as an important goal in its own right, although the pursuit of a range of aims and objectives makes this difficult to achieve in practice. As one example, Box 1.1 shows the vision, principles, aims and objectives for social security recently set out by the Scottish government (see page 8).

Therefore a number of different purposes and goals can be identified for social security policy. Harris (2013, p 4) notes that, 'The key areas of state welfare provision all rest on very simple ideas, or at least are intended to meet straightforward objectives, as for example conceptualised in Beveridge's notion of slaying the "five giant evils" of Want, Disease, Ignorance, Squalor and Idleness.' He goes on to quote the definition put forward by the International Labour Organization (ILO) (Ghai, 2002), which gives three main aims, 'reducing destitution, providing for social contingencies, and promoting greater income and consumption equality'. Or, in other words, social security is about reducing poverty, covering risks and creating a more equal society.

What benefits do we have, and how do they differ?

Just as there are many possible aims, there are also many forms of social security provision. In some countries, in-kind provision is an important element, for example, food stamps in the US, but, as in previous editions of the book, we focus on cash benefits (see Chapter 8). These can be grouped into three main types, differentiated by the method of funding and the main conditions for receipt:

• *Universal*, or *categorical, benefits* are funded by general taxation; they take no account of income and are paid to those who fit the designated category (Child Benefit for all children was the main UK example, until 2013, when higher earners were excluded).

- *Social insurance*, or *contributory, benefits* are in part funded by contributions from workers, employers and the government (see Chapter 9, this volume), and cover interruptions or loss of earnings for specified reasons (retirement, unemployment, sickness and, for women, widowhood).
- *Social assistance*, or *means-tested, benefits* are funded by general taxation and are paid to people with low incomes, taking account of their particular circumstances and family situation. These include benefits for people with no other sources of income as well as various other benefits intended to meet particular needs (for example, housing costs) or circumstances (for example, low wages, large families).

To this list we must add *tax credits*. The Working Tax Credit and Child Tax Credit are administered by HM Revenue & Customs (HMRC) and not by the Department for Work and Pensions (DWP) (see further discussion below). But these tax credits follow the same logic as means-tested benefits – funded from general taxation and paid to people with a low income, taking account of their circumstances. So these tax credits can be discussed alongside benefits such as Income Support, Pension Credit, Housing Benefit and Universal Credit.

Looking beyond the state provision of cash benefits, the *tax system* is also a vehicle for income support, through provisions such as tax allowances and tax exemptions. These increase income by reducing tax deductions. *Occupational benefits* are paid by employers, for example, occupational pension schemes, but regulated (and sometimes subsidised) by government. They also include some schemes that employers are obliged to provide, such as statutory sick pay and statutory maternity pay. The *private market* also plays a role, particularly in respect of pensions, with membership of private pensions schemes encouraged by state subsidies and regulated by government. And *charities or voluntary bodies* may also provide support, in cash or in kind. The growth of foodbanks in recent years (Garthwaite, 2016) is one example of this.

Finally, it should also be noted that the *family* plays a major role in income transfers, and that defining family obligations – who should be required to support whom – is an important aspect of social security policy. The assumption that married women would be financially dependent on their husbands was, for example, central to the postwar National Insurance benefit system. Married women were largely excluded from these benefits on the grounds that they could rely on their husbands for financial support. Married men received allowances for their wives as dependants. This established a particular structure that had wide-reaching and long-term implications for gender divisions (see Chapter 6, this volume).

How much do we spend on social security?

As noted above, public expenditure on benefits and tax credits is a significant element in total government expenditure. DWP benefits expenditure in 2015/16 was about £173 billion, including £2 billion on children, £54 billion on working-age people and £117 billion on pensioners (DWP, 2016a, Benefit summary). HMRC expenditure in the same year was about £11 billion on Child Benefit and about £28 billion on tax credits (DWP, 2016a, non-DWP welfare).

Hood and Oakley (2014) provide a detailed 'survey of the GB benefit system', including benefits and tax credits, and dividing expenditure by type of recipient. Figure 1.1 shows that spending on older people makes up the largest single element (45 per cent), with spending on three other groups (families with children, people with low incomes, sick and disabled people) each at about 17 or 18 per cent. Spending on unemployed people accounts for just 2 per cent of total expenditure (there is also a category of bereaved people, less than 1 per cent, not shown in the figure).

In terms of spending on specific DWP benefits, in 2015/16 the largest was Basic State Contributory Pension (about £90.5 billion), Housing Benefit (about

Figure 1.1: Social security expenditure, Great Britain, 2013-14

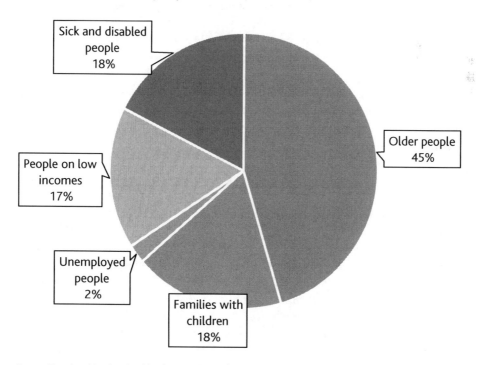

Source: Based on Hood and Oakley (2014, Table 3.1)

£24.6 billion), Disability Living Allowance (about £13.4 billion), Employment and Support Allowance (about £14.4 billion), Pension Credit (about £6 billion) and Attendance Allowance (about 5.5 billion) (DWP, 2016a, Table 1b). HMRC expenditure incudes Child and Working Tax Credit (£27.5 billion) and Child Benefit (£11.2 billion) (DWP, 2016a, non-DWP welfare spending).

It is also important to consider the funding of this expenditure, which is through taxation and National Insurance contributions (see Chapter 9, this volume). Hills (2017) analyses both what people pay into the system (through income and expenditures taxes and National Insurance contributions) and what they receive (through benefits, tax credits and services, including health and education). His analysis shows that, 'even in a snapshot' (2013/14), benefits and services are 'spread across the income distribution'. Just over £12,000 annually goes to the lowest income decile, about £15,000 to the 2nd to 4th decile, then the amount falls until the top decile receive just over £7,000, as Hills puts it, 'still quite a substantial amount' (2017, p 34). Looking over the life course, he concludes that, 'most of us get back something at least close to what we pay in over our lives to the welfare state' (p 269).

The level of expenditure in the UK is not out of line with other comparable countries. The Organisation for Economic Co-operation and Development (OECD) produces regular estimates of 'social spending'. This is wider than social security benefits/tax credits, as it is defined as public spending on 'cash benefits, direct in-kind provision of goods and services, and tax breaks with social purposes' (OECD, 2016). On average, across the 38 OECD counties, in 2016 this amounted to 22 per cent of Gross Domestic Product (GDP). The UK is almost exactly at that level, but many European countries are at higher levels, including France, Finland, Belgium, Sweden, Germany and others. In all countries it is pensions and health that make up the largest proportion of social spending (OECD, 2016).

Who delivers social security?

The UK has a highly centralised system of social security, unlike some other countries where local government is much more central to delivery (Walker, 2005). The DWP is responsible for the administration of the majority of benefits. HMRC is responsible for the administration of Child Benefit, the Guardian's Allowance and the Working Tax Credit and Child Tax Credit. Local government is responsible for the administration of Housing Benefit and Council Tax Benefit. However, both Tax Credits and Housing Benefit are being abolished and merged into Universal Credit (see Chapter 3, this volume), and administered by the DWP.

Since 2013, local authorities have also been responsible for 'local welfare provision'. Up to that point, the Social Fund (administered by DWP) had included discretionary payments in the form of crisis loans and community care grants, which were intended to provide emergency support or help in exceptional circumstances. These were abolished by the Welfare Reform Act 2012 (see further discussion below), with the intention that local authorities would set up their own discretionary schemes. This was at the time of reductions in core funding to local government from central government. A report by the National Audit Office (2016) found that overall spending fell, that local authorities were very cautious in allocating funds to this area because of reduced resources and competing pressures, that charities reported increased demand, and raised doubts as to whether this local provision effectively met needs.

Wales, Scotland and Northern Ireland also have local welfare funds to replace the discretionary Social Fund. But the extent to which the devolved administrations have wider responsibility for social security policy and provision varies considerably (Birrell and Gray, 2016). In Wales there is no devolved authority for social security. The Northern Ireland government has always had responsibility for social security, but under the 'parity principle [that] operates on the basis that Northern Ireland has the same range of social security benefits which are paid at the same rates and subject to the same conditions as in Great Britain' (NI Assembly, 2011). Thus Northern Ireland legislation traditionally followed and matched that of Great Britain. However, this approach came under great pressure in relation to the 2012 Welfare Reform legislation, which was controversial in Northern Ireland and was eventually enacted via Westminster (Bowers et al, 2015).

In Scotland, powers over some benefits have been devolved under the Scotland Act 2016. This includes 11 benefits in total: Disability Living Allowance, Personal Independence Payment, Attendance Allowance, Winter Fuel Payment, Carer's Allowance, Severe Disablement Allowance, Industrial Injuries Benefits, Discretionary Housing Payment, Cold Weather Payment, Funeral Payment, Sure Start Maternity Grant. The Scottish Government (2016) has set out its vision and principles that it proposes to apply to social security policy (see Box 1.1).

Who receives social security?

As noted above, about 30 million people in the country receive one or more social security benefits or tax credits. Table 1.1 (see page 9) shows the benefits/tax credits with around 1 million or more claimants, with Income Support at just under 1 million to Basic State Pension at almost 13 million. These claimants and their families are, in many cases, relying on social security for most or all of their incomes. There are also many people in receipt of support through Winter Fuel Payments (12.5 million) and over-75s TV licences (4.4 million).

Most of those who are supported by the social security/tax credit system are people who are outside of the labour market, by virtue of their age – pensioners and children. Pensioners are, of course, long-term recipients. For people of working age, however, there is movement on and off benefits and tax credits, as circumstances change. This varies across benefits; for example, Jobseeker's

Allowance includes people with relatively short spells of unemployment while Employment and Support Allowance receipt tends to be more long term.

The unemployment rate for minority ethnic groups was 9.9 per cent in 2015 compared with 5.4 per cent for the overall population (DWP, 2016b). However, there is little information on benefit receipt by ethnicity. The Universal Credit equality impact assessment (DWP, 2011) provided some analysis of the 7.9 million

---

Box 1.1: 'A new future for social security in Scotland'

Our Vision: Social Security is important to all of us and able to support each of us when we need it.

Principles
1. Social security is an investment in the people of Scotland.
2. Respect for the dignity of individuals is at the heart of everything we do.
3. Our processes and services will be evidence based and designed with the people of Scotland.
4. We will strive for continuous improvement in all our policies, processes and systems, putting the user experience first.
5. We will demonstrate that our services are efficient and value for money.

Our *fundamental aim* is to create a fairer society, using these new social security powers as a springboard to maximise life chances and opportunities for those people that rely on our help. Our social security powers can contribute to our goal of tackling poverty and inequality. A top priority will be to use our powers to help people move into or stay in work, where this is possible for the individual....

To support this overarching aim, we will work towards the following *outcomes*.

In the short to medium term we will ensure that:

- Recipients are treated with respect and dignity.
- Benefits are administered in a swift and streamlined manner that meets the varying needs of recipients.
- People can access help and advice to claim the benefits to which they are entitled.
- Benefit take-up is maximised.
- There is efficiency for Scottish taxpayers.
- Scottish social security works well alongside other services.
- Benefit recipients have positive experiences of Scotland's social security.

Source: Scottish Government (2016, pp 10-13)

Table 1.1: Claimants of selected social security benefits and tax credits, Great Britain, 2015-16

Benefit	Numbers of claimants (in millions)
Basic State Pension	12.8
Child Benefit	7.2
Housing Benefit	4.8
Child Tax Credit	3.9
Disability Living Allowance	3.0
Working Tax Credit	2.4
Employment and Support Allowance	2.4
Pension Credit	2.1
Attendance Allowance	1.5
Jobseeker's Allowance	0.7
Income Support	0.7

Source: Based on Hood and Keiller (2016, Table 3.1)

working-age households likely to be within the range of Universal Credit (which includes people out of work and people in lower-paid employment). This showed an over-representation of women, of people with disabilities and of non-white people. (See also DWP, 2016c, for some analysis in relation to the Equality Duty 2010.)

Do we pay the 'right' benefit to the 'right' people?

This can mean a number of different things. Benefits are not automatic but must be claimed, and so it is always possible that not everyone who is entitled to benefits is actually claiming. This is measured in two ways – by the number of people who are in receipt as the proportion of the total eligible population (caseload take-up) and by the amount claimed as a proportion of the total amount that could have been claimed (expenditure take-up). Table 1.2 shows the take-up rates in 2014/15 for various means-tested benefits. As is clear, although most eligible people do claim, there are significant numbers who do not, and thus a substantial amount of money goes unclaimed every year. The reasons for non-take-up are complex, including lack of information, barriers in the system and attitudes (Eurofound, 2015; Baumberg, 2016).

On the other hand, some benefits are not paid to the right people, or at the right amount, due to fraud and error in the system. Getting accurate estimates of fraud and error is not straightforward, and the DWP and HMRC define and measure fraud and error in slightly different ways (NAO, 2016a, b). The DWP distinguishes between official error (mistakes by the department), claimant error

Table 1.2: Take-up rates, 2015/16

Benefit/Tax Credit	Caseload take-up rate (%)	Expenditure take-up rate (%)	Number of non-claiming families (millions)	Amount unclaimed (£ billions)
Pension Credit	61	67	1.4	3.3
Housing Benefit	77	85	1.6	4.8
Jobseeker's Allowance[a]	56	59	0.5	1.6
Income Support/ Employment and Support Allowance[a]	84	87	0.5	2.7
Child Tax Credit[b]	86	92	0.6	2.4
Working Tax Credit[b]	65	85	1.2	3.0

Notes: [a] Income-based; [b] 2014/15 central point of estimated range.
Sources: HMRC (2016); DWP (2017a)

(genuine mistakes by claimants) and fraud (people intending to mislead). They estimate both overpayments (where the claimant receives more than they are entitled to) and underpayments (where the claimant receives less). For the DWP benefits fraud and error was at about 2.9 per cent of total expenditure, about £5.1 billion (DWP, 2017b; estimates are for 2016/17). This was mainly overpayments (2.0 per cent) rather than underpayments (0.9 per cent). Of the overpayments, it is estimated that 1.2 per cent is fraud, 0.5 per cent is claimant error and 0.4 per cent is official error. Failure to declare earnings and other income, and failure to declare living with a partner are the most common factors, although, as Griffiths (2017) discusses, the latter is a complex and gendered issue (see also Chapter 6, this volume).

HMRC uses the terms 'error and fraud favouring the claimant' for overpayments and 'error and fraud favouring HMRC' for underpayments. For Child and Working Tax Credits, error and fraud was at about 6.2 per cent of total expenditure, about £1.8 billion (HMRC, 2017, estimates are for 2015/16). Most of this was overpayments (5.5 per cent) rather than underpayments (0.7 per cent).

The concept of the right benefit could also be taken to refer to the amount of benefit, and whether it is enough to live on. Hirsch (2015) compares benefit levels with a *Minimum Income Standard*, based on views of the public about what is necessary to 'achieve a minimum socially acceptable standard of living'. This shows a decline in the adequacy of benefits (measured in this way) between 2008 and 2015, and that the shortfall is greatest for families with children and lowest for pensioners. Qualitative research with people living on benefits highlights problems of debt and difficulties making ends meet (Patrick, 2017; and see Chapter 11, this volume).

People may also be left without benefit income or with reduced income for periods of time. This can be for various reasons, including waiting days at the start of a claim, lack of appropriate information to verify claims, delays to decisions or delays to payment, and sanctions. Sanctions can mean the loss of all or part of benefits for 4 or 13 weeks, and possibly for three years. The number of people affected by benefit sanctions has been rising in recent years, as work requirements have been tightened and applied to more people (see Chapters 3 and 12, this volume). The House of Commons Work and Pensions Committee (2015) recommended that more should be done by the DWP to mitigate the risk of severe hardship caused by loss of income. The report concluded that there was some evidence that sanctions were a factor in increased foodbank use. Loopstra and Lalor (2017) found that over one-third of their sample of households using foodbanks was waiting for a benefit payment or benefit decision.

The social security and tax credit system is extensive, complex and fulfils multiple purposes. Having outlined some of the key features of the UK system, we now turn to key policy developments since 2010, in the landscape of austerity and 'welfare reform'.

Austerity and 'welfare reform'

Since the second edition of this book in 2009, the closely connected issues of austerity and 'welfare reform' have dominated the policy agenda. The first 'austerity budget' from the Conservative/Liberal Democrat coalition government in 2010 aimed to reduce the spending deficit and balance the national budget within five years. (The main measures introduced at that time and in the coalition years are outlined in more detail in Hills et al, 2016 and McKay and Rowlingson, 2016.) Key measures included:

- Changes to benefit and tax credit uprating – the 'triple lock' protects pensions (see Chapter 5, this volume). Working-age benefits were increased by just 1 per cent annually from 2013 to 2015, with a two-year cash freeze from April 2016. Child Benefit was frozen for three years from 2011/12, and increased by just 1 per cent in 2014/15.
- Various reforms to tax credits, including the freezing of the 'family element' in Child Tax Credit, the abolition of the 'Baby Tax Credit' and increases in withdrawal rates as earnings increase.
- Tighter conditions and stricter administration of benefits, including more use of financial sanctions for non-compliance with, for example, job search requirements (see Chapter 3, this volume).
- The 'welfare cap', introduced in the 2014 budget, puts a cash limit on overall spending on certain social security benefits and tax credits (not to be confused with the 'benefit cap' discussed below). This excludes pensions and Jobseeker's

Allowance, but includes tax credits, Child Benefit and disability benefits (Keep, 2017). The welfare cap means that if the costs of certain benefits rise, other benefits will have to be cut to stay within the overall total limit.

The Welfare Reform Act 2012 introduced a number of significant changes:

- The centrepiece is the introduction of Universal Credit, replacing six existing means-tested benefits and tax credits for people of working age with a single system (see Chapter 3, this volume).
- A cap on the amount of benefits working-age people can receive. The cap applies to most out-of-work benefits and is intended to ensure that those not in work should not receive more than those in work.
- Reductions in Housing Benefit for social housing tenants whose accommodation is deemed to be larger than they need (often called the 'Bedroom Tax').
- The introduction of Personal Independence Payments to replace the current Disability Living Allowance, and limiting the payment of contributory Employment and Support Allowance to a 12-month period (see Chapter 4, this volume).
- The abolition of the discretionary Social Fund (as discussed above).

There are also a number of other measures in the 2012 Act, including changes to child maintenance, increased measures to tackle fraud and changes to local housing allowance rates. The timetable for the introduction of the various changes is quite complex and the Act also includes provision for the use of delegated powers (which means that some measures can be introduced by regulations and rules and do not require legislation to be passed by Parliament).

The Welfare Reform and Work Act 2016 was also aimed at reducing expenditure in order to 'help to achieve a more sustainable welfare system' (note 2 from the Welfare Reform and Work Bill presented to Parliament). This Act repeals the Child Poverty Act 2010, makes further cuts to benefits and tax credits, introduces another benefits freeze and replaces support for mortgage interest with loans for mortgage interest (CPAG, 2015; Kennedy et al, 2016). This Act also imposed a two-child limit in Child Tax Credit. A family with a child born after April 2017 will not receive the child element for that child unless they have just one child already or are exempt (for example, some adoption cases and the controversial 'non-consensual conception exemption') (see Chapter 2, this volume).

It is estimated that about £17 billion per year was taken out of the social security budget between 2010/11 and 2015/16 (Browne and Hood, 2015). Assessing the long-term cumulative impact of these spending reductions on household income is complex as the impact also depends on other factors, such as employment participation rates and the level of the National Living Wage. But the various estimates suggest a highly differentiated impact, with some groups in society likely to be particularly affected, including women, people with disabilities, minority ethnic groups and those with the lowest incomes (Cracknell and Keen, 2016; Hills et al, 2016; Portes and Reed, 2018). For those with 'intersecting inequalities', such as Black and minority ethnic (BME) women, the 'gender inequalities intersect with and compound racial inequalities making these women particularly vulnerable to cuts in benefits, tax credits and public services' (Hall et al, 2017, p 1).

Hood and Waters (2017a) conclude that the largest cuts are still to come, particularly affecting low-income families with children. Beatty and Fothergill (2016) estimate that the post-2015 welfare reforms will take almost £13 billion a year from claimants by 2020. This falls unevenly across the country, with less impact in southern England and most impact in the most deprived local authority areas, especially those with higher than average proportions of large families and the Asian ethnic origin population. Families with dependent children and tenants in the social rented sector are also most likely to lose income. Overall, they conclude that, 'A key effect of welfare reform is to widen the gap in prosperity between the best and worst local economies across the country' (2016, p3). Poverty rates are likely to increase. Hood and Waters (2017b) estimate that the rate of poverty (after housing costs) will rise from 21.3 per cent in 2014-15 to 23.6 per cent in 2021-22, with tax and benefit changes accounting for about one-third of this increase. These issues are further discussed in the chapters that follow.

There has been controversy over various elements of these provisions, in particular in respect of the Bedroom Tax, the two-child limit and the benefit cap. The Child Poverty Action Group (CPAG) (2017) has pursued legal challenges against all three, on the grounds of discrimination. A High Court ruling in June 2017 held that the benefit cap is discriminatory, causing 'real damage' to lone-parent families, and that 'real misery is being caused to no good purpose' (Peaker, 2017; see also CPAG, 2017).

The language of 'welfare reform' is, not surprisingly, popular with politicians, and these measures have been presented not just as necessary to cut the deficit, but also as fair, in particular in focusing support for people who work and who show responsible behaviour. McKay and Rowlingson (2016, p 190) point to 'particular ideological motives that influenced the nature of reform', but also argue that 'there are some long-running continuities in social security policy since 1979, regardless of whether governments have been Conservative, Labour or coalition' (2016, p 197). We return in the final chapter to discuss the meaning and extent of 'welfare reform', as we reflect on the more detailed analysis that now follows in the book's individual chapters.

Reading this book

The book is divided into two main sections. The first examines people and policies over the lifecycle. Tess Ridge maps the changing support for children in the social security system, exploring the shift from the 'End Child Poverty' agenda of the Labour government to the retrenchment and austerity measures since 2010. Jane Millar examines social security provisions for people in and out of work, tracing the changes in tax credits, in work obligations and the emergence of Universal Credit. Roy Sainsbury examines provision for people with disabilities and those who care for them. In particular, he examines the evolution of extra costs benefits and income replacement benefits for carers. Stephen McKay looks at provision for pensioners, a group who have been well protected by social security, but where there are significant challenges ahead. Fran Bennett explores the position of women and men in relation to the main types of social security benefits/tax credits, and discusses the challenges of gender analysis of policy, both in the short and long term. Finally in this section, Emma Carmel and Bożena Sojka discuss the complex, and often controversial, relationship between social security and migration.

The second section focuses on key issues in policy and practice. Nicola Yeates explores the global dimensions of social security policy, provision and administration and relates them to the UK. Kevin Farnsworth and Zoë Irving take a broad view in order to examine the mixed economy of financial support that is channelled through the tax and social security system, not just to individuals and households, but also to companies and corporations. In particular they consider what this means for distributional outcomes. John Hudson examines the complexity of understanding public attitudes to 'welfare' in the UK over time, and how attitudes feed into the policy-making process. Ruth Patrick, Margaret Mbaikaize and Sue Watson examine the lived experience of 'getting by' on benefits, particularly at a time of substantial cuts in support. Dan Finn discusses the delivery of social security benefits, tax credits and employment services through job centres and contracted providers. Luke Martinelli introduces a potential radical reform, universal basic income, and discusses whether and how this could work in practice.

The last chapter looks to the future and discusses the issues that will shape social security in the next decades. As will be clear, this book focuses on social security policy and delivery in the UK. While there is some discussion of provision in other countries in various chapters, this is not a cross-national comparative book, and so we do not seek to compare policy developments here and elsewhere. Nor do we seek to explore how the UK fits into broad typologies of welfare state provision and development. Following Esping-Andersen (1990) there is a substantial literature on 'welfare state regimes', which locate the UK in the 'liberal' model, characterised by residual and means-tested provision. The impact of the recession on welfare regimes and policy trajectories is explored further in Schröder (2017) and Taylor-Gooby et al (2017).

Conclusion

The social security system is one of the most important and powerful economic and social policy instruments at the government's disposal. As discussed, it can be used in pursuit of a wide range of policy goals and to address a variety of social and economic challenges and problems. For example, the UK is a very unequal society, with high levels of poverty, and the social security system is one of the most important instruments for income redistribution. Social security also plays an important role in helping to smooth incomes over the life course, with people making contributions or withdrawals depending on circumstances and need. And social security provisions may have an impact on how people live their lives, in their decisions about jobs, about savings, about retirement, about family formation and about family dissolution.

As we pointed out in both previous editions of this book, the term 'social security' may seem increasingly outdated. There is no longer a government department with this name, and the term 'welfare' is increasingly used, even in the legislation (for example, in the Welfare Reform Act 2012). However, the phrase 'social security' captures other important issues, apart from institutional arrangements. The word 'social' indicates that this is a shared system. We are all part of it – as contributors, as recipients, as taxpayers, as citizens – and social security provisions involve various forms of redistribution that are an expression of our values as a society and our commitments to social and economic justice. The word 'security' also highlights an important value, which is that people should not be simply at the mercy of the market, but should be enabled to meet needs now and to plan for the future. The need for social security is as strong, if not stronger, than ever.

Understanding social security is therefore not just the title of this book. There are important ongoing and emerging debates about current provision and about the future shape and purpose of social security. This affects us all. The more we understand the current system, the better we can contribute to these debates about the future.

References

Baumberg, B. (2016) 'The stigma of claiming benefits, a quantitative study', *Journal of Social Policy*, vol 45, no 2, pp 181–99.

Beatty, C. and Fothergill, S. (2016) *The uneven impact of welfare reform: The financial losses to places and people*, Sheffield: Centre for Regional Economic and Social Research, Sheffield Hallam University.

Birrell, D. and Gray, A.M. (2016) 'Social policy, the devolved administrations and the UK Coalition government', in H. Bochel and M. Powell (eds) *The coalition government and social policy: Restructuring the welfare state*, Bristol: Policy Press, pp 325–46.

Bochel, H. and Powell, M. (eds) *The coalition government and social policy: Restructuring the welfare state*, Bristol: Policy Press.

Bowers, P., Kennedy, S., Parkin, L., Armstrong, H. and Wilson, W. (2015) *A fresh start: The Stormont Agreement and Implementation Plan and the Northern Ireland (Welfare Reform) Bill 2015-16*, London: House of Commons Library.

Browne, J. and Hood, A. (2015) *Options for reducing spending on social security*, IFS Green Budget 2015, Chapter 9, London: Institute for Fiscal Studies.

Cooper, V. and Whyte, D. (2017) *The violence of austerity,* London: Pluto Press.

CPAG (Child Poverty Action Group) (2015) *Welfare Reform and Work Bill 2015* (http://cpag.org.uk/content/welfare-reform-and-work-bill-2015).

CPAG (2017) *Revised benefit cap* (www.cpag.org.uk/content/revised-bene t-cap-cpag-ds-and-others-v-secretary-state-work-and-pensions).

Cracknell, R. and Keen, R. (2016) *Estimating the gender impact of tax and benefits changes*, House of Commons Library Briefing Paper No SN06758.

DWP (Department for Work and Pensions) (2011) *Universal Credit – Equality impact assessment*, London: The Stationery Office (www.gov.uk/government/publications/universal-credit-equality-impact-assessment).

DWP (2016a) *Benefit expenditure and caseload tables 2016, Outturn and forecast: Autumn statement 2016*, London: The Stationery Office (www.gov.uk/government/publications/benefit-expenditure-and-caseload-tables-2016).

DWP (2016b) *Labour market status by ethnic group*, London: The Stationery Office.

DWP (2016c) *DWP equality information 2016: Customer data*, London: The Stationery Office (www.gov.uk/government/statistics/dwp-equality-information-2016-customer-data).

DWP (2017a) *Income-related benefits: Estimates of take-up*, London: DWP (www.gov.uk/government/uploads/system/uploads/attachment_data/file/645577/income-related-benefits-estimates-of-take-up-2015-16.pdf).

DWP (2017b) *Fraud and error in the benefit system: Financial year 2016/17 preliminary estimates*, London: DWP.

Esping-Andersen, G. (1990) *The three worlds of welfare capitalism*, Cambridge: Polity.

Eurofound (2015) *Access to social benefits: Reducing non-take-up*, Luxembourg: Publications Office of the European Union.

Garthwaite, K. (2016) *Hunger pains: Life inside foodbank Britain*, Bristol: Policy Press.

Ghai, D. (2002) *Social security priorities and patterns: A global perspective*, Geneva: International Labour Organization.

Griffiths, R. (2017) 'No love on the dole: The influence of the UK means-tested welfare system on partnering and family structure', *Journal of Social Policy*, vol 46, issue 3, pp 543-61.

Hall, S.-M., McIntosh, K., Neitzert, E., Pottinger, L., Sandhu, K., Stephenson, M.-A., et al (2017) *Intersecting inequalities: The impact of austerity on Black and minority ethnic women in the UK*, London: Women's Budget Group and Runnymede Trust with RECLAIM and Coventry Women's Voices.

Harris, N. (2013) *Law in a complex state: Complexity in the law and structure of welfare,* Oxford: Hart.

Hills, J. (2017) *Good times, bad times: The welfare myth of them and us* (Revised edn), Bristol: Policy Press.

Hills, J., De Agostini, P. and Sutherland, H. (2016) 'Benefits, pensions, tax credits and direct taxes', in R. Lupton, T. Burchardt, J. Hills, K. Stewart and P. Vizard (eds) *Social policy in a cold climate,* Bristol, Policy Press, pp 11–34.

Hirsch, D. (2017) *A minimum income standard for the UK in 2015,* York: Joseph Rowntree Foundation

HMRC (Her Majesty's Revenue & Customs) (2016) *Child Benefit, Child Tax Credit and Working Tax Credit take-up rates 2014-15,* London: HMRC.

HMRC (2017*) Child and Working Tax Credits annual error and fraud statistics, 2015-16,* London: HMRC.

Hood, A. and Keiller, A.N. (2016) *A survey of the UK benefit system,* Briefing Note (BN13), London: Institute for Fiscal Studies.

Hood, A. and Oakley, L. (2014) *A survey of the GB benefit system,* IFS Briefing Note (BN13), London, Institute for Fiscal Studies.

Hood, A. and Waters, T. (2017a) *The impact of tax and benefit reforms on household incomes,* Briefing Note (BN196), London: Institute for Fiscal Studies (www.ifs. org.uk/publications/9164).

Hood, A. and Waters, T. (2017b) *Living standards, poverty and inequality in the UK: 2016-17 to 2021-22,* Report (R127), London: Institute for Fiscal Studies (www. ifs.org.uk/publications/8957).

House of Commons Work and Pensions Committee (2105) *Benefit sanctions policy beyond the Oakley Review, Fifth report of Session 2014–15* (https://publications. parliament.uk/pa/cm201415/cmselect/cmworpen/814/814.pdf).

Keep, M. (2017) *The benefit cap,* House of Commons Library Briefing Paper No 06852.

Kennedy, S. (2015) *Welfare Reform and Work Bill [Bill 51 of 2015-16],* House of Commons Library Briefing Paper No 07252.

Loopstra, R. and Lalor, D. (2017) *Financial insecurity, food insecurity, and disability: The profile of people receiving emergency food assistance from The Trussell Trust foodbank network in Britain,* Salisbury: The Trussell Trust.

Lupton, R., Burchardt, T., Hills, J., Stewart, K. and Vizard, P. (eds) (2016) *Social policy in a cold climate: Policies and their consequences since the crisis,* Bristol: Policy Press.

McKay, S. and Rowlingson, K. (2016) 'Social security under the coalition and the Conservatives: Shredding the system for people of working age; privileging pensioners', in H. Bochel and M. Powell (eds*) The coalition government and social policy: Restructuring the welfare state,* Bristol: Policy Press, pp 179-200.

NAO (National Audit Office) (2016a) *Understanding fraud and error in benefits and tax credits: A primer,* London: NAO.

NAO (2016b) *Fraud and error stocktake,* HC 267, London: NAO.

NI (Northern Ireland) Assembly (2011) *Parity and social security in Northern Ireland*, Research and Information Service Briefing Paper 99/11 (www.niassembly.gov.uk/globalassets/Documents/RaISe/Publications/2011/Social-Development/9911.pdf).

OECD (Organisation for Economic Co-operation and Development) (2016) *Society at a Glance 2016: Social spending* (https://data.oecd.org/socialexp/social-spending.htm).

Patrick, R. (2107) *For whose benefit? The everyday realities of welfare reform*, Bristol: Policy Press.

Peaker, G. (2017) 'Real misery is being caused to no good purpose', *DA & Ors, R (On the Application Of) vs Secretary of State for Work and Pensions (2017)* EWHC 1446 (Admin) (https://nearlylegal.co.uk/2017/06/real-misery-caused-no-good-purpose/).

Portes, J. and Reed, H. (2018) *The cumulative impact of tax and welfare reforms*, London: Equality and Human Rights Commission.

Royston, S. (2017) *Broken benefits: What has gone wrong with welfare reform?*, Bristol: Policy Press.

Sainsbury, R. (1999) 'The aims of social security', in J. Ditch (ed) *Introduction to social security*, London: Routledge, pp 34-47.

Schröder, M. (2017) 'Varieties of capitalism and welfare states: Eroding diversity?', in P. Kennett and N. Lendvai-Bainton (eds) *Handbook of European social policy*, Cheltenham: Edward Elgar, pp 46-59.

Scottish Government (2016) *Creating a fairer Scotland: A new future for social security in Scotland*, Edinburgh: Scottish Government.

Taylor-Gooby, P., Leruth, B. and Chung, H. (2017) *After austerity: Welfare state transformation in Europe after the great recession*, Oxford: Oxford University Press.

Walker, R. (2005) *Social security and welfare: Concepts and comparisons*, Oxford: Oxford University Press.

Part One
People and policies across the life course

2

Social security support for children

Tess Ridge

Summary

At the very end of the 20th century the Labour government pledged to eradicate childhood poverty in the UK by 2020. Their commitment to addressing childhood poverty in 20 years resulted in a significant period of policy interest in low-income children and their families and a series of major welfare reforms, including the passing of the Child Poverty Act 2010. Central to those policy measures were changes in support for children and their families through the tax and benefit system. Following the Labour governments of 1997-2010, and during a period of recession and austerity, the coalition government (2010-15) and following Conservative governments (2015-16/17) introduced significant changes to benefits and tax credits. These changes have redrawn the landscape of social security support for children. To examine the nature and implication of these changes, this chapter will:

- explore how and why the state provides social security support for children and reflect on the challenge of delivering support to children via their families;
- consider the impact of 21st-century social security reforms on children's lives and wellbeing in working and workless families;
- explore the changing nature of child poverty policy and legislation, and the implications for children of changes in measurement, adequacy and entitlement.

Introduction

At the start of the 21st century, the debate in the UK about how best to provide state protection and support for children was high on the policy agenda. The Labour governments from 1997-2010 had pledged to eradicate child poverty within 20 years, and that promise and the legislation that followed it breathed new life into the ongoing debate about the type and level of financial support that society and the state should be providing for children and their families. Central to that debate was the issue of where the balance should be struck between state support for children and state intervention in the private realm of family life. Too much support for children may encourage people to have more children (considered a legitimate use of the social security system in some countries), or might increase the risk of family dissolution; too little support, and children would be left to the vagaries of individual family circumstances without any recognition of their social rights and values. Provision of financial support for children and their families is therefore 'linked to deep-rooted moral and ideological questions of freedom, dependency, care and mutual responsibility' (Smith, 1998, p 16).

Social security provisions have an impact on many areas of children's lives, and there is a considerable diversity in the type and level of support that is provided. Benefits for children fall into several different categories, and these may have different rules, aims and intentions, and treat children differently according to age or number of siblings, for example. Box 2.1 shows that state involvement in the provision of support for children can range from Child Benefit, the public acknowledgement of society's interest in sharing the costs of raising all children, to child maintenance, which is concerned with enforcing financial obligations within the family. Children are also supported through Child Tax Credits, which are payments to help low-income families raise their children. Children can also receive non-cash benefits such as free school meals and the Pupil Premium (a payment to the school to be used to support a child's education) if their parents are on the lowest level of means-tested benefits, for example, Income Support.

Box 2.1: State provision for children

- *Child Benefit:* previously universal, now excluding those with higher incomes, a benefit to acknowledge the costs of raising children.
- *Child Tax Credit:* a payment to help with the costs of bringing up a child for working and non-working families on a low income. Payments limited to two children only, from 2017.
- *Universal Credit:* a single benefit replacing adult means-tested benefits and incorporating Child Tax Credit for families in and out of work. To be fully implemented by 2020.
- *Childcare costs:* included in Working Tax Credit is a childcare element that pays up to 70 per cent of childcare costs for low-income working families.
- *Welfare-in-kind:* means-tested provision of non-cash benefits for some low-income children, for example, free school meals and the Pupil Premium linked to receipt of Income Support.
- *Child maintenance:* no cash provision but direct involvement of the state in the 'private' realm of family relationships when parents live apart. Intended to ensure non-resident parents pay child maintenance for their children, if private agreement cannot be made.

Benefits for children: numbers in receipt and expenditure

Social security plays a significant role in most children's lives, and increased income testing draws more children and their families into means-tested state provision (Walker and Howard, 2000). Most parents with children under the age of 16 are entitled to Child Benefit for their children, and many children's economic security and wellbeing also depends on other areas of social security provision. Box 2.2 shows the numbers of children living in families that receive financial support from the state in the form of in-work tax credits or out-of-work benefits in 2014/15. This shows that a substantial proportion of children live in families where social security support has an essential role to play in supporting their needs. Out-of-work payments are vital for over 2 million children, especially those under five. But the highest number of children in need of additional support from the state are the almost 5 million living in working families. For these families, inadequate and insecure wages need to be supplemented by the state through tax credits.

Box 2.2: Social security support for children in 2014/15

In total:

- In 2015, over 12.9 million children were living in 7.4 million families who received a weekly payment of Child Benefit (HMRC, 2015).
- Nearly 7 million children (over half of all children under the age of 16 in the population) lived in low-income families who received means-tested social security benefits or tax credits.

Of these:

- Over 4.9 million children lived in working families in receipt of in-work means-tested payments through Working Tax Credit and/or Child Tax Credit.
  - Of these, 3.1 million were living in couple families and 1.8 million were living in lone-parent families (HMRC, 2016).
- 2 million children lived in families that were in receipt of means-tested out-of-work benefits – including Income Support, Employment Support Allowance and Jobseeker's Allowance (DWP, 2016a).
  - One-third of these was aged under five, and the majority (over 1 million) were in households receiving Income Support (DWP, 2016a).

In respect to spending on children, the Institute for Fiscal Studies (IFS) estimated that in 2015-16 the cost of social security benefits in Great Britain was over

£211 billion (Hood and Waters, 2017). Government expenditure that is clearly targeted on children comes mainly from Child Tax Credits (£21.7 billion) and Child Benefit (£11.2 billion), and overall in 2015/16, benefits and tax credits for families with children amounted to nearly £36 billion. In addition to these targeted payments for children other expenditure is also intended to support them through payments to support their parents, including in-work supplements through Working Tax Credits, unemployment support through Income Support and Jobseeker's Allowance, and payments covering periods of sickness and disability. Expenditure on housing and other services also benefits children.

Responsibility for providing support for children is separated out from adult payments and lies mainly with HM Revenue & Customs (HMRC). This means that £11.2 billion on Child Benefit and £21.7 billion in Child Tax Credits are administered by HMRC, although the Department for Work and Pensions (DWP) still plays a significant role in children's lives through the administration of social security benefits for adults – that is, their parents. Children cannot be divorced from the financial circumstances of their parents, so their circumstances are still affected by the adequacy of adult benefits and the rules and regulations governing social security payments provided for parents – for example, the compulsion on lone parents to seek employment when their youngest child reaches a certain age that is attached to receipt of Jobseeker's Allowance.

Why does the state provide support for children?

Children are beneficiaries of social security benefits that are mainly targeted at their parents, and so the nature and level of support is determined by issues that apply to the adults, including labour market concerns (for example, maintaining work incentives and keeping down wage demands), and family and gender issues (such as providing an income for mothers or reinforcing parental responsibility). Fiscal, moral and political concerns of the state can also dominate the issue of benefits and support for children. For example, means-tested benefits for families without a wage earner have traditionally been set at a low level to ensure the maintenance of work incentives. This principle of 'less eligibility' has severe implications for children living in unemployed families whose benefits consequently fall below the threshold of adequacy for a minimum acceptable standard of living (Hirsch, 2014).

Therefore, in general, children themselves are rarely the main focus of social security provision. Furthermore, when they *are* the main focus, the underpinning aims of that provision may be quite diverse, and informed by very different notions of children and childhood. Box 2.3 shows the possible aims and intentions of social security policies directed towards children.

Box 2.3: Possible aims of social security support for children

- The relief of poverty
- Investment in children
- Recognition of the costs of children
- Redistribution of resources
- Citizenship and children's rights
- Incentive payments

The relief of poverty

The relief of childhood poverty is a core principle behind the provision of social security for children and their families. Childhood poverty is a significant concern in the UK despite the country's affluence. In 2015 the UK was ranked as the fifth richest country in the world, but also as one of the most unequal (IMF, 2016). This inequality is evident in the numbers of children living in poverty. In 2015 there were 3.9 million children living in poverty in the UK, representing nearly one-third of all children (CPAG, no date). Children are at greater risk of experiencing poverty than adults (Main and Bradshaw, 2015).

The development of benefits for children began in the early 20th century when the extent and severity of child poverty began to emerge as a serious cause for concern, and the welfare of children became an important policy issue (see Macnicol, 1980, for an overview of the development of Family Allowances and early benefit provision for children). Social security can play a vital role in supporting children when they and their families are at risk of experiencing poverty through low wages, unemployment, family separation, sickness, disability or bereavement. Different social, economic and demographic factors affect the likelihood of children experiencing poverty. These include living in a lone-parent family, living in a minority ethnic household, living in large families, living in families where there is an adult or a child with a long-term sickness and/or disability, and living in either a workless household or one dependent on low pay – over half of all children living in poverty live in families where at least one member works (Main and Bradshaw, 2015; CPAG, no date). These are not discrete factors but elements of disadvantage that can intersect and reinforce each other (Ridge, 2002). However, although these characteristics are important, the extent of child poverty is also dependent on an individual country's labour supply and earnings, and the tax and benefit packages that countries provide to support parents with the costs of raising children (Bradshaw and Barnes, 1999). All economically developed countries provide support for children through the tax and benefit system and, as Bradshaw (1999, p 396) argues, 'child poverty is not inevitable – countries make more or less explicit choices about how far they employ social and fiscal policies to mitigate the impact of pre-transfer forces.' (See below for further discussion of the Labour pledge to 'end child poverty'.)

Investment in children: the social investment approach

Another reason for which the state might also provide fiscal support for children is as a form of investment in the future. The notion of children as 'investments' is a common and pervasive theme in UK and European social policy (Bourget et al, 2015). In the UK it has its origins in times of national renewal and concerns about the future. Labour's approach to social investment was to greatly increase payments targeted at children and to improve children's services (see below). The appeal of 'investing' in children lies not so much in providing for the best interests of children, but in the overriding interests of future economic prosperity and social stability. However, focusing on children as adults-to-be can lead to policies taking particular forms that focus more on the outcomes of childhood than on addressing the needs and experiences of children during childhood (Ridge, 2002).

Recognition of the costs of children

Social security can also be provided to families in recognition of the costs of having children and the value that society places on them. However, providing benefits that recognise the costs of raising children again poses questions about the adequacy of current benefits and the appropriate balance between parental and state support. Although state expenditure on children is increasing, parents meet the main bulk of the direct costs of children. An assessment of children's needs can be obtained from a list of socially perceived necessities, things that people recognise as being essential for a child growing up in the UK today. The national Poverty and Social Exclusion Survey (Gordon et al, 2013) lists a diverse range of needs from adequate food and clothing to social participation, developmental stimulation and environmental wellbeing.

This 'consensual' list of necessities has been used to construct an index of childhood deprivation, which classified children as poor if they lacked one or more of the essential items on the list (see Main and Bradshaw, 2014). Historically, the level of social security support provided for children falls well below the estimated costs of raising children (see Middleton et al, 1997).

Redistribution of resources

Social security can also be used to redistribute resources between different groups in society. 'Vertical redistribution' between high-income groups to low-income groups plays an important role in supporting children in low-income families. However, children's interests are also served by 'horizontal redistribution', the distribution of resources from those without children to those with them (see Sainsbury, 1999). It is crucial to find the right mix between vertical and horizontal redistribution as well as the redistribution of resources on other dimensions to ensure that the interests of children are met.

Citizenship and children's rights

More radical agendas propose that support for children should be based on the principle of equity, the notion of citizenship and children's rights, recognition that society has an obligation towards sharing the costs of children and supporting children as individuals in their own right. To approach social security benefits from a children's rights perspective would again raise the issue of adequacy, as children and young people would have a right to social protection and an adequate standard of living regardless of their parents' income and circumstances. Lister (1990, p 59) has argued that Child Benefit, for many years a universal benefit for all children, should be seen as the child's 'badge of citizenship'. However, the fortunes of Child Benefit and its predecessor Family Allowances have ebbed and flowed since their inception (see Macnicol, 1980). Nonetheless, Child Benefit has played a vital role for many low-income families, providing support and stability in times of crisis and need (Bradshaw and Stimson, 1997). Yet Child Benefit has rarely been viewed simply as a benefit for children; it has been bound up with gender and employment issues, the debate about motherhood and 'purse and wallet' debates about how resources are distributed within the household (Bennett and Dornan, 2006). Where it has been seen as a benefit for children it has invariably been concerned with children as future investments rather than as a significant element of children's rights and citizenship during childhood. Since 2013 Child Benefit has been taxed in families where one of the parents has an individual income of over £50,000. However, the policy is unequal in its effect as, for example, a single parent on £60,000 a year will lose all of their Child Benefit but a couple on £50,000 each will keep all of theirs. This shows the challenges of maintaining equity between children within the social security system.

Incentive payments

Finally, social security benefits for children might be used as an incentive to encourage or reward particular types of behaviour. While this is not uncommon for adult claimants, the use of benefit incentives for children and young people is rare. The Labour government, in its provisions for low-income children, did introduce a range of new incentivised polices. These included the Education Maintenance Allowance and Child Trust Fund, both intended to encourage and reward children and young people for particular behaviours.

The Child Trust Fund was linked to financial education in the National Curriculum and used to encourage financial competence and the development of regular savings habits in children (and their parents). Children were to be given a lump sum at birth, to be placed in a savings account to which access was restricted until the child was 18. Children, and their parents, were encouraged to add to their savings and to develop the habit of saving regularly. For low-income families the state promised to provide further endowments at key life stages, for example, 5, 11 and 16 years. However, the Child Trust Fund was abolished in 2010 when a change of government from Labour to the coalition ushered in an era of welfare cuts and austerity measures.

The Education Maintenance Allowance faced a similar fate, introduced by Labour to encourage low-income young people to stay on at school. The incentive was linked to a Learning Agreement in terms of attendance and course work, and payments were then made directly to the young person. Despite evidence to show that following their implementation they had increased staying-on rates and improved attainment rates for 16- to 18-year-olds from the poorest families, the coalition government abolished the Education Maintenance Allowance in 2011 (Chowdry and Emmerson, 2010), although it continued in Scotland, Northern Ireland and Wales.

Changing the landscape: benefits for children in the 21st century

This section summarises the key measures introduced by the Labour government and examines what happened to these in the following years when Labour lost power and was replaced by the coalition and then Conservative government.

Labour and support for children

When Labour came to power in 1997 following a 20-year period of Conservative free market economic policies, child poverty rates were high, and children had disproportionately suffered from changes in economic conditions and demographic structures (Oppenheim and Harker, 1996; Walker and Walker, 1997; Millar, 2001). In 1998, in recognition of spiralling child poverty rates, Prime Minister Tony Blair announced that his government would eradicate child poverty within the next 20 years (Blair, 1999).

Labour's commitment to eradicate child poverty placed children and their families at the centre of the policy process, and resulted in a major reconstruction of the welfare system. At the heart of the government's reforming agenda were policy measures to promote paid work (for example, the Minimum Wage and New Deal programmes), coupled with a radical overhaul of the tax and benefits system to ensure that paid work was rewarded and extra resources were targeted at those who were in the most need (HM Treasury, 1999, 2000). These reforms fundamentally changed the way in which children were supported by the state. Box 2.4 outlines the main changes to social security and fiscal support for children between 1997 and 2010.

Box 2.4: Key changes to social security and fiscal support for children between 1997 and 2010

- *Increased Child Benefit*, the (then) universal payment for all children.
- *Increases in Income Support rates* for children, including the removal of age-related differences between under-11s and under-16s.
- *Increases in the Maternity Grant* from £100 to £500. Called the Sure Start Maternity Grant, this was means-tested, and in order to receive it the mother, or her partner, must have received information about child healthcare from their doctor, midwife or health visitor.
- *Replacement of Family Credit with Working Families' Tax Credit (later renamed Working Tax Credit)*, paid at a higher rate, including a Childcare Tax Credit to offset the costs of childcare.
- *Child Tax Credit*, a single tax credit to replace children's rates of Income Support, Jobseeker's Allowance, Disabled Persons' Tax Credit and Working Families Tax Credit.
- *Education Maintenance Allowances*, means-tested support paid directly to children aged 16-18 who attend full-time courses at school or college.
- *Reform of the child support system*, with the introduction of a simpler formula, ultimately fully disregarded for Income Support recipients.

Labour's welfare-to-work polices and children

Central to Labour's policy agenda was the promotion of paid work to lift children in 'workless' families out of poverty. Many parents, especially lone parents and families where there are disabilities, experience considerable barriers to entering paid employment (Millar and Ridge, 2001). Labour brought in welfare-to-work policies including a New Deal for Lone Parents that encouraged lone parents into employment and set out to 'make work pay' and 'make work possible'. Central to this was the introduction of new Working Families Tax Credits for in-work support and Child Tax Credits to provide seamless support for children in workless and low-income working families. A National Childcare Strategy was launched and a Childcare Tax Credit was created to help with the costs of childcare.

Payments for children in 'workless' families were also increased and inequities between different ages of children were addressed in line with research evidence that had shown that Income Support rates for children, especially younger children, were inadequate (Middleton et al, 1997). A series of Labour budgets progressively uprated child payments and abolished age-related payments so that all children under the age of 16 were paid the same (HM Treasury, 2001), resulting in an 80 per cent rise in real terms between 1997 and 2001 (Lister, 2001).

Changes in the tax and benefits system during the Labour administrations resulted in the redistribution of income towards families with children and increased support for children in the benefit system, and these changes were underpinned by a social investment approach (Lister, 2001). However, there were ongoing concerns about adequacy as the payments for parents were not correspondingly increased and remained substantially below the 60 per cent of median income poverty line used by the government (Piachaud and Sutherland, 2001). Children's needs and payments cannot be separated out from overall family income, and therefore the increases for children were diluted by lack of increased support for the adults in their families. Overall, however, childhood poverty was placed at the centre of policy during the Labour administrations, and there was a significant increase in targeted and means-tested resources given to disadvantaged children and families (Waldfogel, 2010). Despite a damaging global recession, child poverty levels fell, and ultimately nearly 1 million children were lifted out of poverty during Labour's time in office. Although Labour's child poverty targets were not met, they made substantial advances in reducing child poverty. By the end of their period in office, childhood poverty, measured before housing costs, had fallen from 3.4 million children in 1998/99 to 2.5 million in 2010/11 (DWP, 2012).

Child Poverty Act 2010

A key element of Labour's policy provision for children was the development of the Child Poverty Act 2010, formulated to drive policy along towards the target of eradicating childhood poverty by 2020. The Act was one of the final measures of the Labour government, passed through Parliament before the 2010 election and the coalition government that followed. The Act set out the duties of central government, local authorities and devolved administrations to measure child poverty across four dimensions – relative poverty, combined income and poverty, absolute poverty and persistent poverty – and to produce an annual child poverty strategy to meet poverty reduction targets. Box 2.5 sets out the key features of this legislation that came into force after Labour lost power.

The Child Poverty Act was inherited as a duty by the incoming coalition government, which did not have the same policy approach to child poverty. Ultimately the Child Poverty Act had a short life and, on the heels of increasing austerity and cuts to social security and welfare provision brought in by first the coalition government and then the Cameron Conservative government, it was abolished within six years following the passing of the Welfare Reform and Work

> **Box 2.5: Key features of the Child Poverty Act 2010**
>
> **Purpose of the Act**
> - Enshrine in law the Labour government's commitment to end child poverty by 2020.
> - Develop process by which targets can be identified and met.
>
> **Key elements**
> 1. Every successive government was required to produce a child poverty strategy to make progress towards 2020.
> 2. Four measures of childhood poverty.
> 3. Annual report to Parliament – each government to be held to account on progress towards child poverty targets.
> 4. Child Poverty Commission to be established to oversee progress.
> 5. Duty on local authorities and their partners in service delivery to tackle child poverty and to develop their own child poverty strategies.

Act 2016. This removed the targets to reduce child poverty, the duty to produce a Child Poverty Strategy and the measure of poverty based on family income. The UK government is now only committed to producing an annual statistic on the number of children in workless families.

In many ways the Child Poverty Act can be seen as an aspirational backdrop to a period in which childhood poverty and the role of social security in supporting low-income children and their families was at the forefront of government policy. The period from 2010 onwards represents a very different political landscape that began with the formation of the coalition government (2010–15) and the beginning of severe welfare cuts and the withdrawing of benefits and services from low-income children and their families (Ridge, 2013).

Coalition government 2010-15

The coalition government was formed in 2010 between the Conservatives and the Liberal Democrats against a backdrop of recession and economic crisis, and the policy direction taken was one of austerity and severe reductions in public spending. As deficit reduction took priority, changes in welfare provision, particularly in social security support, had a significant impact on low-income children's lives. Starting with an emergency budget in June 2010, a public spending review in October 2010 and the passing of the Welfare Reform Act in 2012, there was a significant withdrawal and reduction of financial support for children and their families through substantial cuts to social security benefits and tax credits (Ridge, 2013). In 2013 the Child Poverty Action Group (CPAG) compiled a list of 42 social security changes to highlight the unprecedented number and complexity of cuts to social security benefits, and identified cuts totalling over £22 billion a year by 2014-15 (CPAG, 2013).

Children were particularly vulnerable to the measures taken that affected support received by their parents, as well as support targeted at the children themselves. Cuts that affected children through their parents included the cutting of Local Housing Allowance and Housing Benefit; a welfare cap on the amount of benefits a family could receive, which had a particular impact on larger families; reductions in support through Working Tax Credit; and the imposition of an under-occupancy penalty (commonly known as the Bedroom Tax) on families in social rented housing deemed to have a spare bedroom. These measures were coupled with changes in the delivery of Council Tax Benefit and Social Fund loans, which were relocated from central to local government, with significantly reduced budgets. Cuts in capital spending also led to increasing unemployment and redundancies in local authorities and the public sector where women made up a significant proportion of the workforce (see Ridge, 2013, for an overview of social security cuts and their effect on children).

There were also a substantial number of cuts to provision directly targeted at children. Box 2.6 sets out some of the changes that directly affected children's social security entitlements.

Box 2.6: Coalition (2010-15) social security cuts affecting children and young people

- Scrapping of Labour's plans to extend free school meals to children in low-income working families.
- Abolition of the Child Trust Fund.
- Baby element of Child Tax Credit removed.
- Childcare support cut from 80 to 70 per cent of costs.
- Abolition of Health in Pregnancy Grant.
- Sure Start Maternity Grant limited to the first child only.
- Child Benefit Rates frozen from 2011-14.
- Taxing of Child Benefit.
- Removal of a planned supplement to Child Tax Credit for toddlers.
- Scrapping of the Education Maintenance Allowance.

Taken together, these cuts represented a severe and significant reduction in welfare support for low-income children who are particularly dependent on social security. The UK Children's Commissioner, in a report to the United Nations (UN) Committee on the Rights of the Child, found that 'the best interests of children were not central to the development of these policies', and the UK government had failed to protect disadvantaged children and had breached their rights (UK Children's Commissioner, 2015, p 1).

The Cameron Conservative government (2015-16) continued with welfare cuts, culminating in the passing of the Welfare Reform and Work Act 2016. This Act effectively abolished the Child Poverty Act, further lowered the benefit cap reducing support for children in larger families, and placed a freeze on working-age social security and tax credits for four years, which included individual child elements of Child Tax Credit. The first child premiums for Universal Credit were also abolished and the family premium in Housing Benefit was withdrawn. The May Conservative government (2016-17) that took power following the Brexit referendum did not reverse the £12 billion cuts set in motion by the previous Cameron government, and as a result, the cumulative impact of social security and tax credit cuts imposed during the period from the coalition onwards has resulted in a sharp rise in child poverty, with figures for 2015/16 showing that nearly 4 million children are living in poverty in the UK (DWP, 2016b). Large families are particularly hit by these measures, and so this means that children in black and minority ethnic (BME) groups are disproportionately affected. Around 30 per cent of White British children live in large families (with three or more children) compared with 51 per cent of Black African children, 64 per cent of Bangladeshi children and 65 per cent of Pakistani children (Hall et al, 2017).

Two child – or one sibling – policies

Of particular interest and concern with regards to social security provision for children during the coalition period onward has been the development of two child (or one sibling) policies. These measures have the effect of restricting children's support in relation to the number of siblings they have. First, the Sure Start Maternity Grant was limited to the first child only, and then the Welfare Reform and Work Act 2016 brought in limitations in entitlement to the child element of Child Tax Credits and Universal Credit to a maximum of two children in each household. This is a highly controversial change, and although there are exceptions, these are also themselves contentious, particularly the 'non-consensual conception' exception category (a birth resulting from rape, for example), which will be highly complex and sensitive to administer equitably. These changes in entitlement are extremely significant for children, and signal the breach of several key principles of social security support for all children, including equity between children, the relief of poverty, investment in children, recognition of the costs of children, and the recognition of all children's citizenship rights. The benefit cap, coupled with restrictions in entitlement, mean that children's vulnerability to poverty will in future be at risk of substantially increasing depending on how many brothers and sisters they have. This means that some children effectively become non-citizens with regard to social security support and entitlement in their own right.

Conclusion

This chapter has shown the important role that social security and tax credits play in supporting children's lives. For low-income children adequate and reliable financial assistance at times of need play a critical part in ensuring that their families, both in and out of work, can manage financially. However, the chapter has also shown that payments for children can be complex and subject to changes in rules, adequacy and entitlement. Their payments are not protected and they can be disproportionately vulnerable to policy change, benefit cuts and austerity measures. What is especially apparent are the ways in which different political agendas, changes in government and changes in social security provision can have profound implications for childhood poverty. A strong policy agenda to eradicate childhood poverty backed by legislation, as developed by the Labour governments of 1998-2010, brought considerable resources into social security for children and made significant headway in reducing child poverty. Since 2010, the austerity policies and welfare retrenchment imposed by the coalition and subsequent Cameron and May Conservative governments reversed the trend in falling child poverty figures, and resulted in rising numbers of children experiencing poverty. It is projected that the impact of sustained severe cuts in social security provision could result in 5 million children being in poverty in the UK by 2020 (IFS, 2017). This is a far cry from the aspirational 2020 target of eliminating child poverty set by Labour at the start of the century.

Overview

Social security for children can be informed by very different and sometimes competing discourses of family and childhood, and benefits for children can be underpinned by different aims and intentions.

There is an ongoing tension between parental responsibility for children and the interests and obligations of society and the state towards ensuring the wellbeing of children.

Labour's commitment to eradicating child poverty resulted in an attempt to fundamentally change the way in which children are supported by the state and a redistribution of resources towards children and their families.

Austerity measures and cuts in social security support for children and their families have had a significant impact on financial support for children.

Benefits for children such as Child Benefit have moved away from a 'universal' model of support for all children as a citizen right towards a system of taxation and means testing.

Changes in entitlement to social security support for children based on the number of children in each family have significant consequences for children in terms of equity and citizen rights.

Social security for children should respond to the needs and rights of children. However, while children may have different needs to adults, they must still be considered within the context of their households.

Questions for discussion

1. Why and how does the state provide social security for children?
2. What was policy aim of the Child Poverty Act 2010 and why was it repealed?
3. What has been the impact of 21st-century social security reforms on children's lives?

Key reading

Main, G. and Bradshaw, J. (2015) 'Child poverty in the UK: Measures, prevalence and intra-household sharing', *Critical Social Policy*, vol 36, no 1, pp 38-61.

Ridge, T. (2013) '"We're all in this together": The hidden costs of poverty, recession and austerity policies on Britain's poorest children', *Children & Society*, vol 2, no 5, pp 406-17.

Waldfogel, J. (2010) *Britain's war on poverty*, New York: Russell Sage Foundation.

Website resources

www.cpag.org.uk
   Child Poverty Action Group

www.jrf.org.uk
   Joseph Rowntree Foundation

www.endchildpoverty.org.uk
   End Child Poverty Coalition

www.gov.uk/browse/benefits/families
   Government, Benefits for families

http://ec.europa.eu/social/main.jsp?catId=1044
   European Commission, Social investment

References

Bennett, F. and Dornan, P. (2006) *Child Benefit: Fit for the future*, CPAG Policy Briefing, August (http://cpag.org.uk/sites/default/files/CPAG-Child-Benefit-Fit-Future-0806.pdf).

Blair, T. (1999) 'Beveridge revisited: A welfare state for the 21st century', reproduced in R. Walker (ed) *Ending child poverty*, Bristol: Policy Press.

Bourget, D., Frazer, H., Marlier, E., Sabato, S. and Vanhercke, B. (2015) *Social investment in Europe: A study of national policies, 2015*, Luxembourg: Publications Office of the European Union.

Bradshaw, J. (1999) 'Child poverty in comparative perspective', *European Journal of Social Security*, vol 1, no 4, pp 383-406.

Bradshaw, J. and Barnes, H. (1999) 'How do nations monitor the well-being of their children?', Paper to the LIS Child Poverty Conference, York: Social Policy Research Unit, University of York.

Bradshaw, J. and Stimson, C. (1997) *Using Child Benefit in the family budget*, Social Policy Research Centre, London: The Stationery Office.

Chowdry, H. and Emmerson, C. (2010) *An efficient maintenance allowance?*, London: Institute for Fiscal Studies (www.ifs.org.uk/publications/5370).

CPAG (Child Poverty Action Group) (2013) 'Factsheets' (www.cpag.org.uk/sites/default/files/CPAG_factsheet_the%20cuts_May13.pdf).

CPAG (no date) 'Child poverty facts and figures' (www.cpag.org.uk/child-poverty-facts-and-figures).

DWP (Department for Work and Pensions) (2012) *Households Below Average Income: A statistical analysis 1994/95-2010/11*, Leeds: Corporate Document Services.

DWP (2016a) *Children in out-of-work benefit households*, London: DWP (www.gov.uk/government/uploads/system/uploads/attachment_data/file/540077/children-in-out-of-work-households-report-may-2015.pdf).

DWP (2016b) *Households Below Average Income: A statistical analysis 1994/95-2015/16* Leeds: Corporate Document Services.

Gordon, D., Mack, J., Lansley, S., Main, G., Nandy, S., Patsios, D. and Pomati, M. (2013) *The impoverishment of the UK: Poverty and Social Exclusion first results: Living standards* (www.poverty.ac.uk/pse-research/pse-uk-reports).

Hall, S.-M., McIntosh, K., Neitzert, E., Pottinger, L., Sandhu, K., Stephenson, M.-A., et al (2017) *Intersecting inequalities: The impact of austerity on Black and minority ethnic women in the UK*, London: Women's Budget Group and Runnymede Trust with RECLAIM and Coventry Women's Voices.

Hirsch, D. (2014) *The cost of a child in 2014*, London: Child Poverty Action Group (CPAG).

HMRC (Her Majesty's Revenue & Customs) (2015) *Child Benefit statistics, August 2015*, A National Statistics publication.

HMRC (2016) *Child and Working Tax Credits statistics, UK. Finalised annual awards in 2014-15*, A National Statistics publication.

HM Treasury (1999) *Supporting families through the tax and benefit system*, London: HM Treasury.

HM Treasury (2000) *Budget, March 2000*, London: Public Enquiry Unit.

HM Treasury (2001) *Tackling child poverty: Giving every child the best possible start in life*, London: HM Treasury.

Hood, A. and Waters, T. (2017) *Living standards, poverty and inequality in the UK: 2016–17 to 2021–22*, Report (R127), London: Institute for Fiscal Studies (https://www.ifs.org.uk/publications/8957).

IMF (International Monetary Fund) (2016) *World Economic Outlook Database, October 2016* (www.imf.org/external/pubs/ft/weo/2016/01/weodata/index.aspx).

Lister, R. (1990) *The exclusive society: Citizenship and the poor*, London: Child Poverty Action Group.

Lister, R. (2001) 'Doing good by stealth: The politics of poverty and inequality under New Labour', *New Economy*, July, pp 65-70.

Macnicol, J. (1980) *The movement for Family Allowances, 1918-1945: A study in social policy development*, London: Heinemann.

Main, G. and Bradshaw, J. (2014) *Child poverty and social exclusion: Final report of 2012 PSE study*, Poverty and Social Exclusion.

Main, G. and Bradshaw, J. (2015) 'Child poverty in the UK: Measures, prevalence and intra-household sharing', *Critical Social Policy*, vol 36, no 1, pp 38-61.

Middleton, S., Ashworth, K. and Braithwaite, I. (1997) *Small fortunes: Spending on children, childhood poverty and parental sacrifice*, York: Joseph Rowntree Foundation.

Millar, J. (2001) 'Benefits for children in the UK', in K. Battle and M. Mendelson (eds) *Benefits for children – A four country study*, Ottawa, Canada: The Caledon Institute of Social Policy, pp 187-25.

Millar, J. and Ridge, T. (2001) *Families, poverty, work and care: A review of the literature on lone parents and low-income couple families with children*, DWP Research Report No 153, Leeds: Corporate Document Services.

Oppenheim, C. and Harker, L. (1996) *Poverty: The facts*, London: Child Poverty Action Group.

Piachaud, D. and Sutherland, H. (2001) 'Child poverty: Aims, achievements and prospects for the future', *New Economy*, June, pp 71-6.

Ridge, T. (2002) *Childhood poverty and social exclusion: From a child's perspective*, Bristol: Policy Press.

Ridge, T. (2013) '"We're all in this together": The hidden costs of poverty, recession and austerity policies on Britain's poorest children', *Children & Society*, vol 27 no 5, pp 406-17.

Sainsbury, R. (1999) 'The aims of social security', in J. Ditch (ed) *Introduction to social security: Policies, benefits and poverty*, London: Routledge, pp 34-47.

Smith, R. (1998) 'Who pays for children', *Benefits*, issue 21, January.

UK Children's Commissioner (2015) *UN Committee on the Rights of the Child* (www.niccy.org/media/1489/uk-ccs-uncrc-examination-of-the-fifth-periodic-report-july-2015.pdf).

Waldfogel, J. (2010) *Britain's war on poverty*, New York: Russell Sage Foundation.

Walker, R. and Howard, M. (2000) *The making of a welfare class: Benefit receipt in Britain*, Bristol: Policy Press.

Walker, A. and Walker, C. (1997) *Britain divided: The growth of social exclusion in the 1980s and 1990s*, London: Child Poverty Action Group.

3

Social security and work obligations

Jane Millar

Summary

Until fairly recently, paid employment and social security benefits were assumed to be alternative sources of income for working-age people. Starting from the 1970s, accelerating from the late 1990s, two main trends have undermined this separation:

- An increasingly central focus on the goal of promoting employment for all, which has included stricter work requirements for out-of-work benefit recipients and a widening definition of who should be available for work.
- More employed people have been gradually brought into the social security system, at first through an in-work benefit for low-paid families with children, and then through a system of tax credits that also includes single people and childless couples.

The phased introduction of Universal Credit, which started in 2010, takes these developments even further by merging out-of-work and in-work benefits into a single means-tested benefit and with a further extension of work obligations.

This chapter examines how work obligations have become increasingly central to social security provision for all people of working age. The first section outlines the changes to out-of-work benefits, the second examines the development of in-work benefits and the third traces the emergence of Universal Credit.

Introduction

Beveridge's 1940s plan for social security set out a scheme with three main elements (Beveridge, 1942). These were: *national insurance benefits* (funded by contributions from workers, employers and the government, intended as a replacement for earnings loss through identified contingencies including unemployment, sickness, widowhood and retirement); *national assistance benefits* (funded from general taxation, means-tested support for non-working people with low incomes); and *family allowances* (funded from general taxation, paid at the same rate for all families, regardless of income level). Thus, with the partial exception of family allowances, the main function of social security benefits was clearly to replace lost earnings, not to pay benefits to working people.

This system operated with little change through the 1950s and 1960s, when unemployment was low. But the insurance-based system was not well suited to the higher levels of unemployment from the 1970s, not least because this excluded groups without insurance cover, including long-term unemployed people (who exhausted their contribution) and young unemployed people (with no contribution record). Other non-working (sometimes called 'inactive') groups were increasing in number, including lone parents and people with long-term sickness or disability. And the number of working families in poverty was also increasing. Here we start by looking at changes to benefits for unemployed and non-working people, then consider benefits and tax credits for people in work, and in the final section we look at how these have come together in the form of Universal Credit. This chapter focuses on social security benefits and tax credits, and the work obligations attached to these. Chapter 12 (this volume) covers employment services and welfare-to-work measures.

Social security: unemployment and jobseeking

In this section we summarise the key changes to work requirements attached to social security benefits for non-working people. There are three main groups to consider: unemployed people, lone parents and people with long-term sickness or disability.

Unemployed people

Full employment (for men) was one of the central underlying assumptions of the Beveridge report (1942). In that context, unemployment was seen as a short-term status and the purpose of unemployment benefit was to provide a wage replacement, to maintain income and living standards for the period out of work, and also to enable unemployed people to look for work. Initially this was a flat-rate benefit paid for 12 months. It was a contributory benefit so available to those who had met the contribution conditions through the national insurance system. But there were also requirements to be available for, and seeking, work. For longer-term unemployment, or those without the required contributions, the national assistance scheme provided means-tested support. This was later replaced by Supplementary Benefit (1966-88) and Income Support (1988 onwards). These benefits also included work obligations for claimants.

The rising unemployment rate was an important political issue from the 1970s, when unemployment started to increase significantly. The 'claimant count' of numbers receiving unemployment benefit reached 1 million in early 1976, 2 million in 1981, and peaks of 3 million in 1985 and 1993, then falling until the post-recession rise from around 2008 (ONS, 2016a, Figure 13). Long-term unemployment (over 12 months) remained high and reached a peak in the early 1990s, accounting for about two-fifths of unemployed people (Leaker, 2009). It was during this time that the term 'dependency culture' was increasingly used by many on the political right, to argue that the benefit system was encouraging laziness and a lack of engagement with paid work (Dean and Taylor-Gooby, 1992).

In was in this context that Jobseeker's Allowance was introduced by the Conservative government in October 1996. This replaced the existing system with two types of Jobseeker's Allowance – contributory and income-based – so this was not dissimilar to the previous system. But the name change – Jobseeker's Allowance – was symbolic of the much increased focus on work requirements. There was a substantial increase in the evidence that claimants had to provide to demonstrate that they were looking for work, set out in a signed Jobseeker's Agreement.

Jobseeker's Allowance has continued as the main benefit for unemployed people, and will be until Universal Credit is fully implemented. In May 2017 there were about half a million recipients of Jobseeker's Allowance, mainly income-based (DWP, 2017c).

Lone parents

The increase in the number of lone-parent families has been one of the most significant changes in family patterns in the second half of the 20th century (Kiernan et al, 1998). Lone parents had not been included in the postwar national insurance system and so, if they were not working, were only eligible for means-tested benefits. Lone parents were not required to be available for work, or to do anything to seek work, if their youngest child was under the age of 16. This enabled lone parents to be full-time carers for their children, but also meant that they were not provided with any support if they did want to take up paid work.

In the late 1980s, the Conservative governments started to target lone parents for employment, but it was only after the 1997 election of the Labour government that there was a clear focus on increasing employment rates for lone parents. A target of 70 per cent employment was set. The approach was initially on a voluntary basis and the benefit rules remained unchanged, with no work requirements for lone parents, until 2008. From that date, there was a series of steps progressively moving non-employed lone parents from Income Support to Jobseeker's Allowance. This meant that these lone parents were required to fulfil work obligations, and thus treated in the same way as any other unemployed jobseeker. The age of the youngest child still provided the cut-off point, as shown in Box 3.1. Lone parents with younger children may also be required to attend regular 'work-focused' interviews, to discuss their work plans for the future, and/ or prepare for work by, for example, training or writing CVs. Whitworth and Griggs (2013) analyse the changes in the underlying arguments for compulsion to work for lone parents, from a generally paternalistic approach under the Labour governments to a more contractual approach under the coalition and Conservative governments.

Box 3.1: Lone parents and work obligations

Moved to Jobseeker's Allowance and therefore required to be available for, and seeking, work:

- From 2008: when youngest child is aged 12
- From 2009: when youngest child is aged 10
- From 2010: when youngest child is aged 7
- From 2012: when youngest child is aged 5

Income Support work-focused interviews:

- From 2001-14: work-focused interviews for all at time of claim and annual, six-monthly or quarterly depending on age of youngest child.
- From 2014: Lone parents with a youngest child aged 3 or 4 are required to undertake work-related activities, such as improving basic skills and preparing CVs. These are intended to be flexible, tailored and reasonable.

Source: DWP (2017a)

Employment rates for lone parents have increased substantially, from 44 per cent in 1997 to 67 per cent in 2016 (ONS, 2016b). Among lone parents not in work, the policy changes brought more lone parents into Jobseeker's Allowance. In mid-2008 there were about 7,000 lone parents receiving Jobseeker's Allowance; this rose to over 150,000 by late 2012, and has since fallen to about 64,000 in mid-2017 (DWP, 2017b). There were also about 390,000 lone parents in receipt of Income Support in early 2017 (DWP, 2017c).

People with long-term sickness and disability

Long-term sickness and disability benefits have been a feature of the UK social security system since 1948. In principle they are intended to support people who have been out of work because of sickness or disability for periods typically of over six months. The system of benefits for long-term sickness and disability is very complex, with national insurance benefits, benefits for extra costs and benefits for compensation (see Chapter 4, this volume). Over the years, this has created a set of overlapping benefits, often difficult to negotiate, some of which have included work tests. As with lone parents, the increased focus on increasing employment intensified under the post-1997 Labour governments, again starting with a more voluntary approach.

The introduction of the Employment and Support Allowance in 2008 was a key change. This replaced the existing Incapacity Benefit for non-working people. Like Jobseeker's Allowance it has both contributory and means-tested elements. The major innovation was the new 'Work Capability Assessment', carried out by external providers (see Chapter 12, this volume). The first part of the assessment is to judge whether there is a 'limited capability for work'. Those judged fit for work can claim Jobseeker's Allowance, with the required Jobseeker's Agreement. Those judged to have a limited capability for work are further assessed and divided into two groups: the 'work-related activity' group, who must attend work-focused interviews on a regular basis and possibly fulfil other work conditions, and the 'support group', who have no work requirements.

The operation of the Work Capability Assessment has been controversial, with concerns raised about delays, accuracy and fairness of the assessments, especially as they are carried out by private contractors. Being assessed as 'fit for work' is the most common reason why people dispute decisions (DWP, 2016). There have also been concerns about the level of support provided and the complexity of the system, with different basic amounts and premiums for claimants of Employment and Support Allowance, Jobseeker's Allowance and Income Support. There were significant cuts to Employment and Support Allowance in the 2015 Budget (see Chapter 1, this volume, and also Grover, 2015). And claimants of disability benefits and premiums will also lose income in the switch to Universal Credit. The Personal Independence Payment and Disability Living Allowance (see Chapter 4, this volume) will continue to be paid to Universal Credit claimants, but the disability premiums attached to existing benefits will not continue (Royston and Royston, 2012). Some claimants will be protected by transitional arrangements, but these end if there are any changes in circumstances, so this does not provide ongoing protection.

In introducing the Employment and Support Allowance, there was an explicit aim to reduce the numbers of people receiving incapacity benefits (Holmes et al, 2015), not least because it was felt that incapacity benefits were, in practice, supporting many people who were indeed capable of work. However, the number of recipients of Employment and Support Allowance has remained high, at 2.4 million in early 2017 (DWP, 2014c). For a detailed analysis of disability benefits and welfare reform, including comparisons with other European countries, see Lindsay and Houston (2013).

Social security: in-work benefits and tax credits

The extension of the social security system to include people in low-paid work started from the 1970s. In their influential study in the mid-1960s, Abel-Smith and Townsend (1965) found that poverty was much more widespread than had been thought, and also that it was increasingly a problem for working families, with one in five poor families with children being working families. But there was little support for measures such as a national minimum wage (Brown, 1983). A proposal for a refundable 'tax credit' scheme (House of Commons Social Security Select Committee, 1997) almost reached the legislative stage before being rejected as too costly. Thus, neither wage regulation nor tax reform was seen as able to provide a solution to the problem of poverty among working families. Instead, attention turned to the social security system, and the start of the modern development of in-work benefits in the UK. These were a new departure for the Beveridge wage replacement system. But looking further back, there is a clear connection to the Speenhamland system. This operated in the late 18th and early 19th centuries, and provided means-tested wage supplements set by the number of children and price of bread. For a historically located account of 'social security and wage poverty', see Grover (2016).

In-work benefits are intended to supplement wages in order to enhance work incentives and to tackle working poverty (see Box 3.2). But these are not necessarily compatible aims, especially in a means-tested system in which benefits/ tax credits are withdrawn as earnings rise. The design details of the means test (for example, the rate at which benefit is withdrawn and the treatment of other earners in the family) are thus very important. The Institute for Fiscal Studies (IFS) provides regular analysis of these issues (see, for example, Adam and Browne, 2013).

As Box 3.2 shows, the government statements about aims are very much focused on the individual and the decision by that person to work, or to work more hours. But in-work benefits can also be seen as supporting employers, rather than employees, by supplementing and thus institutionalising low wages (Grover, 2016; see also Chapter 9, this volume). The obligations on people to seek work or work more hours are not matched by parallel obligations on UK employers to offer employment contracts with a minimum number of hours or to offer extra hours (Rubery et al, 2016). Estimating the number of zero hours contracts is not straightforward, but based on a survey of UK businesses this was put at about 1.4 million in May 2017 (Pyper and Browne, 2017).

Box 3.2: In-work benefits: definitions and aims

There are various ways in which income in work may be boosted through the social security and tax systems, including child benefit/family allowances, housing benefits, tax thresholds, lower rates of tax, childcare and other costs of working subsidies, and so on. Statutory Minimum Wages also provide a floor for earnings. While all these will make a difference in income and living standards in work, in this chapter we focus on the benefits/tax credits that are targeted at people in work and that are specifically intended to top up wages.

In the UK in-work benefits have usually been aimed at improving work incentives and at tackling working poverty. Thus, for example:

- *Family Credit:* 'to provide extra support to these families in accordance with their needs; to ensure that as far as possible they are better off in work; and to see that they can achieve improvements in family income by greater effort without losing all benefit' (DHSS, 1985, p 29).
- *Working Families Tax Credit:* 'promoting work incentives, reducing poverty and welfare dependency, and strengthening community and family life' (HM Treasury, 1998a, p 5).
- *Working Tax Credit/Child Tax Credit:* 'supporting families with children, recognising the responsibilities that come with parenthood; tackling child poverty, by offering the greatest help to those most in need, such as low-income families; helping to make sure that work pays more than welfare and that people have incentives to move up the earnings ladder' (HM Treasury, 2002, p 3).

Since the 1970s, there have been four main versions of in-work benefits in the UK (see Millar, 2009, for a more detailed discussion) up to the introduction of Universal Credit:

1971-88 Family Income Supplement: this was available to families with dependent children, with an employed parent working at least 30 hours per week or 24 hours for lone parents. Once awarded, Family Income Supplement continued in payment for 12 months.

1988-99: Family Credit: this was available to families with dependent children, with an employed parent working at least 24 hours per week. Once awarded, Family Credit continued in payment for six months. A similar in-work benefit (Disability Working Allowance) for people with disabilities was introduced in

1992, and there was a pilot scheme (Earnings Top-Up) for single people and couples without dependent children.

1999-2003: Working Families Tax Credit/Disabled Persons Tax Credit: this was available to families with dependent children, with an employed parent working at least 16 hours per week. Once awarded, it continued in payment for six months. The Disabled Persons' Tax Credit was similar in structure. The National Minimum Wage, introduced in 1999, was also intended to reduce the risk of in-work poverty. These two tax credits were thus not very different from Family Credit, albeit more generous. But one key change was that these were designated as 'tax credits' in order to 'reduce the stigma associated with claiming in-work support ... [the] clear link with employment should demonstrate the rewards of work over welfare' (HM Treasury, 1998b, p 3).

From 2003: Working Tax Credit/Child Tax Credit: Working Tax Credit is available to all low-paid workers, with different weekly hours thresholds (16 for lone parents, people with disabilities, people aged over 60; 24 hours for couples with children; and 30 hours for single people and childless couples aged 25-59). Child Tax Credit is available to families with dependent children, and includes both working and non-working families. There were also some major changes to the way the means test operated. These included delivery through the tax system and an annual assessment of entitlement with provisional awards based on the previous tax year and then reconciled with actual income in the current year. This change caused some difficulties with administration (Millar, 2009).

The number of working people receiving in-work benefits/tax credits has risen significantly over the past four decades. Family Income Supplement included less than 100,000 working families with children in the late 1970s, Family Credit extended to about 0.7 million by the mid-1990s, and Working Families Tax Credit to about 1.3 million by the early 2000s (Millar, 2009). By 2015/16 there were about 3 million in-work recipients of Working Families and/or Child Tax Credits, including about 0.5 million with no children (HMRC, 2017). This is not a true time series, being based on different data sources and definitions, and the increased numbers reflect changes in labour market conditions, in family structure and in policy. But the extent to which these means-tested wage supplements have become embedded into the working population is clear. The annual entitlement to tax credits for people in work rose from around £11.3 billion in 2003-04 to around £20.5 billion in 2015/16 (HMRC, 2017). For many working people these tax credits are an important component of income.

The UK is not alone in this shift towards wage supplementation in social security. The US system also dates back to the 1970s, and reaches a significant number in the working population. Other countries have also introduced in-work benefits, making this an increasingly important policy area, as discussed in Box 3.3.

Box 3.3: In-work benefits: international comparisons

Using cash transfers and tax credits to supplement wages has become an increasingly central part of social security systems in many countries. Immervoll and Pearson (2009) identified 16 out of 30 OECD countries as having some form of in-work benefits, although with much variation in their design of these. They concluded that there was a policy shift from seeing such benefits as 'interesting but unusual' in the 1990s to being mainstream by the 2000s – 'to be considered as a matter of course by countries seeking to have a dynamic labour market' (Immervoll and Pearson, 2009, para 31).

The UK and US both introduced in-work benefits in the 1970s. The Earned Income Tax Credit has been in operation in the US as a federal scheme since the mid-1970s, and is now a large programme received by about 29 million families in 2013 (Falk and Crandall-Hollick, 2016). It is mainly targeted at families with children, although it is also available to childless and to single people. It is a refundable credit, which initially rises as earnings rise, is then paid at a maximum rate over a wide range of income, and finally is reduced as earnings increase until it reaches zero. Payments are made annually as a lump sum. Sykes et al (2015) find that recipients value Earned Income Tax Credit as a reward for work, and conclude that this promotes dignity and social inclusion.

Alongside the schemes in the UK and US, Kenworthy (2015, p 5) also identifies more recent schemes in other European countries (Austria, Belgium, Denmark, Finland, France, Germany, Ireland, the Netherlands, Portugal and Sweden) and elsewhere (Australia, Canada, Japan, South Korea and New Zealand).

Universal Credit

By the early 21st century, benefits for people of working age in the UK were generally conditional on stringent work requirements, and there was an extensive and well embedded system of in-work financial support. But debates continued about the system of social security support for working people. There was concern in particular about the complexity of the system of benefits and tax credits in and out of work, and the potential impact of this on effectiveness (NAO, 2005; Public Accounts Committee, 2006). It was argued that the system was hard to understand and therefore to access, and that making the transition between out-of-work and in-work benefits was difficult and was thus limiting work incentives.

There was also some concern about people churning between unemployment and low-paid jobs and about progression in work.

Sainsbury and Stanley (2007) put forward a proposal for a 'single working-age benefit', which would merge most out-of-work earnings replacement benefits, and thereby ease the movement between, for example, benefits for incapacity and benefits for unemployment and vice versa. Freud (2007) endorsed this in his review of future options for welfare to work. The House of Commons Work and Pensions Committee (2007) looked in detail at the issue of benefit simplification, and concluded that there should be further work and debate on the concept of a 'single working-age benefit', including in-work benefits. The Centre for Social Justice (2009) report, *Dynamic benefits*, made the case for a 'universal' benefit to create a system that would be simpler, cost-effective and improve work incentives. That report was in part a technical analysis of the perceived failings of the system, examining issues such as marginal tax rates and complexity. But it was also strongly focused on the need to change behaviour, arguing that promoting work, and a working lifestyle, was key to positive behaviour change.

In the event it was the Centre for Social Justice's proposal that most closely shaped the initial blueprint for Universal Credit, including the transformational goals (see Box 3.4). Following the 2010 election, Iain Duncan Smith was appointed Secretary of State for Social Security. He was co-founder of the Centre for Social Justice, and had written the preface to *Dynamic benefits*. A Green Paper and a White Paper swiftly followed (DWP, 2010a, b), setting out the proposal for Universal Credit. Legislation followed in 2011, and the first payments were made in April 2013.

The concept is simple, bringing the out-of-work and in-work systems together into one single benefit. Universal Credit replaces six existing means-tested benefits and tax credits (Income-based Jobseeker's Allowance, Housing Benefit, Working Tax Credit, Child Tax Credit, Income-Related Employment and Support Allowance, and Income Support). Universal Credit will, when fully implemented, include around 7 to 8 million households (House of Commons Work and Pensions Committee, 2014). The intention is for 'a simple structure designed to: provide a basic income for people out of work, covering a range of needs; make work pay as people move into and progress in work; and help lift people out of poverty' (DWP, 2010b, p 14). Universal Credit will, the government anticipates, simplify the benefit system and thus make it easier to understand, to access and to administer, increasing take-up and reducing fraud and error.

The complexity of the current system was, as discussed above, already an area of concern, and so this focus on simplification has generally been welcomed. For example, the Resolution Foundation, a think tank that has been closely following the Universal Credit story, notes that 'Simplifying six benefits with different eligibility and withdrawal criteria into one benefit with a single withdrawal rate that is more easily understood makes sense.... As such, it appears there is considerable support for the underlying goals of Universal Credit across the political spectrum' (Finch et al, 2014, p 6).

The delivery of Universal Credit has, however, proved to be complex and slow. The initial plans were that Universal Credit would be introduced between April 2013 and the end of 2017, starting in specific areas with new claims from single people, then moving on to couples and families with children, and finally to the transfer of existing claimants (House of Commons Work and Pensions Committee, 2014). But there have been serious delays and several changes to the timetable. On the original timetable there should have been almost 8 million households in receipt by the end of 2017, but there were only around half a million recipients in June of that year (DWP, 2017d). The revised timetable is for full implementation by 2022 (House of Commons Hansard, 2016).

Box 3.4: Universal Credit as transformational change

The two politicians most closely associated with Universal Credit – Iain Duncan Smith and Lord David Freud – have been clear about the nature of the transformational change that they believe Universal Credit should be seeking to achieve. In the preface to *Universal Credit at work, spring 2015*, they write:

> ... what Universal Credit is really about is a *sweeping cultural change*....

> For *jobcentres* ... vastly improved administration ... reduced levels of fraud, error ... allowing Work Coaches to focus on the real task of helping people enter and progress in work....

> For *local authorities* ... new local partnerships ... joining up services for the most vulnerable to deliver holistic support that helps people get online and better manage their money....

> For *businesses* ... recruiting someone part-time, for extra shifts or over-time suddenly becomes a real possibility, in turn reinvigorating growth....

> And *above all ... for individuals*, Universal Credit marks a complete shift in the whole nature of welfare, no longer trapping people in dependency but providing the incentive and support to secure a better future for themselves and their families.... (DWP, 2015, p 3, emphasis added)

Duncan Smith and Freud also played an important part in keeping Universal Credit alive when the problems of implementation looked almost overwhelming (Timmins, 2016).

The delays have been the result of major problems with the IT system, with project management and with the need to develop processes that work with employers, local authorities and housing associations (Timmins, 2016). Iain Duncan-Smith and David Freud have also argued that these delays reflect a careful approach to 'test and learn', trying out the system in specific areas and for specific groups before going live (see, for example, Freud's evidence to the House of Commons Work and Pensions Committee, 2017). Others have argued, however, that the difficulties and delays are not just administrative problems, but arise from flaws in the aims and design (Millar and Bennett, 2017).

The structure of Universal Credit is similar to the existing means–tested benefits in that it consists of a basic allowance (different rates for single/couple, above/below age 25) with additional elements (for children, childcare costs, limited capability for work, carer, housing costs). The maximum amount may be reduced by the benefit cap (which sets a limit on the total that can be received; see Chapter 1, this volume). There is a 'work allowance', which means that people in work can earn a certain amount before the benefit is reduced. The level of this varies according to household circumstances, and whether the maximum award includes housing costs. Beyond the work allowance, the maximum amount is reduced by 63 per cent (from April 2017) for every £ of net earnings. All recipients – in and out of work, both partners in a couple – must sign a 'claimant commitment' that states their work obligation. Universal Credit is paid as single monthly payment.

There have been some significant changes to the original proposal, not least in respect of the level of support that will be offered. For example, in 2015, three main changes were announced (Keen and Kennedy, 2016). These were:

- Reductions in the 'work allowances' for most claimants from April 2016.
- Limiting the child element to two children for new claims and births after April 2017.
- Removal of the first child premium for new claims from April 2017.

Questions have therefore been raised about whether Universal Credit will be able to meet its stated objectives (Finch, 2015a; Brewer et al, 2017), and what this major change will mean for the millions of people who will be affected (Millar and Bennett, 2017).

We now look at each of the three main goals (improving work incentives, reducing working poverty and benefit simplification) in turn. We also discuss the extension of conditionality.

Improving work incentives

Increasing employment by improving work incentives is at the heart of Universal Credit. The intention is both to stimulate more people to enter work (work participation) and for those in work to increase their hours (work intensity). The integrated payment means there is no need to make a new claim when starting work or increasing hours, and the level of the work allowance and the single withdrawal rate were intended to ensure that work pays more than non-work, and extra work hours means more money. Estimates of the initial proposals suggested that this would be the case (Brewer et al, 2011). But latter estimates, taking account of the actual design, were more cautious. Overall, there are likely to be fewer households with very high marginal tax rates (Browne et al, 2016). But the work incentives for lone parents, people who rent and second earners in couples have been reduced by the 2015 changes outlined above (Finch, 2015a). The impact on the work incentives for 'second earners' is particularly problematic for women in couples, with a potential impact on their longer-term employment and incomes (see Chapter 6, this volume). The early evidence on the impact on employment (DWP, 2017d) finds that Universal Credit claimants are more likely to be in work at any point within six months of their claim than a matched group of Jobseeker's Allowance claimants (63 per cent compared with 59 per cent). However, this analysis relates only to single unemployed claimants without children. There is some research from the formal DWP evaluation on the 'claimant journey' for families (DWP, 2017f). But estimates of the employment outcomes for the much larger population of couples and people with children will only become available as the scheme is rolled out.

Reducing working poverty

The second key goal is to reduce in-work poverty. As with work incentives, there was initially an upbeat assessment by the government of the likely impact on poverty. But the changes to Universal Credit introduced by the Coalition government in 2015, as outlined above, included cuts that would directly impact working families with children. Some of these cuts would be offset by the rise in the National/Living Wage, but nevertheless it has been estimated that working households with children would lose an average of £1,300 in 2020 (Keen and Kennedy, 2016). Finch (2015b) estimates that, taking account of all the benefit changes, about 600,000 more children will be in poverty by 2020, with two-thirds of this increase among children in working households.

There has also been concern that other aspects of the design may cause difficulties with budgeting and potentially create hardship. The first payments take several weeks to come through, possibly leaving people with no immediate source of income. The monthly payments in arrears are likely to be problematic for some, as people on low incomes often manage their money over shorter time periods. There is no flexibility of different payments being received on different days of the week or month, as previously. The increase in foodbank use has been attributed to delays in payments (The Trussell Trust, 2017), and housing associations report significant rises in rent arrears (House of Commons Work and Pensions Committee, 2017). The requirement for all of Universal Credit to be paid into one account also raises concerns about women's access to family income (Millar and Bennett, 2017; see Chapter 6, this volume). By autumn of 2017, concerns about implementation, especially the impact of the scheme, and measures to reduce waiting days were announced in the 2017 Budget (Brewer et al, 2017; Kennedy et al, 2017).

Benefit simplification

The promise of simplification has been an important factor in the general political support for Universal Credit, with the replacement of six benefits by one appearing to result in a much simpler system. The 'digital by design' approach – claiming, providing evidence of jobseeking and reporting changes in circumstances online – is also intended to streamline the system. So, too, is the automatic provision by employers of real-time information on changes in earnings. But in practice, these systems have to work with the realities of how people live, the changes in their circumstances over time, and how they interact with the benefit system. Millar and Bennett (2017) argue that many of the key design features – the monthly assessment, the direct payments, the digital systems – are far from simple for claimants and out of line with the research evidence about how people on low incomes live, and that this is likely to cause ongoing problems. Harris (2013, p 250) concludes that, 'the legal framework [for Universal Credit] remains … one of the most complex across the whole field of public law, reflecting in part the complexity of the underlying policy.' Universal Credit may be a simplification of the system, but that does not, in itself, make it a simple system.

Extending conditionality

Financial incentives are not the only route to increased work participation and intensity. The rules about availability for work, jobseeking and increasing hours of work are also important. These form the basis for the claimant commitment, which all must sign, including both members of a couple. The aim is to place people into one of four groups: (i) no work-related requirements; (ii) work-focused interviews; (iii) work preparation; or (iv) all work-related requirements. The first three groups are confined to those with work and work-related activity limitations (for example, disability, caring for very young children). The fourth is the default group into which most people are expected to be placed. Failure to comply with the terms of the claimant commitment can result in financial sanctions in the form of a reduction or loss of benefits for a specified length of time.

Universal Credit also extends work requirements to some people already in work who are required to seek extra hours or increased pay if they are working part time and earning below the equivalent of 35 hours at National Minimum/Living Wage (special rules apply to the self-employed). There are two main justifications for this in-work conditionality. The first is that it is necessary to prevent people from just choosing to work a few hours a week with income topped up by the state (a sort of 'working dependency'). Prior to Universal Credit, eligibility for in-work benefits required meeting a weekly hours threshold (16 or 24), which set a limit to the level of part-time work that was possible. The second is that people should aim to progress in work, to improve their situations by working more hours, in current or additional jobs. The DWP 'work coaches' are there to provide support in order to help people make this progress in work. But work coaches also apply the sanctions, so there is a potential tension in their roles and relationships with claimants. Even in the early implementation, the imposition of in-work requirements on working people has been met with some perplexity and confusion by those affected, who feel they are already meeting their obligations (Wright et al, 2016).

Dwyer and Wright (2014, p 33) conclude that 'the type and scale of the conditionality changes within Universal Credit (particularly in combination with the Work Programme) represent a fundamental change to the principles on which the British welfare state was founded.' They identify a shift from a shared social contract to 'a new ubiquitous conditionality' that puts the onus on to individuals, without any similar obligations on the state or employers. By blurring the distinction between people out of work and people in work, the legitimacy of support for both groups may increasingly come under challenge.

Conclusion

The policy measures discussed in this chapter have, over the course of the past 30 or so years, reconstructed the social security benefit system for people of working age. Social security as wage *replacement* has increasingly become social security as wage *supplement*. Most working-age adults are now subject to work obligations as a condition of receiving support, and this includes groups who in the past would not have been designated as potentially in work. Lone parents, for example, are no longer supported as full-time carers unless they have very young children or significant caring responsibilities. Both members of couples, including families with children, are expected to be in work. People with disabilities must meet stringent tests of work capability. Some people in work must also seek to increase their work activity in order to receive support. Conditionality in respect of availability for work, jobseeking and increasing work intensity has become central to the system, affecting millions of people both in and out of work.

Overview

Social security support for people out of work has become a mainly means-tested system of support with benefit receipt dependent on fulfilling stringent conditions of availability for work and job search.

These work obligations are required for most people of working age, including lone parents and people with disabilities. Some people in part-time work are also subject to work obligations, as part of the requirements for Universal Credit.

In-work wage supplements have become a central element in the UK system of social security.

Universal Credit, when fully implemented, will include about 7 to 8 million households. This is a major change to the social security system, and it is intended to transform not just the systems, but also the behaviour of people in receipt.

Questions for discussion

1. Why has there been such a strong, and continuing, focus on work obligations in the social security system?
2. How well is Universal Credit meeting the original goals? What are the key factors in this?
3. What is the case for and against increased work conditionality in relation to (a) lone parents and (b) disability benefit claimants?

Key reading

For a historical perspective, see Grover, C. (2016) *Social security and wage poverty: Historical and policy aspects of supplementing wages in Britain and beyond*, London: Palgrave Macmillan.

For an account of the politics of Universal Credit, see Timmins, N. (2016) *Universal Credit: From disaster to recovery?*, London: Institute for Government.

For more on Universal Credit, see Millar, J. and Bennett, F. (2017) 'Universal Credit: Assumptions, contradictions and virtual reality', *Social Policy and Society*, vol 16, no 2, pp 169-82 and Dwyer, P. and Wright, S. (2014) 'Universal Credit, ubiquitous conditionality and its implications for social citizenship', *Journal of Poverty and Social Justice*, vol 22, no 1, pp 27-35(9).

Website resources

http://researchbriefings.parliament.uk
  House of Commons Library, Research briefings

www.gov.uk/government/organisations/department-for-work-pensions/about/statistics
www.gov.uk/government/collections/universal-credit-statistics
  DWP statistics

www.ifs.org.uk/research_areas/116
  Institute for Fiscal Studies, Tax and benefit system

www.resolutionfoundation.org
  Resolution Foundation

http://revenuebenefits.org.uk/universal-credit
  Revenue Benefits

References

Abel-Smith, B. and Townsend, P. (1965) *The poor and the poorest*, London: Bell & Sons.

Adam, S. and Browne, J. (2013) *Do the UK government's welfare reforms make work pay?*, IFS Working Papers W13/26, London: Institute for Fiscal Studies.

Beveridge, W. (1942) *Social insurance and allied services*, Cmnd 6404, London: HMSO.

Brewer, M., Browne, J. and Jin, W. (2011) *Universal Credit: A preliminary analysis*, IFS Briefing Note 116, London: Institute for Fiscal Studies.

Brewer, M., Finch, D. and Tomlinson, D. (2017) *Universal remedy: Ensuring Universal Credit is fit for purpose*, London: Resolution Foundation.

Brown, J.C. (1983) *Family Income Supplement: Family Income Support – Studies of the social security system Part 1*, London: Policy Studies Institute.

Browne, J., Hood, A. and Joyce, R. (2016) *The (changing) effects of universal credit*, IFS Green Budget, London: Institute for Fiscal Studies.

Centre for Social Justice (2009) *Breakthrough Britain: Dynamic benefits – Towards welfare that works*, London: Centre for Social Justice.

Dean, H. and Taylor-Gooby, P. (1992) *Dependency culture: The explosion of a myth*, London: Routledge.

DHSS (Department of Health and Social Security (1985) *The reform of social security*, London: HMSO.

DWP (Department for Work and Pensions) (2010a) *21st century welfare*, Green Paper, Cm 7913, London: The Stationery Office (www.gov.uk/government/uploads/system/uploads/attachment_data/file/181139/21st-century-welfare_1_.pdf).

DWP (2010b) *Universal Credit: Welfare that works*, White Paper, Cm 7957, London: The Stationery Office (www.gov.uk/government/uploads/system/uploads/attachment_data/file/48897/universal-credit-full-document.pdf).

DWP (2015) *Universal Credit at work*, London: DWP.

DWP (2016) *Employment and Support Allowance: Work Capability Assessments, mandatory reconsiderations and appeals*, London: DWP.

DWP (2017a) *Income Support lone parent regime statistics*, London: DWP.

DWP (2017b) *Lone parents receiving JSA: Monthly claimant count* (www.gov.uk/government/statistics/lone-parents-receiving-jsa-monthly-claimant-count).

DWP (2107c) *Quarterly statistics,* London: DWP.

DWP (2017d) *Universal Credit statistics to June 2017*, London: DWP.

DWP (2107e) *Universal Credit employment impact analysis: Update, September 2017*, London: DWP.

DWP (2107f) *Universal Credit test and learn evaluation: Families*, London: DWP.

Dwyer, P. and Wright, S. (2014) 'Universal Credit, ubiquitous conditionality and its implications for social citizenship', *Journal of Poverty and Social Justice*, vol 22, no 1, pp 27-35(9).

Falk, G. and Crandall-Hollick, M.L. (2016) *The Earned Income Tax Credit (EITC): An overview*, Washington, DC: Congressional Research Service.

Finch, D. (2015a) *A budget for workers?*, London: Resolution Foundation.

Finch, D. (2015b) *A poverty of information: Assessing the government's new child poverty focus and future trends*, London: Resolution Foundation.

Finch, D., Corlett, A. and Alakeson, V. (2014) *Universal Credit: A policy under review*, London: Resolution Foundation.

Freud, D. (2007) *Reducing dependency, increasing opportunity: Options for the future of welfare to work*, London: The Stationery Office.

Grover, C. (2015) 'Employment and Support Allowance, the summer budget and less eligible disabled people', *Disability & Society*, vol 30, p 10.

Grover, C. (2016) *Social security and wage poverty: Historical and policy aspects of supplementing wages in Britain and beyond*, London: Palgrave Macmillan.

Harris, N. (2013) *Law in a complex state: Complexity in the law and structure of welfare*, Oxford: Hart Publishing.

HMRC (HM Revenue & Customs) (2017) *Child and Working Tax Credits statistics, UK: Finalised annual awards in 2015-16*, London: HMRC.

HM Treasury (1998a) *The modernisation of Britain's tax and benefit system, Number 2, Work incentives: A report by Martin Taylor*, London: HM Treasury.

HM Treasury (1998b) *The modernisation of Britain's tax and benefit system, Number 3, The Working Families Tax Credit and work incentives*, London: HM Treasury.

HM Treasury (2002) *The modernisation of Britain's tax and benefit system, Number 10, Child and Working Tax Credits*, London: HM Treasury.

Holmes, E., Pickles, C. and Titley, H. (2015) *Employment and Support Allowance: The case for change*, London: Reform.

House of Commons Hansard (2016) *Welfare reform: Written statement*, HCWS96, Damian Green, July, London: House of Commons.

House of Commons Social Security Select Committee (1997) *Social security first report: Taxes and benefits*, London: The Stationery Office.

House of Commons Work and Pensions Committee (2007) *Benefits simplification, Second report of session 2005-06*, London: The Stationery Office.

House of Commons Work and Pensions Committee (2014) *Universal Credit implementation: Monitoring DWP's performance in 2012-13*, HC 1209, London: The Stationery Office.

House of Commons Work and Pensions Committee (2017) *Universal Credit update inquiry*, London: House of Commons.

Immervoll, H. and Pearson, M. (2009) *A good time for making work pay? Taking stock of in-work benefits and related measures across the OECD*, OECD Social, Employment and Migration Working Papers No 81, Paris: OECD Publishing.

Keen, R. and Kennedy, S. (2016) *Universal Credit changes from April 2016*, House of Commons Library Briefing Paper no CBP7446, London: House of Commons Library.

Kennedy, S., Keen, R. and Wilson, W. (2017) *Universal Credit roll-out: Autumn/winter 2017*, House of Commons Library Briefing Paper no 8096, London: House of Commons Library.

Kiernan, K., Land, H. and Lewis, J. (1998) *Lone motherhood in twentieth-century Britain: From footnote to front page*, Oxford: Oxford University Press.

Kenworthy, L. (2015) *Do employment-conditional earnings subsidies work?*, ImPRovE Working Paper No 15/10, Antwerp: Herman Deleeck Centre for Social Policy, University of Antwerp.

Leaker, D. (2009) 'Unemployment: Trends since the 1970s', *Economic & Labour Market Review*, vol 3, no 2, pp 37-41.

Lindsay, C. and Houston, D. (eds) (2013) *Disability benefits, welfare reform and employment policy*, Basingstoke: Palgrave Macmillan.

Millar, J. (2009) 'Tax credits', in J. Millar (ed) *Understanding social security* (2nd edn), Bristol: Policy Press, pp 233-251.

Millar, J. and Bennett, F. (2017) 'Universal Credit: Assumptions, contradictions and virtual reality', *Social Policy and Society*, vol 16, no 2, pp 169-82.

NAO (National Audit Office) (2006) *Dealing with the complexity of the benefits system*, HC592, London: The Stationery Office.

ONS (Office for National Statistics) (2016a) *UK labour market statistics: Nov 2016* (www.ons.gov.uk/releases/uklabourmarketstatisticsnov2016).

ONS (2016b) *Working and workless households in the UK: Apr to June 2016* (www.ons.gov.uk/releases/workingandworklesshouseholdsintheukaprtojune2016).

Public Accounts Committee (2006) *Tackling the complexity of the benefits system*, HC765, London: The Stationery Office.

Pyper, D. and Brown, J. (2017) *Zero hours contracts*, House of Commons Library, Briefing paper number 06553, London: House of Commons Library.

Royston, S. and Royston, S. (2012) *Disability and Universal Credit*, London: Citizen's Advice/The Children's Society/Disability Rights UK.

Rubery, J., Keizer, A. and Grimshaw, D. (2016) 'Flexibility bites back: The multiple and hidden costs of flexible employment policies', *Human Resource Management Journal*, vol 26, issue 3, pp 235-51.

Sainsbury, R. and Stanley, K. (2007) 'One for all: Active welfare and the single working-age benefit', in J. Bennett and G. Cooke (eds) *It's all about you: Citizen-centred welfare*, London: Institute for Public Policy Research, pp 43-56.

Sykes, J., Kritz, K., Edin, K. and Halpern-Meekin, S. (2015) 'Dignity and dreams: What the Earned Income Tax Credit (EITC) means to low-income families', *American Sociological Review*, vol 80, no 2, pp 243-67.

Timmins, N. (2016) *Universal Credit: From disaster to recovery?*, London: Institute for Government.

Trussell Trust, The (2017) *Early warnings: Universal Credit and foodbanks*, Salisbury: The Trussell Trust.

Whitworth, A. and Griggs, J. (2013) 'Lone parents and welfare-to-work conditionality: Necessary, just, effective?', *Ethics and Social Welfare*, vol 7, no 2, pp 124-40.

Wright, S., Dwyer, P., McNeill, J. and Stewart, A.B.R. (2016) *First wave findings: Universal Credit*, York: University of York.

4

Disabled people and carers

Roy Sainsbury

Summary

The UK social security system is somewhat unusual in its provisions for disabled people and the people who care for them compared with other countries. In addition to income replacement benefits for people outside the labour market, since the 1970s there have been benefits that address the extra costs of being disabled and the loss of income from work for carers. These benefits have been through a series of reforms in subsequent decades, but were not included in the major social security changes from 2010 onwards that saw the introduction of Universal Credit.

This chapter will:

- explain the evolution of extra costs and benefits for carers from the 1970s to the present day;
- explore the rationale, aims and objectives of these benefits;
- look at how extra costs and benefits for carers are addressed in other countries;
- explore the role these benefits play in the lives of the recipients;
- explain some contemporary issues, including adequacy, and the relationships of these benefits with employment;
- reflect on how these benefits might evolve in the future.

Introduction

Having a long-term health or disabling condition has a range of possible economic consequences such as being out of the labour market and having a reduced standard of living compared with others in the population. The UK social security system recognises the reduced earning capacity of disabled people through a range of income replacement benefits including Employment and Support Allowance and more recently Universal Credit (see Chapter 3, this volume). However, disability or long-term sickness is also known to generate extra costs for everyday items such as heating, food, transport, and personal care and assistance.

The economic impacts of disability do not only fall on to disabled people themselves, of course. Family, friends and neighbours who contribute in some way to the care of a disabled person can all be affected, and those who contribute large amounts of time to caring for others experience the greatest financial effects.

In this chapter we examine how the UK social security system responds to the extra financial needs of disabled people and the financial disadvantages faced by carers. We look at the evolution of benefits, their rationale, their use by claimants and the issues and problems that persist. We will see how much these provisions cost and how they compare with our European neighbours. The overall story that emerges is one of general consensus, progress and expansion from the 1970s until the onset of the global economic crisis in 2008, after which the story becomes more one of controversy, retrenchment and contraction.

The evolution of extra needs benefits

Personal Independence Payment is the current principal extra needs benefit for disabled people. This was first introduced in 2012 for new claimants, followed by a rolling programme over several years of 'migrating' recipients of its predecessor benefit, Disability Living Allowance, on to the new benefit. Disability Living Allowance itself was the product of merging two earlier benefits, Attendance Allowance and Mobility Allowance, first introduced in the 1970s.

It is important to note that from the first introduction of extra needs benefits in the 1970s eligibility has been based on an assessment of people's needs only. Benefits have always been non-contributory and non-means-tested, with no work conditionality attached to their receipt. They can be paid to rich and poor, and to people who are in work or unemployed, and are therefore as close to a universal benefit (see Chapter 1, this volume) as we have in the UK social security system.

The evolution of extra needs benefits has therefore essentially taken place in three phases, as set out in Box 4.1.

Phase 1: Attendance Allowance and Mobility Allowance (1970s)

The emergence of extra needs benefits in the 1970s was one of the policy outcomes of a major survey of disabled people carried out by the Office of Population Censuses and Surveys (OPCS) in 1968-69. Among other things this survey revealed much higher levels of disability among the UK population than previously thought, with large numbers of people reported as requiring help to deal with the demands of everyday living. Although the Labour government of the time lost power before it could act on the findings, the incoming Conservative government picked up the policy and introduced Attendance Allowance in 1971 for people needing attention or supervision during both the day and night. In 1972 a new lower rate of Attendance Allowance was introduced for people whose needs occurred in the day *or* the night, thus creating a structure for the benefit that endured for the next 20 years.

Box 4.1: The evolution of extra needs benefits: three phases

Phase 1: 1970s
- Attendance Allowance, 1971
- Mobility Allowance, 1975

Phase 2: early 1990s
- Replacement of Attendance Allowance and Mobility Allowance in 1992 with:
  - Disability Living Allowance (for children and working-age claimants)
  - Attendance Allowance (for people over 65)

Phase 3: post-2010
- Replacement of Disability Living Allowance with Personal Independence Payment

The history of Mobility Allowance followed a different course. Mobility assistance for disabled people dates from 1921 when ex-service personnel injured in the First World War were given motorised bath chairs. A one-person, three-wheel vehicle (popularly known as the 'trike') gradually replaced the bath chairs, and after the Second World War eligibility was extended to civilians (in response to the large numbers of people disabled in the war). An alternative cash allowance was also available to enable people to buy adapted cars (the forerunner of the Motability scheme still in operation in 2017). The trike was, however, notoriously dangerous, could only carry one person and effectively excluded people who were, for a variety of reasons, unable to drive one. The policy response was to introduce a cash benefit, Mobility Allowance, to replace the trike scheme. Mobility Allowance was introduced in 1975.

Phase 2: Disability Living Allowance and Attendance Allowance (early 1990s)

The OPCS carried out further major surveys of disabled people in the UK between 1985 and 1988. One important finding was that although *severely* disabled people were well served by the existing Attendance Allowance and Mobility Allowance schemes, a large group of *moderately* disabled people did not qualify for either benefit but nevertheless incurred (sometimes considerable) extra costs. The policy response from the then Conservative government was to reform Attendance Allowance and Mobility Allowance. A new benefit, Disability

Living Allowance, was created by the amalgamation of Attendance Allowance and Mobility Allowance for people under 65 (including children). Disability Living Allowance had two components, a *care* and *mobility* component, but each had an additional, lower level of award, in recognition of the needs of people with moderate disabilities. Hence the care component now had three levels, paid at a higher, middle or lower rate, and the mobility component was paid at either a higher or lower rate. Claimants could claim either or both of the components.

Attendance Allowance was retained for claimants over 65 but only assessed on their care needs; there was no entitlement to any financial help with their mobility needs. (Under the former Mobility Allowance scheme, older people up to the age of 80 were eligible, such that the 1992 reforms represent a level of retrenchment for people of pension age.)

Phase 3: Personal Independence Payment (post-2010)

Extra needs benefits were further reformed by the coalition government of 2010-15 in the wake of the global economic crisis that began in 2008. As part of a wave of austerity measures, the government sought to reduce the costs of Disability Living Allowance by £2 billion as part of a wider programme of cuts to the social security budget. It chose to do this by replacing Disability Living Allowance with a new benefit called Personal Independence Payment. Two crucial reforms were intended to produce the required savings: first, the lower level of the care component was abolished, and second, the new eligibility criteria were tighter than for Disability Living Allowance. The care component was renamed the 'daily living component' while the 'mobility component' retained its name (both are paid at either a 'standard' or 'enhanced' rate).

Attendance Allowance for the over-65s was not reformed at the same time. It remained essentially in its 1992 form.

The evolution of benefits for carers

Benefits for carers have primarily been intended as income replacement benefits for people who forgo earnings when they provide substantial amounts of care. They are non-contributory and have never been *fully* means-tested in the way that other income replacement benefits (such as Income Support and Universal Credit) have been. Recipients have been allowed to work, but benefit entitlement is lost if earnings reach a defined threshold. Benefits for carers place no work conditionality requirements on recipients.

The story of benefits for carers is less complicated than for extra needs benefits. From the introduction of Invalid Care Allowance in the 1970s to its replacement by Carer's Allowance in 2003 we see more of a succession of gradual policy changes rather than any kind of fundamental shift in direction. Box 4.2 shows the main milestones in the evolution of benefits for carers.

Box 4.2: The evolution of benefits for carers: two phases

Phase 1: 1970s
- Invalid Care Allowance, 1975

Phase 2: early 1990s
- Carer's Allowance, 2003

Phase 1: Invalid Care Allowance (1975)

In 1974 a government White Paper, *Social security provision for chronically sick and disabled people* (DHSS, 1974), concluded that there was 'a strong case for the provision of a non-contributory benefit' for people who acted as carers for sick and disabled people. Legislation followed in 1975 to create a new benefit, Invalid Care Allowance. Although restricted initially to single men and women who could not undertake full-time work because of their caring role for a relative, entitlement was later extended to people caring for non-relatives (in 1981) and to married women (in 1986).

Phase 2: Carer's Allowance (2003)

Following a major review of policy on caring (DH, 1999) the Labour government considered changes to Invalid Care Allowance to extend its coverage. In consequence, the benefit became available in 2002 to people over 65 and claimants were able to receive payments for eight weeks after the death of the person they were caring for. At the same time, the name of the benefit was changed to Carer's Allowance, thus removing the outmoded language of 'invalid' to refer to a disabled person.

Under current rules (in 2017) Carer's Allowance can be claimed by people providing 35 hours or more care a week for a severely disabled person in receipt of one of a range of qualifying benefits (including Attendance Allowance or the daily living component of Personal Independence Payment). Claimants can keep any earnings they receive up to a ceiling (£116 a week at 2017–18 rates). If they earn above this amount, they lose all entitlement to Carer's Allowance.

How eligibility conditions for extra needs benefits have developed

Eligibility for Personal Independence Payment is primarily based on how disability affects someone's capacity to carry out activities associated with 'daily living' and with 'getting about'. A claimant's health or type and severity of disability is not a determinant of eligibility; rather, it is the effects of these that are relevant. This approach is consistent with the *social model of disability* which proposes that 'disability' is the result of systemic barriers, negative attitudes and exclusion by society rather than being inherent to an individual because of any impairment they might have (Barnes, 1991; Oliver and Barnes, 1998).

The influence of the social model can be seen in the changes to the eligibility criteria in the three phases of development described in Box 4.1. Originally, Attendance Allowance was assessed on a person's need for personal assistance during the day and night. With the introduction of Disability Living Allowance in 1992, the criteria were based on what functions a person could do (such as lifting, reaching, washing and dressing) (Sainsbury et al, 1995). This approach was maintained under Personal Independence Payment. Entitlement to Mobility Allowance was originally based on whether a person was unable, or virtually unable, to walk. Under Disability Living Allowance claimants could also qualify if they needed assistance from another to walk outdoors. Under Personal Independence Payment, eligibility has been further extended to people who find it difficult to navigate a journey from one location to another (for example, because of a learning difficulty or mental health problem).

These changes can be seen as a reflection of the increasing understanding of disability as a social construct and how extra needs benefits can enhance social inclusion.

Uses of extra needs benefits

One often misunderstood aspect of extra needs benefits is that they are not intended to be used in any particular way, or to pay for particular goods and services. Because entitlement is based on an assessment of care (or 'daily living') and mobility needs, it is sometimes assumed that the money should be earmarked by the recipient to pay for care services or transport assistance. However, this has never been an explicit policy objective. Personal Independence Payment and its predecessors have always been presented in policy documents and debates as benefits intended to *contribute to the extra costs of disability* (see, for example, Tibble 2005). There are two aspects of extra costs: *increased* costs for things we all buy or pay for, and *additional* costs that are specific to individual disabled people. Examples of increased costs might include extra heating (because of a medical condition), extra laundry costs (because clothes and bedding need washing more frequently) or extra transport costs (because it is not possible to take cheaper options such as public transport). Additional costs might include personal care, special foods (because of specific dietary requirements), equipment (such as stair lifts, hoists, specially adapted kitchen equipment) or (again) transport (because of the need to attend hospital appointments).

Although it is possible to discuss in the abstract the potential costs of disability, it is equally useful to examine evidence on what benefit recipients actually *spend* their benefit income on and what impacts they experience as a result. In a qualitative study of the uses of Disability Living Allowance and Attendance Allowance by Corden et al (2010), a wide range of expenditures were found, but a number of other effects were described by the research participants that can be categorised as *enabling* and *preventive*. Box 4.3 summarises the study's findings.

Box 4.3: Uses of extra needs benefits

Spending on goods and services

- Residential care
- Personal care at home
- Transport
- Food
- Fuel
- Home maintenance/cleaning/ gardening
- Medical supplies/equipment
- Telephones/computers
- Social activities
- Clothes and bedding
- Treatment/tuition (for children)
- Activities/toys (for children)
- Giving presents, gifts and 'treating'

Enabling uses

- Helping money management
- Enabling people to live at home
- Enabling people to keep in touch with family/friends
- Keeping part of society/social inclusion
- Enabling paid work
- Enabling saving

Preventive effects

- Avoiding moves into residential care or nursing homes
- Avoiding deterioration in health
- Making fewer demands on formal health and social care services
- Providing a financial safety net
- Helping debt management

Source: Corden et al (2010)

What is striking from Box 4.3 is the range and diversity of the uses made of Disability Living Allowance and Attendance Allowance, and that most of these are not directly related to care or mobility needs. If it is possible to identify a common characteristic of all these uses it is that they all, in different ways, contribute to improvements in the quality of life and wellbeing of the recipients and their families. Box 4.4 presents two case studies of some imaginative and innovative uses of extra needs benefits.

Box 4.4: Using Disability Living Allowance and Attendance Allowance

Paying for pets

For some children, communication and language skills are enhanced by interaction with or observation of a cat or dog; for others, touching an animal can calm moods or stimulate positive reactions. One parent explained how their little girl continually tried to balance and walk because she wanted to follow her pet dog into the garden. One Attendance Allowance recipient explained she used her benefit to pay a dog walker. Her dog provided much-valued companionship and increased her quality of life and wellbeing, but she could not walk the dog herself because of her disability.

Paying for telephones

Ownership of a telephone was often described as 'absolutely essential' for keeping in touch with family, friends and accessing social opportunities. Having a mobile phone also meant people felt safer going to the shops on their own, because they could summon help quickly if necessary. Some people said they made heavy use of a phone in their home, using it to order taxis, give shopping orders, contact GPs and other health services etc.

Source: Corden et al (2010)

The evidence on how disabled people spend their benefit income and the wide range of positive outcomes they can achieve provides a compelling argument for at least their continuation and possibly their extension.

Trends in the numbers of extra needs benefits and benefits for carers

Data on numbers and trends in receipt of extra needs benefits and benefits for carers are not easy to summarise or interpret, not least because of changes in eligibility criteria that have at different times aimed to expand the potential claiming population or to reduce it. The general picture, however, is of a consistently increasing number of claimants over time.

In 1992, when Disability Living Allowance was introduced, there were 1.1 million claimants. Numbers grew rapidly in the next five years in line with policy intentions to expand the coverage of the benefit to people with moderate levels of disability. By 1997, there were 2 million claimants. Since then, and until the introduction of the Personal Independence Payment in 2014, there were annual increases of between 3 and 5 per cent per year, resulting in a total claiming population of 3.3 million in 2013. From 2014 onwards the combined total of new Personal Independence Payment claimants and existing Disability Living Allowance claimants has continued to rise, reaching 3.6 million in 2015 (TUC, 2011; DWP, 2016).

In 2003, when Invalid Care Allowance was renamed Carer's Allowance with expanded eligibility, there were 400,000 recipients of the benefit. Since then, numbers have more than doubled to 803,000 in 2016 (DWP, 2016).

Extra needs benefits and benefits for carers in an international context

In this section we look at how other countries in Europe address the extra costs of disabilities and the financial effects experienced by the people who care for them.

Extra needs benefits in Europe

By ratifying the UN Convention on the Rights of Persons with Disabilities in 2009, UK governments have been committed to a wide range of aims and responsibilities regarding disabled people concerning, among other things, independent living, employment, education and social security. In particular, Article 28(2)(c) of the Convention requires signatories to take 'appropriate steps' to ensure 'access by persons with disabilities and their families living in situations of poverty to assistance from the State with disability-related expenses....' (UN, 2006). As with many international agreements and conventions, there is no real detail about what its terms actually mean or how governments are meant to address and satisfy their responsibilities. There is no specification, for example, of what 'disability-related expenses' cover.

A review in 2016 (Sainsbury and Lawson, 2017) of how European countries are meeting the requirements of Article 28 found that in addition to payments through countries' social security systems (which was not common), assistance with disability-related expenses takes several different forms:

- cash transfers
- reimbursements of expenses
- grants for specific expenditures
- direct provision of services
- discounts or exemptions from taxes or charges.

Interestingly, there was widespread recognition among European countries of the extra costs of mobility for disabled people (in comparison with other types of need), but governments have responded in a variety of ways. Assistance through national benefit systems that give recipients the freedom to decide how to access transport opportunities is restricted to a handful of countries other than the UK (including the Czech Republic, Sweden, Cyprus, Greece, Ireland and Latvia). More commonly mobility is provided by more direct means. Free travel on public transport or some level of fare subsidy or reduction is provided in a number of countries (including Hungary, Portugal and the Czech Republic). Free or subsidised car parking provisions have been made in, for example, Cyprus, the Netherlands and Austria. (The UK has its own familiar 'Blue Badge' scheme administered by local authorities.) Assistance with the purchase of an adapted car or with paying for adaptations to an existing car is made in Iceland, Croatia and the UK. A range of taxes and charges that are normally applied to car users are discounted in some way for disabled people in a number of countries (including Malta, Austria, Romania and Croatia).

Benefits for carers in Europe

There is great variation in how different countries recognise and support the costs of caring for disabled adults and children within their systems of social security. In some countries (Latvia, Denmark and Austria, for example) there are provisions for making payments directly to a disabled adult as a contribution to the costs of their personal care. Although in the UK Personal Independence Payment can be paid to people with relatively moderate disabilities, some countries only pay extra needs benefits to more severely disabled people. For example, in Greece, the Paraplegia/Tetraplegia Benefit is available only to people with a tightly defined level of physical disablement, while in Cyprus the Care Allowance Scheme is restricted to quadriplegic claimants only.

In some countries separate provision is made for parents as carers of disabled children (for example, in Denmark, Slovenia and Sweden). An alternative form of support to parents of disabled children is in the Netherlands, where they can receive double the basic rate of Child Benefit for each disabled child (although this is means-tested). Similarly in Hungary parents can receive enhanced family allowances for a disabled child.

Countries with provision that resembles the UK Carer's Allowance include Ireland, Croatia and Sweden. Ireland has a similar Carer's Benefit and in addition pays recipients an annual Carer's Support Grant originally intended to allow for respite care services. In Croatia 'caretakers' looking after a disabled child or adult who is completely dependent on them for care and assistance can qualify for a monthly allowance. In Sweden the regular Care Allowance can be supplemented by a Care Allowance for additional expenses if parents of a disabled child incur particularly large expenses associated, for example, with medicines or a change of residence.

In comparison with most European countries, therefore, UK provision for carers can be viewed as more established (having been in place since 1975) even if it can be criticised for not being particularly generous (see below).

Disability and carers' benefits and employment

As mentioned above, Personal Independence Payment (and its predecessors) can be claimed by people in or out of work. There has been some controversy over the years about whether or not extra needs benefits act as a disincentive to people getting work.

Beatty et al (2009) explored the overlaps between people receiving long-term sickness benefits and Disability Living Allowance. They found that of the 1.7 million working-age recipients of Disability Living Allowance, 74 per cent also claimed a long-term sickness benefit. This should not be surprising given the stringent eligibility conditions for both sets of benefits. People receiving extra needs benefits are by definition disabled, and therefore will be disadvantaged in the labour market. A smaller proportion claimed a combination of Disability Living Allowance and other benefits (6 per cent), while 20 per cent claimed Disability Living Allowance alone, most of whom were in work.

A study of the relationship between Disability Living Allowance and work (Thomas and Griffiths, 2010) found that one in five respondents in a survey of recipients of Disability Living Allowance thought that their benefit would be affected if they were working. The authors inferred from this that some people saw Disability Living Allowance as an out-of-work benefit similar to means-tested unemployment benefits, which would be reduced or stopped if they had earnings from work, thus creating a work disincentive effect.

The coalition government of 2010–15 made use of these findings as part of its rationale for replacing Disability Living Allowance with Personal Independence Payment. In its consultation paper, *Disability Living Allowance reform* (DWP, 2010a, p 10), it argues that:

> Evidence suggests that DLA [Disability Living Allowance] can also act
> as a barrier to work, when it should enable people to lead independent

lives, including having or getting a job. DLA is widely perceived to be an out-of-work benefit and receiving it appears to reduce the likelihood of being in employment, even after allowing for the impact of health conditions or impairments. There is evidence that people who receive DLA have lower work expectations.

This is a distinctive change in the discourse around extra needs benefits from the presentation of Disability Living Allowance as something wholly positive (in helping disabled people with the inevitable extra costs they face) to becoming a problem, discouraging and preventing people from having 'independent lives' through paid work. We return to the implications of this shift in the debate in the conclusion to this chapter.

The relationship between Carer's Allowance and paid work is different. As described earlier, recipients of Carer's Allowance can earn up to £116 a week (equivalent to 15 hours at the National Living Wage of £7.50 an hour in 2017). However, it should be remembered that to be eligible for Carer's Allowance a person must be providing care for at least 35 hours a week, that is, already equivalent to a full-time job. Figure 4.1 presents data on the proportion of carers who work either full or part time or in self-employment. One striking feature is the proportion of people who not only provide over 35 hours of care a week (the threshold for Carer's Allowance) but who also hold down jobs, half of which are full time.

Figure 4.1: Carers and work: proportion of working-age carers in employment

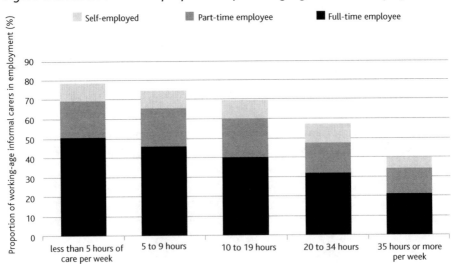

Source: Aldridge and Hughes (2016, p 22)

Adequacy of Disability Living Allowance/Personal Independence Payment and Carer's Allowance

Disability Living Allowance and Personal Independence Payment

As mentioned earlier, in policy documents dating back to the 1970s, extra needs benefits such as Disability Living Allowance and Personal Independence Payment have always been described as 'contributing to the extra costs of disability'. This wording is not accidental. These benefits are not presented as *meeting* extra costs. (The arguments underpinning Child Benefit are similar. No policy-maker has ever claimed that Child Benefit meets the costs of raising children; only that it contributes to meeting those costs.)

Debates about the adequacy of extra needs benefits have always been problematic primarily because of the difficulty (or, arguably, the impossibility) of putting a figure on the 'extra costs of disability'. For individuals these vary enormously, from a few pounds a week to thousands of pounds for people needing high levels of intensive support. The types of extra costs generated by different disabling conditions also vary enormously (consider, for example, the extra costs generated by deafness or blindness compared with those that result from a severe physical disability). Nevertheless, a commission set up by the disability charity Scope estimated that across all disabilities the average costs for disabled people were £550 a week, compared with an average income of £360 a week (Scope, 2015). A claimant receiving the maximum award from Personal Independence Payment in 2017–18 would receive £140 a week. Although the Scope figures are estimates, they give a sense of the magnitude of the gap between real costs and the level of the 'contribution' by Disability Living Allowance and Personal Independence Payment. The Scope review also reinforces the conclusion of Zaidi and Burchardt (2005, p 112) that, '... the extra costs of disability are substantial, especially for disabled people living alone, and ... such extra costs rise with severity of disability.'

Levels of extra needs benefits are clearly not set with any reference to the actual costs and expenses incurred by disabled people. Like Child Benefit, the levels are a reflection of what the government of the day decides are appropriate and affordable. Such decisions are fundamentally political and economic rather than rational or evidence-based.

Carer's Allowance

The level of Carer's Allowance (and Invalid Care Allowance before it) has always been a subject of controversy since the 1970s. The value of Invalid Care Allowance was originally set at 60 per cent of other income replacement benefits. The justification for this was that non-contributory benefits had to be lower than contributory benefits in order to maintain people's motivation and support for paying their National Insurance contributions (Brown, 1984). The extent to which this argument is valid 40 years later seems rather doubtful, particularly when some benefits with contributory and non-contributory elements (such as Employment and Support Allowance) are paid at the same basic rate.

The criticism that Carer's Allowance has been paid at a persistently low level can be easily illustrated if we compare it with the level of the National Living Wage, as shown in Table 4.1 using 2017–18 rates.

Table 4.1: Comparing Carer's Allowance and wages (2017-18 rates)

	Basic rate	Weekly amount (@ 35 hours)
National Living Wage	£7.50 an hour	£262.50
Carer's Allowance	(Equivalent to £1.80 an hour for 35 hours caring)	£62.70

As Table 4.1 shows, if Carer's Allowance was paid at the rate of the National Living Wage, claimants would receive over £260 a week for 35 hours' caring. However, they actually receive £62.70, the equivalent of an hourly rate of £1.80. And for many Carer's Allowance recipients providing more than 35 hours care, the equivalent rate falls much lower. In a review of carers in the UK by the New Policy Institute in 2016 (Aldridge and Hughes, 2016), it was estimated that there were over 700,000 carers providing 50 hours or more of care each week. At 50 hours, Carer's Allowance provides an equivalent hourly income of £1.25.

Where next for extra needs benefits and benefits for carers?

Despite the changes to extra needs benefits in the period since their introduction in the 1970s, the basic template remains in place with a clear line of development from the original Attendance Allowance to the daily living component of Personal Independence Payment and from Mobility Allowance to the mobility component of Personal Independence Payment. Successive governments have never claimed that the benefits go beyond contributing to meeting people's extra costs, and hence their value has no connection with the actual costs incurred by disabled people. Up until 2010 governments seemed to show a marked reluctance to antagonise or alienate disabled people's organisations, perceived as a powerful political force in society. However, faced with the increasing costs of Disability Living Allowance and the pressures of tackling the deficit in public finances after 2008, the coalition government changed tack. Although they held back from absorbing Disability Living Allowance into Universal Credit (the Minister for Welfare Reform, Lord Freud, said he did not want to 'go to war with everyone' over Universal Credit; see Timmins, 2016), the reform of Disability Living Allowance represented an undeniable decline in provision for disabled people.

In reality, the intended reduction in the numbers of claimants and expenditure on Personal Independence Payment had failed to materialise by 2016 some four years after its introduction (DWP, 2016). While the underlying structure of extra needs benefits seems well established, having endured for over 40 years, debates about coverage and levels of payment continue. Furthermore, some commentators have warned about a worrying shift in government attitudes towards disability policy. As the disability academic Jenny Morris wrote, referring to the period after 2010, 'the current direction of policy and public debate is undermining the legitimacy of an additional costs benefit' (Morris, 2013, p 61).

In contrast, benefits for carers, it seems, have always posed different policy challenges that arguably have never been fully addressed. For example, two important and influential public bodies have highlighted some fundamental issues with Carer's Allowance. The House of Commons Work and Pensions Committee (2008a, p 36) questioned the role and purpose of Carer's Allowance:

> ... as the scope of the Allowance has been increased, to include married women initially and then to include people over pensionable age, Carer's Allowance has become almost a hybrid. On the one hand it is an earnings replacement benefit, on the other it becomes an additional costs compensation, and it fails on both scores because of that.

In a similar vein, the National Audit Office set out the terms of an almost existential crisis at the heart of Carer's Allowance...

> ... some carers have unmet expectations in terms of whether the Allowance is a wage for caring, a reward for caring, compensation for the costs of caring, or a reflection of the extent of care they provide. (NAO, 2009, p 11)

Before 2010 some stakeholders grasped this policy challenge and in particular tried to address the implications of the dual nature of Carer's Allowance as an income replacement benefit and as compensation for extra costs borne by carers as a result of their caring. The House of Commons Work and Pensions Committee came out with firm proposals in a report in 2008:

> We ask DWP to give urgent and detailed consideration to replacing Carer's Allowance with a two-tiered benefit for carers.... A *Carer Support Allowance*, to be paid at the same rate as Jobseeker's Allowance, with the opportunity to earn a modest amount in a paid job ... and a *Caring Costs Payment*, available to all carers in intensive caring roles (35+ hours per week, consistent with existing Carer's Allowance)... (House of Commons Work and Pensions Committee, 2008b, p 12)

In the debates and discussions that informed the development of Universal Credit from 2010, the coalition government appeared to duck the challenge posed by these reports despite the fact Carer's Allowance is as much a working-age benefit as Jobseeker's Allowance, Employment and Support Allowance, Income Support and so on. In its Universal Credit White Paper, it stated:

> The Government is carefully considering whether changes to Carer's Allowance will be necessary to take account of the introduction of Universal Credit and provide clearer, more effective support for carers. (DWP, 2010b, p 19)

Despite this, at the time of writing in 2017, there seems to have been no outcome to whatever 'careful considerations' have been taking place. For example, there was no reference at all to Carer's Allowance in the Conservative Party manifesto prior to the 2017 general election. (In contrast, the Labour Party manifesto promised to increase Carer's Allowance to the level of Jobseeker's Allowance.)

Conclusion

At one level, the support to disabled people and carers through the UK social security system can be portrayed as a success story. We are one of few countries giving disabled people a universal benefit based only on an assessment of need derived from the social model of disability. However, the consensus, progress and expansion that characterised policy developments up until the global economic crisis of 2008 onwards has given way to controversy, retrenchment and contraction.

There is no doubt that extra needs benefits can make a huge difference to the lives of disabled people and are used in a wide range of ways to promote their health, wellbeing and social inclusion. Carer's Allowance also contributes positively to the incomes of carers. However, their value has been repeatedly criticised as being too low to meet the full costs of disability or to be a meaningful level of compensation for having a reduced, or no, capacity for paid employment.

In 2017 arguments continue to be held about what the purposes of Personal Independence Payment and Carer's Allowance should be. For example, the debate about the relationship between extra needs benefits and work highlights a fundamental tension in trying to reconcile the policy aims of increasing levels of employment in the population (including among those with health and disabling conditions) and supporting those who are not in work. However, a policy discourse that suggests that Disability Living Allowance and Personal Independence Payment create disincentives to work gives a clear indication about where post-2010 governments have seen the emphasis.

Finally, we must acknowledge that answers to questions about the future development of extra needs benefits and benefits for carers depend on answers to more fundamental questions about how we assess the 'right' relationship between the state and disabled people and the people who care for them. What rights should both groups be able to claim, and what responsibilities should be placed on them in return? Addressing these questions reminds us that social security is at heart a deeply normative and moral area of social policy.

Overview

The UK social security system has recognised the extra costs of disability and the financial disadvantages faced by carers since the 1970s.

The UK has wider provision for disabled people and for carers compared with most European countries.

Reforms to extra needs benefits and benefits for carers up to 2010 were generally characterised by a gradual expansion of coverage to, for example, people with learning difficulties and mental health problems (for Disability Living Allowance and Personal Independence Payment), and to married women and retirement pensioners (for Carer's Allowance).

After 2010 the introduction of Personal Independence Payment has reduced coverage (by excluding people with moderate disabilities) and tightened eligibility criteria as part of wider government austerity cuts.

Questions for discussion

1. Do you think society, through the social security system, treats disabled people and their carers fairly?
2. If you were Secretary of State for Work and Pensions, what changes would you like to see made on extra needs and carers benefits?
3. How do you assess the arguments for and against maintaining Carer's Allowance at a lower level compared with other income replacement benefits such as Income Support, Employment and Support Allowance and Universal Credit? Is a 'two-tier' Carer's Allowance the way forward?

Key reading

Aldridge, H. and Hughes, C. (2016) *Informal carers and poverty in the UK*, London: New
     Policy Institute.

Sainsbury, R. and Lawson, A. (2017) *Social protection for disabled people in Europe:
     Synthesis report*, Utrecht: Academic Network of European Disability Experts (ANED).

Scope (2015) *Driving down the extra costs disabled people face – Extra Costs Commission
     Interim report*, London, Scope.

Website resources

www.disability-europe.net
  ANED (Academic Network of European Disability Experts)

www.gov.uk/government/organisations/department-for-work-pensions
  Department for Work and Pensions

www.carersuk.org
  Carers UK

www.carers.org
  Carers Trust

www.disabilityrightsuk.org
  Disability Rights UK

www.parliament.uk/business/committees/committees-a-z/commons-select/work-and-
pensions-committee
  House of Commons Work and Pensions Select Committee

References

Aldridge, H. and Hughes, C. (2016) *Informal carers and poverty in the UK*, London:
     New Policy Institute.

Barnes, C. (1991) *Disabled people in Britain and discrimination: A case for anti-
     discrimination legislation*, London: Hurst & Company.

Beatty, C., Fothergill, S. and Platts-Fowler, D. (2009) *DLA claimants – A new
     assessment: The characteristics and aspirations of the Incapacity Benefit claimants who
     receive Disability Living Allowance*, DWP Research Report 585, London, The
     Stationery Office.

Brown, J. (1984) *The disability income system*, London: Policy Studies Institute.

Corden, A., Sainsbury, R., Irvine, A. and Clarke, S. (2010) *The impact of Disability
     Living Allowance and Attendance Allowance: Findings from exploratory qualitative
     research*, DWP Research Report No 649, London: The Stationery Office.

DH (Department of Health) (1999) *Caring about carers: A national strategy for carers*,
     London: DH.

DHSS (Department of Health and Social Security) (1974) *Social security provision
     for chronically sick and disabled people*, HC 276, London: HMSO.

DWP (Department for Work and Pensions) (2010a) *Disability Living Allowance reform*, Cm 7984, London: The Stationery Office.

DWP (2010b) *Universal Credit: Welfare that works*, Cm 7957, London: The Stationery Office.

DWP (2016) *Quarterly statistical summary: November 2016*, London, DWP.

House of Commons Work and Pensions Committee (2008a) *Valuing and supporting carers*, HC 485-I, London: The Stationery Office.

House of Commons Work and Pensions Committee (2008b) *Valuing and supporting carers, Government response to the Committee's fourth report of session 2007–08,* HC 105, London: The Stationery Office.

Morris, J. (2013) 'Do as you would be done by: Poverty and disability', in J. Derbyshire (ed) *Poverty in the UK: Can it be eradicated?*, London/York: Prospect/Joseph Rowntree Foundation, pp 60-4.

NAO (National Audit Office) (2009) *Supporting carers to care*, HC 130, London: The Stationery Office.

Oliver, M. and Barnes, C. (1998) *Disabled people and social policy: From exclusion to inclusion*, London: Longman.

Sainsbury, R. and Lawson, A. (2017) *Social protection for disabled people in Europe: Synthesis report*, Utrecht: Academic Network of European Disability Experts (ANED).

Sainsbury, R., Hirst, M. and Lawton, D. (1995) *Evaluation of Disability Living Allowance and Attendance Allowance*, DSS Research Report No 41, London: The Stationery Office.

Scope (2015) *Driving down the extra costs disabled people face – Extra Costs Commission Interim report*, London: Scope.

Thomas, A. and Griffiths, R. (2010) *Disability Living Allowance and work: Exploratory research and evidence review*, DWP Research Report 648, London: The Stationery Office.

Tibble, M. (2005) *Review of existing research on the extra costs of disability*, DWP Working Paper 21, London: Department for Work and Pensions.

Timmins, N. (2016) *Universal Credit: From disaster to recovery?*, London: Institute for Government.

TUC (Trades Union Congress) (2011) 'Why are there more DLA claimants?', Touchstone blog (http://touchstoneblog.org.uk/2011/08/why-are-there-more-dla-claimants/).

UN (United Nations) (2006) *The United Nations Convention on the Rights of Persons with Disabilities* (www.un.org/development/desa/disabilities/convention-on-the-rights-of-persons-with-disabilities.html).

Zaidi, A. and Burchardt, T. (2005) 'Comparing incomes when needs differ: Equivalization for the extra costs of disability in the UK', *Review of Income and Wealth*, vol 25, no 1, pp 89-114.

5

Protecting pensioners

Stephen McKay

Summary

The UK's system of providing incomes for older people is complex, and includes extensive non-state as well as state elements. In this chapter we explore:

- controversial reforms to increase the state pension age – when the state pension may first be received – while bolstering the amount of the main state pension;
- increases to pensions as part of the so-called 'triple lock', which seem to have helped reduce the number of pensioners on a low income. This positive treatment of state pensions stands in marked contrast to the approach to benefits for working-age people;
- the non-state part of pension income, which remains significant in the UK, and plays a major part in generating the high degree of inequality in pensioner incomes;
- the long-run demographic pressures that focus on the costs of pensions, and other provisions associated with getting older, such as social care.

Introduction

Benefits for older people remain the largest part of the UK social security system. They also represent an area of the social security system that has been unusually well protected since 2010, despite a policy of austerity in the public finances that has seen significant reductions in spending on benefits for those of working age (McKay and Rowlingson, 2016). The benefit freezes and cuts affecting the working population have simply not been applied, in most cases, to those above state pension age.

Most people expect that after a period of time in the labour market, towards the end of their lives they will have some time in retirement, away from a paid job. This raises the question of how they will obtain the incomes on which to live. Prior to the 20th century, people would expect to work until death or incapacity prevented them from doing so, at that point relying on support from their families, or possibly from limited local social support arrangements, unless they could save for themselves. Expectations have changed, and there is an aspiration that people may be retired for a *substantial* number of years or even decades – reflecting increases in life expectancy for older people. Taking this as a starting perspective, the provision of security in retirement must depend on having some access to financial resources other than earnings from paid work, although earnings will remain an option for some older people. This new package of income comprises benefits available from the state (safety net benefits, contributory benefits) and private resources that individuals have managed to save as cash, as assets of various kinds or in the form of occupational or other pension products.

However, in practice, left to their own devices, people may under-save for retirement. This may be the result of low incomes during their working lives, necessitating a need for redistribution to keep them out of poverty. They may also be unaware of their chances of living to a good age, and hence require incentives, or to be compelled to save a satisfactory amount to provide an income when work ends.

It is well known that the UK population is ageing. People are living longer, and there are some 'bulges' in the population that mean that certain larger cohorts will be retiring in the near future while being replaced in the labour market by smaller later cohorts (see Figure 5.1). The 'baby boomers', generally defined as those born from 1945-65, are (in 2018) aged 53-73. The pension costs of this unusually large cohort will begin to fall on those born later, who are among smaller birth cohorts than the baby boomers.

In this chapter, we first describe the nature of benefits for older people in the UK, and how policy has developed since 2010 in particular. We identify the main features of the pensions systems, and how they affect people's incomes in the longer term. We also look at the challenges to be faced in the future.

The UK pensions system

The World Bank (1994) suggested that three pillars of pension provision were required. These were: a flat-rate public pension (to combat poverty); forced savings through the private sector; and voluntary savings on top. About 20 years later, this set of pillars was updated to five, to allow for a more rounded analysis of countries' pension income systems (The World Bank, 2005), as shown in Box 5.1. The new conceptual framework put forward the idea of a wider range of pillars capturing more issues about sustaining living standards in older age.

Figure 5.1: Population structure of the UK, 2015

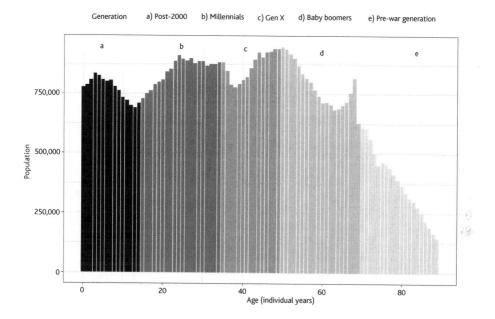

Source: ONS population statistics

Box 5.1: The World Bank's revised multi-pillar pension structure

- A non-contributory pension (or zero pillar).
- A contributory system replacing income (first pillar).
- Forced savings (second pillar) into an individual savings account.
- Further voluntary savings (third pillar).
- In addition, there may be expectations around informal intra-family or intergenerational sources of support, and also mentioned are access to healthcare and housing, within wider social policy.

What this framework helps illustrate is the wide range of different sources of incomes that are likely to be available to older people, and the likely interplay of different elements provided both by the state and private sector organisations, and indeed informally, through the family. Moreover, in looking at the provision of income to older people, we should not ignore the wider needs for care, whether 'social care' or healthcare, and for housing provision, among other areas of social policy.

We see different elements of this framework in the UK system of income and support for older people. The pensions system in the UK is complex; indeed, it has been described as 'the most complex pension system in the world' (Pensions Commission, 2004, p 210), with many different elements resulting from incremental and larger structural reforms occurring at regular intervals in the past. As is common for the UK, but less common in many countries, there is a rather large element provided outside the state (private pensions, which come in various varieties) in addition to a large state component. Moreover, the state regulates non-state provision, and to a large extent incentivises it, though tax reliefs, and mandates it, through auto-enrolment of employees into one of a range of private pensions.

The state provides a main pension that people receive, the Basic State Pension, but this is in the process of moving towards a New State Pension that integrates both the Basic Pension and its additional earnings-related elements. This complicates the description we provide as, commonly with pensions reform, existing rights built up under previous schemes are respected when there are new reforms to future entitlements. A simplified account is presented concerning the newer and older systems, which will each continue for some considerable time.

Contributory state pensions

The contributory state pension arrangements are in a state of flux. The bedrock of the overall pensions system is the **Basic State Pension**, the origins of which can be traced back to the Beveridge report (Beveridge, 1942) that laid the foundations for the postwar welfare state. From April 2016 new pensioners instead received the **New State Pension** (discussed below).

Importantly, the Basic State Pension is a contributory benefit with the aim of providing a subsistence level of income that would, in principle, provide enough to live on, but would not support a more comfortable lifestyle. One of Beveridge's 'guiding principles' was that,

> … in establishing a national minimum, it should leave room and encouragement for voluntary action by each individual to provide more than that minimum for himself and his family. (Beveridge, 1942, p 7)

People accumulate rights to a Basic State Pension by paying National Insurance contributions (NICs) over their working lifetimes – those in paid work earning above a relatively low threshold pay NICs. However, a scheme that based rights only on earnings would exclude those unable to work, such as those who are unemployed, those who have a disability or are raising children. Therefore, those receiving earnings-replacement benefits have their state pension rights maintained through a system of credits, while those caring for children or people with disabilities have to pay in for fewer years to attain the same level of entitlement. The Basic State Pension is paid at a flat rate for those entitled to the maximum amount (that is, there is an upper value that no one exceeds, although those with gaps in their employment history may get less than this maximum). For those reaching State Pension Age before April 2016, the maximum for a single person is around £120 per week (in 2017).

While the pension for single people is flat rate, an additional amount may also be paid for a spouse (that is, a married partner). This may be paid when that spouse has not achieved a similar or larger entitlement to their own pension. Indeed, until 1977 it was possible for married women to pay a much lower rate of NICs (through the 'married women's option') in return for not accumulating rights to the Basic State Pension or other contributory benefits. Instead, they would have an entitlement equivalent to 60 per cent of the basic rate, on the basis of their husband's contributions, when both reached State Pension Age. After 1977, no new women could take this route, but those who had chosen this option were permitted to continue with this approach. Some women are, however, said to be surprised at their lack of personal entitlement on reaching pensionable age (House of Commons Work and Pensions Committee, 2016b; Thurley and Keen, 2017b). The House of Commons report noted that, 'Although there may always be communication issues between government and citizens when laws change, more could and should have been done, especially between 1995 and 2009' (House of Commons Work and Pensions Committee, 2016b, p 3).

For those retiring by 2016, the Basic State Pension could also be topped up by a range of state-provided earnings-related provisions. The idea behind these has been to emulate the system of non-state pensions (see below) for those whose employment does not permit access to a good private pension. This means that the level of pension from the state, overall, moves closer to lifetime earnings rather than being simply flat rate. Provisions have changed over time, with greater and lesser degrees of ambition (from the 1960s Graduated Retirement Benefit, to the 1970s State Earnings-Related Pension Scheme [SERPS], to the 2000s State Second Pension [S2P]). There was therefore an attempt to include provisions that related to the overall size of contributions, but the links have generally been weak, complex, and subject to frequent changes in legislation.

The New State Pension brings together the Basic State Pension with the earnings-related elements, to create a scheme that remains flat rate but is paid at a higher level. The full New State Pension is around £155 per week, or about £35 higher than the older Basic State Pension scheme, through consolidating the separate previously earnings-related amounts. This kind of consolidating reform is beneficial to lower earners, who would have qualified for more limited additional pensions, but less good for middle earners who might have achieved more through their previous state earnings-related provision. In the past, many people on higher earnings elected to 'contract out' of an element of SERPS and instead had a non-state pension with a contribution that would otherwise have gone to such a state additional pension. For this group, the arrangements may be less beneficial than those applying before.

Other state benefits

The state retirement pension, since it replaces earnings, may be not claimed alongside certain other benefits designed to play that role, such as Jobseeker's Allowance (JSA) or Employment and Support Allowance (ESA). However, running alongside the contributory pensions are:

- A general means-tested benefit – Pension Credit – for those with low overall incomes. This continues to exist, because older people are outside of the new Universal Credit scheme for those of working age.
- Other means-tested benefits that are also available to the working-age population, such as Housing Benefit or Council Tax Support.
- Other contingent benefits that are similar to those for younger people although sometimes with some changes (disability benefits, such as Attendance Allowance for those with care needs).
- There are also some separate provisions that are age-related, such as the Winter Fuel Payment, free bus passes, free prescriptions, free eye tests and, for the over-75s, free TV licences.

Pension Credit is income-related and ensures that people achieve a basic minimum level of income. In past years this has been set at a higher level than the Basic State Pension, so that someone with only the Basic State Pension was generally entitled to some element of Pension Credit, plus Housing Benefit if renting, and Council Tax Support. As a means-tested benefit, Pension Credit is subject to several concerns that apply more generally to benefits based on a test of means (income and capital). In particular, it is subject to potential non-take-up, as people are either not aware of the potential benefit to them, or feel it would be stigmatising to claim a benefit that relies on being poor/vulnerable rather than one available as of right, like the contributory Basic State Pension. Various steps have been taken to try to ensure that take-up is high, but the potential for non-take-up remains. There may also be negative effects on incentives to save, a 'pensions trap', which means that those who may expect to rely on Pension Credit have a reduced incentive to make any provision for themselves as it might just eliminate their entitlement to Pension Credit. Others might suggest that a large means-tested benefit serves to undermine part of the principle of a contributory scheme – older people may point to those who have not saved during their lifetimes who then appear to be just as well-off financially as those who have worked and saved into the state pension.

As listed above, older people may also receive means-tested support for the costs of rent, and for Council Tax. These depend on personal circumstances, although sometimes older people receive more favourable treatment. The controversial 'Bedroom Tax', which limits the amount of eligible rent depending on family size, does not apply to older people. Some of the disability benefits available to older people, such as Attendance Allowance, have also avoided some of the cuts and restrictions applied to Disability Living Allowance for the younger population that is transitioning to the Personal Independence Payment (PIP).

Last, there are a few provisions made for older people that may or may not be considered part of social security but that are often controversial when considered for cuts, such as the Winter Fuel Payment, free bus passes and, for the over-75s, free TV licences. Indeed, the last of these forms part of the BBC's budget and policy area. The other elements have proven controversial, partly through being universal – with the idea that richer pensioners 'don't need them'.

Private pensions and savings

People may choose to save into a range of different savings products and investments to help provide for their retirement. In the UK the idea of saving by buying houses, including for private renting, remains a popular concept. However, the vehicles clearly designed for older age are a range of non-state pensions. These may be provided through an employer (occupational or workplace pensions) or taken out as a savings product with a financial provider (personal pensions).

Among employer pensions, products used to be most often provided on a 'defined benefit' basis, where benefits were generally linked to the level of salary at retirement, or increasingly, an average of their salary over their working lives. Over time these have generally been replaced with 'defined contribution' schemes, where the level of pension depends on the amount invested over time and the financial returns. Leaving aside any conceptual differences, in practice, employers nearly always put less money into defined contribution schemes – and often employees do, too (Rowlingson and McKay, 2017, Figure 26).

In most cases, when people join them, they enjoy tax relief on the contributions made (because they are counted as having been made before income is taxed). Any returns on top of the contribution are also untaxed. At retirement people may then generally choose to take one-quarter of the value of the pension fund as a tax-free lump sum. The remainder is then generally (although see below) paid as a regular income or 'pension' during the rest of the person's lifetime. This latter pension is subject to Income Tax for pensioners receiving sufficient income to be in the range of the Income Tax system. So pensions are not free from tax, but there are often tax advantages inherent in pensions. These mostly comprise the lack of tax on the lump sum, and the fact that the tax rate may be lower in older age than in working age. This is a bit different to the tax treatment of relatively tax-privileged savings, like Individual Savings Account (ISAs). These are savings accounts, with options to invest in the stock market, having returns that are free from Income Tax or Capital Gains Tax, but that are invested in from post-tax income. A concern about these tax advantages is that they tend to accrue to richer people, and particularly the small minority of earners who pay higher rates of Income Tax.

Non-state schemes are entirely voluntary – people can choose to join them, or not. However, a new policy of auto-enrolment means that employees are automatically entered into schemes and must explicitly choose to opt out of them, and to continue to do so over time. The state provides a default scheme, the National Employment Savings Trust, but many organisations choose to make their own scheme available, or purchase arrangements from a third party supplier. Auto-enrolment has meant quite large increases in the numbers of employees participating in non-state pensions (Rowlingson and McKay, 2016), although it remains to be seen how many continue to stay in such schemes, and on some evidence, many have ceased making contributions altogether (Rowlingson and McKay, 2017). Even where people remain in the scheme, the overall level of contributions may be lower than is needed for a strong pension income. After all, the compulsory level of contributions is 8 per cent of earnings (4 per cent from work, 3 per cent from the company, 1 per cent in the form of tax relief), whereas older defined benefit schemes entailed contributions around double this.

In the recent past there have been various shocks and scandals in the financial sector, culminating in the 2007/08 global financial crisis and a prolonged recession. Box 5.2 lists a number of these that have had the effect of reducing confidence in pensions and financial products more widely.

Other sources of income

An important source of income for some older people, and indeed a growing number, is earnings from paid work. There is no longer any compulsion to cease work (or to 'retire') in order to receive pension benefits, whether from the state or elsewhere. Some people may choose to keep working, or may feel that their income would be too meagre to meet their needs if they stopped work, and so feel forced to continue in paid work. Legislation makes it illegal to discriminate against people on the grounds of age, although this does not ensure than all such discrimination is prevented (Macnicol, 2006; Riach and Rich, 2010). Older people may also be able to draw on income in the form of rent, if they have properties that they let out. They may have also benefited from increases in house prices, which could be used to release equity, either by downsizing to a cheaper property or by using an equity release product from a financial services provider.

Box 5.2: Failure of trust in pensions and financial products

State pensions

SERPS is paid to widow(er)s on the death of their spouse. The Social Security Act 1986 halved the amount that could be inherited, from 100 per cent of that additional pension to 50 per cent. The Department of Social Security (DSS) did not update the information available to the public, and staff gave wrong information when people asked about SERPS – despite the 14-year lead time for the legislation to take effect. A redress package has now been put in place. In one report:

> ... the Parliamentary Ombudsman finds the Department guilty of maladministration.... I strongly criticise DSS for failing to make their leaflets on retirement pensions and surviving spouses' benefits sufficiently comprehensive and up to date in this important respect following the enactment of the 1986 Act, and for their repeated failure to do so until spring 1996. (Parliamentary Ombudsman, 2000)

A long-term policy to equalise men and women's state pension ages between 2010 and 2020 was sped up for women, with an influential campaign arguing that insufficient notice and information had been provided (see below and Pemberton, 2017).

Private pensions

- *Occupational, the Maxwell scandal (1991):* 20,000 people lost £480 million in pension funds that were used by Robert Maxwell to (temporarily) prop up ailing companies in his group (the missing money was mostly made good by £100 million from government and a settlement for £276 million from financial institutions).
- *Final salary pension transfers – one to watch?* Pensions freedom has given people more options to change their pension arrangements, raising concerns about a possible set of negative implications in the future (FT, 2017), with £50 billion transferred from 'safe' final salary schemes into cash lump sums in the last two years.
- *Personal, the mis-selling of pension products:* during 1988-94, many people who would have been better off in employer pension schemes were wrongly sold personal pensions. A total exceeding £13 billion is expected to be paid out in recompense by the financial services industry (FSA, 2000).

Other financial matters

Among recent issues damaging trust in the financial system, although not strictly about pensions, have been:

- The collapse of the Northern Rock bank, part of the initial stages of the global financial crisis.
- High rates of interest on short-term ('payday') loans, now somewhat restricted in scale.

Policy changes since 2010

The framework of reforms since the mid-2000s to pensions was set during an inquiry under the New Labour government, and led by Adair Turner under the auspices of the Pensions Commission. A series of three reports set out issues and practical interventions. The first report (Pensions Commission, 2004) identified a problem of under-saving for retirement – too few people saving enough to have a good or acceptable standard of living in retirement. The Pensions Commission suggested that there were essentially three things that could be done in response. These were:

* higher taxes to pay for higher state pensions;
* people being forced to save more into non-state pensions;
* people working longer and hence spending less time as retired and dependent on non-labour income.

A fourth option, of doing nothing, was rejected while another approach was to do a little bit of each of the different options. Ultimately the Commission's recommendations were to make progress across each of the possible reforms. In particular, they proposed auto-enrolment into a low cost, non-state pensions product, which was a key element of reforms.

Policy towards pensions has also been affected by later changes by the coalition government. In particular, these include the 'triple lock' that has seen significant spending on state pensions, and 'pensions freedom' that has given people greater options for what to do with their non-state pensions pots.

Increases to the state pension age

Legislation has outlawed employment discrimination on grounds of age, so it is not possible for employers to make people retire simply when they reach a particular age. Hence it makes sense to instead talk in terms of a 'pension age' rather than a 'retirement age'. In practice, people may cease work at, before or after their state pension age.

When the Liberal government introduced state pensions in 1908, the state pension age was established at 70, with a pension that was not based on past contributions. The age at which a pension could be claimed was then reduced to 65 in 1925, but then in 1940 it was further dropped to 60 for women, but not for men, although there are different explanations for why this unequal set of ages was introduced (see Pemberton, 2017). Legislation in the 1970s gave women equal rights in the workplace, which inevitably started to put pressure on the idea of differential pension ages for women and men. Rights to equal pay eventually meant equality in occupational pensions, based on laws around equal pay, since pensions may be regarded as a form of deferred pay. However, the different state pension ages continued to be unchallenged until the Pensions Act 1995, which itself postponed the beginning of closing the pensions age gap until 2010, with the aim of full equalisation in 2020.

However, in the midst of this much-delayed equalisation it was thought necessary to increase state pension ages for everyone, to save costs. Hence the coalition government sped up the timing, and starting in April 2016, moved to push women's state pension age to 65 by November 2018 (Thurley and Keen, 2017a). There are recommendations, following an independent review, to increase the state pension age to 68 during 2037-39 (Cridland, 2017), rather than in the 2040s, as previously envisaged. One reason for the increased attention to increases in state pension age is, of course, longevity. As people live longer, and, crucially, remain in good health, it is argued that it is reasonable to expect them to work longer. Moreover, more people enter higher education, entailing a later start to their working lives, and hence may require longer to acquire sufficient pension rights.

In 2017, increases in state pensions are again becoming a topic of controversy, in terms of how women born in the 1950s have been affected, and the implications for those with lower life expectancies, who are often from poorer backgrounds. There has been a campaign on the former – WASPI (Women Against State Pension Inequality) – challenging the fast rate of increases in pension ages for women born in the 1950s, and (they claim) the limited attempts to communicate these changes to those affected (Pemberton, 2017).

Others point to the relatively low life expectancies in some areas of UK, and among those from poorer backgrounds, which would mean many people dying before they have the opportunity to claim their state pension. Increases to state pension age, both current and planned, may take this age above average life expectancy in some parts of the country.

The triple lock on state pensions

One of the most prominent policies towards state pensions (although not, interestingly, affecting the means-tested Pension Credit for poorer pensioners) is the so-called 'triple lock'. The coalition government introduced this from April 2012. It means that the basic state pension is increased each year by the higher of earnings increases and price inflation, subject to being a minimum of a 2.5 per cent increase each year. This was to help pensioners at least stay in line with changes in earnings. From 1979 until 2011, guaranteed increases in pensions were only linked to changes in prices (the Retail Prices Index, RPI) so that living standards of pensioners reliant mostly on the basic state pension fell behind those of the working-age population, whose earnings tended to rise more quickly than inflation. During the period of the triple lock, however, inflation and wage changes were very low in the period after the financial recession, and hence the 2.5 per cent was often the rate of increase. Over the same period, changes in working-age benefits were generally limited to 1 per cent.

The existence of the triple lock has certainly been part of the clear improvement in levels of pensioner income over time. It has also meant that the costs of increasing the state pension have been considerable. Arguably, the rising costs of state pensions as a result of the triple lock have been one reason for seeking increases in the state pension age. Some commentators are therefore looking at ways to make changes. The Work and Pensions Committee's report on intergenerational fairness suggested that the triple lock come to an end after 2020, to be replaced by an earnings link (House of Commons Work and Pensions Committee, 2016a). As is often the case, once a benefit has been introduced, it is difficult to remove. The 2017 Conservative election manifesto proposed a move to a kind of double lock (inflation or wage increases), but this remains controversial.

Lifetime ISA ('LISA')

It has always been possible for people to save towards their retirement in the form of standard savings products, rather than specifically pensions. For example, Individual Savings Accounts (ISAs) permit saving with the potential for a reasonable rate of return, and with the greater flexibility of instant access. They may also be easier to understand than pensions. Starting in April 2017, a new savings product (Lifetime ISA or 'LISA') means that younger people (under 40) can save money towards either retirement or house purchase. People are able to save up to £4,000 a year, and receive a 25 per cent top-up from the government each year. That process of topping up ceases when a person reaches the age of 50. There are various rules about how the money may be used – for house purchase it needs to be as a first-time buyer, and for a property below certain monetary values; for a pension it needs to be taken at 60 or later.

Pensions freedom

At pensionable age, a person may have built up a sizeable non-state pension fund, and this is used to generate an income for life and the option of an immediate lump sum. It has generally been the case that people can take one-quarter of a non-state pension fund as a lump sum. This makes sense, as it is free of Income Tax. It may be a large sum of money and could be used to pay off any debts at retirement, including mortgages, or to fund holidays or other projects, or to help children financially. The rest of that pension fund, prior to April 2015, then had to be used to buy an 'annuity', a source of income that pays out until death. However, with low interest rates and hence low rates of return, that source of income might appear to be quite small when setting aside a seemingly large sounding pot of money. For example, a pension fund of £75,000 might only yield a monthly income of £165 (index-linked) – although that sum would last for a person's life, no matter how long they lived.

The advent of 'pensions freedom' means that, for defined contribution schemes, people may instead draw from their pension fund over time rather than having to convert it to an annuity. This sounds advantageous, but the amounts taken are often subject to tax at a higher than expected level (for instance, by moving people into a higher tax band). People may also run the risk of running out of money, which could not happen with an annuity that lasts for life. This new policy is clearly only in its early stages, and does not apply to all different kinds of pensions (such as defined benefit schemes), so it is perhaps too early to evaluate.

Incomes and employment of pensioners

Reductions in low incomes among older people

As can be seen from the above discussions, older people can receive incomes from a wide range of different sources. These include the state pension (flat-rate and earnings-related elements); non-state pension products; savings and investments; and employment. Pensions in The World Bank's *zero and first pillar* (the Basic State Pension, Pension Credit and other income-related benefits) are relatively redistributive towards groups experiencing lower earnings during their working age life, and may also be extended to those with gaps in their labour market history for reasons of unemployment or raising children. However, *second and third pillar pensions* (often privately provided in the UK) are paid at levels that relate to the amount of contributions made from earnings while in work – in other words, those additional pensions tend to be higher among those who had higher earnings during their working lifetimes. Those more likely to be out of the labour market, or on lower earnings, will generally have accumulated smaller additional pensions – or none at all. Those most likely to be in this situation are women, some minority ethnic groups, older pensioners and those living in rented housing (Ginn, 2003). Self-employed people are not included in S2P schemes, and so have entitlement only to the Basic State Pension, unless they make separate private provision of their own. Indeed, self-employed people stand to gain considerably from the move to the New State Pension, as they will receive it even though their NICs are lower than employees. An attempt to increase them failed notably as part of the 2017 Spring Budget, and was abandoned.

The risk of having a low income in older age is thus related to work history – men are least likely to be poor if they have worked in professional and clerical occupations; for women, those working in professional, clerical and managerial occupations are most likely to avoid low incomes post-60 years of age (Bardasi and Jenkins, 2002). This is not just a matter of differing levels of earnings from different jobs – access to good workplace pensions may also depend on the size of the employer (larger ones being more likely to provide pensions), and being in the public sector where workplace pensions are effectively universal and with a high level of employer contribution. Overall, the kinds of inequalities found in the labour market – by gender, by minority ethnic status or by disability – may be converted directly into inequalities in older age through their effects on second/third pillar pensions.

The different sources of pensioner income are illustrated in Figure 5.2, for 2015-16. This breaks down the pensioner population into couples and single people, and then shows average amounts of income for different fifths (quintiles) of the income distribution. It is worth noting that single pensioners, poorer than average than couples, include a disproportionate number of women, as they more often outlive their partners. They may also lack non-state provision if they worked in lower-paid occupations and/or took time out to raise children.

Several features should be apparent. First, pensioner couples tend to have much higher incomes than single people. This partly relates to older people having become widows (or widowers), but also that higher earners are more likely to be part of couples. Second, there is considerable inequality of incomes among older people, with the top 20 per cent of pensioners (Q5) being much better off than the next fifth. This inequality arises largely through the unequal distribution of

Figure 5.2: Weekly incomes of pensioner couples and single people

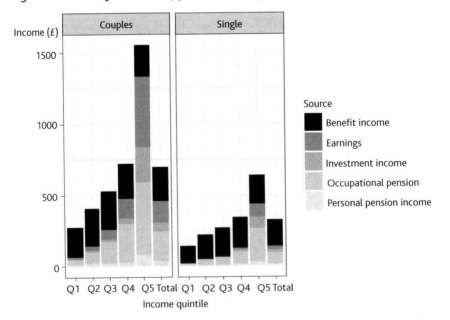

Source: Pensioners' incomes series: An analysis of trends in pensioner incomes: 1994/95 to 2015/16

non–state pension income and income from investments. The average amount of income from state pensions is fairly constant irrespective of overall income, but occupational pensions drive a large amount of the differences between quintiles. Another clear factor is that those in the top 20 per cent are also the most likely to have substantial incomes from earnings. This may indicate a group that is both younger and in better health than average, meaning that they are able to remain in paid work after pensionable age.

These patterns of income show that many pensioners are better off than might be expected, even in comparison with those of working age. The policy of increases to state pensions has meant considerable drops in the proportion of older people on low incomes, and hence drops in their poverty rates. If a popular image of older people was of a group living a hand-to-mouth existence, than that picture needs some revision. Of course, a sizeable proportion of older people *are* still poor, but fewer than among working-age adults in the UK population, and a rather lower proportion than among children (see Figure 5.3). By 2015/16, 16 per cent of older people had incomes below 60 per cent of the median – commonly regarded as a 'poverty line' for the UK – compared with 30 per cent of children and 21 per cent of adults of working age. In the mid-1990s, the incidence of low income among pensioners was somewhat above people of working age, and only a little below that of children.

Figure 5.3: Percentage below 60% of contemporary median income after housing costs

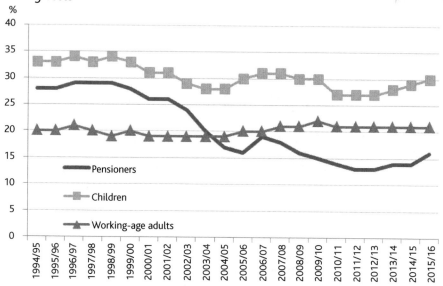

Source: Households Below Average Income: An analysis of the UK income distribution: 1994/95-2015/16

A possible source of disappointment for some older people is that the New State Pension is only being enacted for those reaching state pension age after 2016. Many pensioners, and particularly many poorer ones, would be better off had they had access to the new system rather than the current one.

Rising rates of employment among older people

Increases in state pension age may be expected to encourage – or to force – some people to remain longer in paid work. Increased health among older people may also play a part, and legislation has removed compulsory 'retirement' from jobs. Over the last decade the employment rates of all people have increased, as the UK labour market has proved to be very resilient despite the recession. So the employment rates of men have risen from 60.5 per cent (2001) to reach 62.2 per cent (2016), according to data from the Labour Force Survey. Over the same time, women's employment rates increased from 46.2 to 49.6 per cent. However, among the greatest proportionate increases in rates of working have been those of older people. These are illustrated in Figure 5.4. Employment rates of men remain higher than those of women, despite the ongoing process of equalising the state pension ages. There have been some impressive increases in rates of working for both genders. In 2001, among those aged 65-69, 11 per cent of men and 5 per

Figure 5.4: Employment rates of older men and women, 2001 and 2016

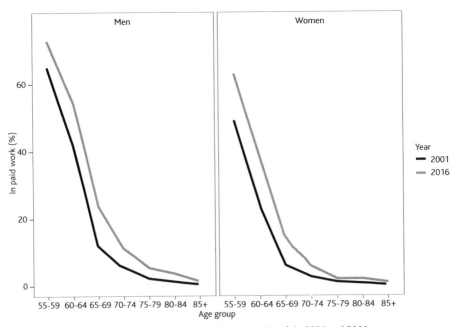

Source: Analysis of Quarterly Labour Force Surveys for January-March in 2001 and 2016

cent of women were in paid work. By 2016 these rates had increased to 24 per cent of men and 14 per cent of women. Among women aged 60-64, between 2001 and 2016 the rate of employment increased from 23 to 38 per cent.

Key policy issues and challenges

This chapter has reviewed the system of income protection for older people – and the provision of pensions in particular. The system is complex. There is a contributory basic pension, on which may be added additional pensions, both through the state and through private providers. There is a means-tested benefit, Pension Credit, for those whose income would otherwise be deemed too low for a satisfactory living standard, with that standard set by government. This very complexity can be a source of concern, with people unable to form a clear idea of their total post-retirement incomes before leaving paid work. For many, there may be entitlement to means-tested support in the form of Pension Credit, but non-take-up remains an issue. Those retiring after 2016 also have relatively more generous state pensions than those retiring earlier, with a higher guaranteed level of support from the New State Pension. Overall, pensioner poverty has been reduced, but there remain important inequalities among pensioners. In particular, groups facing labour market disadvantage, such as women, people with disabilities and some minority ethnic groups may see this disadvantage continued into retirement. There are also specific issues for the self-employed, who lack access to the range of workplace pensions, and, in terms of lower incomes for single people, particularly women who outlive their partners.

The reforms made to non-state pensions, known as 'pensions freedom', offer people more choice with their pension pots. But with that greater set of options comes the possibility of making choices that are not in the person's longer-term interests – the freedom to make bad decisions. It is, however, too early to be sure about the effects of those reforms.

Policy since 2010 has included a commitment to increase the level of the state pension – the triple lock. This has proved quite costly, and its future remains subject to doubt. Moreover, this high level of cost may be one reason for the interest in raising the state pension age at a relatively rapid rate. One danger of this is that the lifetime poor may have lower life expectancies than others, meaning a more short-lived period of retirement even if the state pension is now higher.

UK pensions since 2010 are also the subject of many reforms – the New State Pension, auto-enrolment into non-state pensions, pensions freedom – and the overall evaluation of their impact has yet to take place.

Many chapters in this volume draw attention to the difficult choices made in social security policy, and measures to curtail public spending through tighter entitlement conditions and low rates of benefit increase over time. Pensioners have escaped the austerity affecting other groups of state clients – at least in terms of money benefits, although not in terms of social care spending and pressures on the NHS. This has helped reduce the numbers who are poor, but at a significant cost in overall spending, meaning that the sustainability of higher state pensions will inevitably be subject to close scrutiny.

Overview

The UK pensions system is complex, comprising strong state-provided and privately provided elements.

Some types of income in retirement are universal (or close to it), such as the contributory state pension and the means-tested Pension Credit, while other elements are higher for those who paid in more during their working lifetime (for example, occupational pensions, income from investments).

The level of pensioner income has been rising, and rates of low income falling, although there are ongoing increases in the ages at which it is possible to receive state pensions.

Demographic developments, with the large cohort of the baby boomers moving into lengthy retirements, remain an important backdrop to policy towards pensions and older people.

Questions for discussion

1. What should the role of the state be in respect of pensions, both in making provision and in regulation? Should the state do more than alleviate pensioner poverty?
2. Is it feasible, or desirable, to have commitments to the uprating of future state pensions (such as through the 'triple lock' within state pensions, or links to inflation and/or earnings?)
3. How far will demographic changes force the government to reduce pension levels in the future? How far would increasing the state pension age be better than reducing levels of increases in pension levels?

Key reading

House of Commons Work and Pensions Committee (2016) *Intergenerational fairness: Third report of session 2016-17*.
Pensions Commission (2004) *Pensions: Challenges and choices: The first report of the Pensions Commission*, vol 1, London: The Stationery Office.

World Bank, The (2005) *Old-age income support in the 21st century: The World Bank's perspective on pension systems and reform*, Washington, DC: The World Bank.

Website resources

www.dwp.gov.uk
  Department for Work and Pensions (DWP)

www.ifs.org.uk
  Institute for Fiscal Studies (IFS)

www.pensionspolicyinstitute.org.uk
  Pensions Policy Institute (PPI)

References

Bardasi, E. and Jenkins, S. (2002) *Income in later life: Work history matters*, Bristol: Policy Press.

Beveridge, W. (1942) *Social insurance and allied services*, London: HMSO.

Cridland, J. (2017) *Smoothing the transition: Independent review of the State Pension age (Final report)*, London: The Stationery Office (www.gov.uk/government/uploads/system/uploads/attachment_data/file/602145/independent-review-of-the-state-pension-age-smoothing-the-transition.pdf).

FSA (Financial Services Authority) (2000) 'FSA announces progress and updated redress costs of the pensions review', Press release, FSA/PN/147/2000, 1 December.

FT (*Financial Times*) (2017) 'The great British pensions cash-in', 25 October.

Ginn, J. (2003) 'Parenthood, partnership status and pensions: Cohort differences among women', *Sociology*, vol 37, no 3, pp 495-512.

House of Commons Work and Pensions Committee (2016a) *Intergenerational fairness: Third report of session 2016–17*.

House of Commons Work and Pensions Committee (2016b) *Communication of state pension age changes: Seventh report of session 2015-16*.

Macnicol, J. (2016) *Age discrimination: An historical and contemporary analysis*, Cambridge: Cambridge University Press.

McKay, S, and Rowlingson, K. (2016) 'Social security under the coalition and Conservatives: Shredding the system for people of working age; privileging pensioners', in H. Bochel and M. Powell (eds) *The coalition government and social policy: Restructuring the welfare state*, Bristol: Policy Press, pp 179-200.

Parliamentary Ombudsman (2000) *State earnings-related pension scheme (SERPS) inheritance provisions, Third report for session 1999-2000*, London: The Stationery Office.

Pemberton, H. (2017) 'WASPI's is (mostly) a campaign for inequality', *The Political Quarterly*, Wiley Online Library.

Pensions Commission (2004) *Pensions: Challenges and choices: The first report of the Pensions Commission*, vol 1, London: The Stationery Office.

Riach, P.A. and Rich, J. (2010) 'An experimental investigation of age discrimination in the English labour market', *Annals of Economics and Statistics*, pp 169-85.

Rowlingson, K. and McKay, S. (2016) *Financial inclusion: Annual monitoring report 2016*, Birmingham: University of Birmingham (www.birmingham.ac.uk/Documents/college-social-sciences/social-policy/CHASM/annual-reports/financial-inclusion-monitoring-report-2016.pdf).

Rowlingson, K. and McKay, S. (2017) *Financial inclusion: Annual monitoring report 2017*, Birmingham: University of Birmingham (www.friendsprovidentfoundation.org/wp-content/uploads/2017/09/Financial-Inclusion-Report-2017.pdf).

Thurley, D. and Keen, R. (2017a) *State pension age review*, House of Commons Library (http://researchbriefings.parliament.uk/ResearchBriefing/Summary/SN06546).

Thurley, D. and Keen, R. (2017b) *Increases in the state pension age for women born in the 1950s*, House of Commons Library Briefing Paper Number CBP-07405 (http://researchbriefings.parliament.uk/ResearchBriefing/Summary/CBP-7405).

World Bank, The (1994) *Averting the old age crisis*, Washington, DC: The World Bank.

World Bank, The (2005) *Old-age income support in the 21st century: The World Bank's perspective on pension systems and reform*, Washington, DC: The World Bank.

6

Gender and social security

Fran Bennett

Summary

'Gender' is understood as going beyond biological differences between the sexes to how women and men are positioned and treated in society. The patterns of women and men's lives have been viewed and valued differently by the social security system in the UK, as elsewhere. Moreover, 'welfare reforms' since 2010 – including reductions and restructuring of benefits and tax credits – had gendered implications. This means they affected the relative resources of women and men, as well as their roles, and the relationships between them.

This chapter will:

- explore the position of women and men in relation to the main types of social security benefits/tax credits;
- consider the impact of 'welfare reforms', especially those from 2010 onwards, on women in particular;
- discuss the issues involved in cumulative gender analysis of such measures;
- assess the implications of new and potential social security policies in terms of how they might affect the resources, roles and relationships of women and men, both immediately and in the longer term.

Introduction

The purposes of social security (benefits and tax credits) are discussed in Chapter 1 and other chapters. Gender issues are relevant to redistribution in its various forms – including vertical (between people who may have similar resources but have different needs), horizontal (between people who may have similar resources but have different needs) and over the lifecycle. Social security provision is a key tool of redistribution. But contingencies covered, and eligibility conditions, are closely connected to labour market status and family. Women and men are differently positioned in relation to these. This means they get different benefits and different amounts from the system and are affected differently by changes. (In addition, Black and minority ethnic [BME] women face multiple disadvantages [including racism], and are more likely to be living in low-income households, to be unemployed and to live in households with dependent children, especially large families; see Hall et al [2017]. Measures that affect people in these situations negatively will therefore have a disproportionate impact on them.)

So, although equal treatment is laid down in UK law, in practice, the ways in which the benefits and tax credits systems are structured and implemented do not have gender-neutral consequences. Currently a European Union (EU) directive (EEC, 1979) governs equal treatment for social security for women and men, and, under the Equalities Act 2010, UK public authorities must have regard to the effects of their policies on certain groups, including women (Bennett and Sung, 2013). This chapter considers issues that arise if these commitments are taken seriously. And it widens the lens, as recommended by Daly and Rake (2003), to consider the impact of social security policy not only on the relative resources of women and men, but also on the roles they play and the (power) relations between them. This is seen as essential to carry out a full analysis of the implications of social security policies and 'welfare reforms' based on an understanding of gender not limited to biological differences of sex, but taking account of the positions of women and men in society and how they are treated.

The position of women and men in relation to the main types of benefits/tax credits

Gender issues arise in relation to each form of benefits/tax credits provision (Bennett, 2005). But gender analysis has not been prominent in official UK policy-making, and the differential impact of the system on women and men therefore often goes unrecognised (Bennett, 2005).

The UK's postwar social security system created in the 1940s was largely based on the (stereo)-typical family of a male breadwinner and his dependants. 'Gender difference was built into social security at this key moment' (Pascall, 2012, p 108). While single women could be 'social citizens' with social rights alongside men, most married women paid reduced National Insurance contributions (NICs) and depended on their husbands for most benefits. Many women still receive 'derived benefits' based on their husband's contributions, especially for pensions and widowhood (Pascall, 2012).

If benefits replace earnings from employment, or (like pensions) in part represent savings, or deferred earnings, they tend to reflect market inequalities. So those earning less, including many women, usually receive less benefit (although this can be modified by policy decisions). In addition, in *contributory benefits*, the male is often taken as the norm (Pascall, 2012). So this type of benefit is often based on the (stereo)-typically male pattern of full-time, long-term employment, and is less well attuned to the part-time, low-paid, interrupted work patterns more typical of women's lives (and increasingly men's, too). However, contributory benefits based on the individual rather than the family can give the claimant an independent income.

Benefits based on *categories* – membership of a group, not contributions – can overcome some of these difficulties. For example, Carer's Allowance for someone looking after a disabled person is non-contributory and non-means-tested. It provides an independent income for many women. But categorical benefits replacing earnings tend to be lower than contributory benefits (Pascall, 2012). Categorical benefits can also help with additional costs, such as for children or a disability. There may be a residence test, as an alternative to contribution records, or means testing.

Means testing typically makes the benefit rights of individuals in couples dependent on their partner's presence, resources (income and assets) – and increasingly also behaviour. In the UK, means-tested payments can be paid to replace earnings, as top-ups to other income, or to help meet additional costs. They may compromise incentives for 'second earners' in couples (often women) to enter work or earn more (Pascall, 2012), because their wage is offset by reduced benefits/tax credits, often from the first pound. Many women, and some men, cannot claim means-tested benefits because their partner's income takes joint resources above the qualifying level. And means testing takes no account of unequal resource sharing within the household, or 'hidden poverty' (when someone in a household above the poverty line is nonetheless poor).

The benefits/tax credits system has also been criticised for creating a 'couple penalty' (Adam and Brewer, 2010; Hirsch, 2012). Individuals are alleged to be influenced against cohabitation or marriage because they receive less income as a couple than when living separately. But Griffiths (2017) found in research with lone parents that it was means testing itself – the removal of access to an independent income, and one partner in a couple potentially being dependent on the other – that had influenced their partnering decisions and living arrangements. Box 6.1 examines issues involved in focusing on households/families versus individuals relating to benefits/tax credits.

Women receive a higher proportion of their income from social security compared with men (Pascall, 2012), partly because of their lower incomes, and especially because of interruptions to employment related to caring responsibilities for children and older people and working part time, often in lower-paid jobs. This is particularly likely for BME women (Hall et al, 2017). Roantree and Shaw (2014) argue in addition that being a low-waged parent, particularly a lone parent, is a good indicator for predicting long-term poverty; most such parents are women. But women also tend to be 'conduits' (Daly and Rake, 2003): they receive benefits/tax credits to meet the needs of others (usually children). Such payments can give access to some independent income, but have also been seen as reinforcing women's 'compulsory altruism' – with no choice but to take on caring responsibilities (Land and Rose, 1985).

Box 6.1: Household/family versus individual income

Bennett and Sutherland (2011) argue that individual benefit entitlement can give autonomy (particularly valued by women); facilitate independence, because a partner's presence, resources and actions are not relevant; help prevent 'in-work poverty' if someone in a couple loses their job; give some security of income; and avoid 'couple penalties'.

But means-tested benefits/tax credits, which for couples involve joint assessment of income and needs, are increasingly central to UK provision, particularly for those below pension age. Social security here focuses largely on meeting household/family need in the present, rather than on maintaining an individual's living standard through periods of risk, or on benefits as a right of citizenship for all. This can make it challenging to bring gender issues to the fore, as the focus is on the household/family rather than on (gendered) individuals, and on the situation at one point in time rather than on longer-term impacts.

More generally, analysing the gendered impact of social security policies when income is usually measured on the basis of the household or family unit makes it hard to disaggregate effects on individuals. Researchers may modify this by analysing impact by gender for single-adult households (see, for example, Browne, 2011; WBG, 2016). Such studies tend to find single adult female households losing more from policy changes since 2010 than their male counterparts, largely because most lone parents are women (see De Agostini et al, 2014). The National Equality Panel (Hills et al, 2010, p 159) went further, to examine individual income: '... which gains importance when resources are not equally shared within a couple, for instance'.

We discuss these approaches later. But they are unusual. Most distributional analyses are limited to a snapshot of household income undifferentiated by sex and anchored in a point in time.

Benefits/tax credits must be claimed by someone, and are usually paid into an account nominated by them. Many couples have a joint account, but not all, and such accounts may not always be jointly controlled or accessible equally to both partners. Working Tax Credit is usually paid to the main earner. Joint claims for means-tested benefits/tax credits, including Universal Credit, require a couple to nominate an account for payment. Individual non-means-tested benefits usually go to whoever claims, and Housing Benefit to the tenant. Child Benefit is usually claimed by the mother, and Child Tax Credit by the 'main carer' (in a couple, nominated by them).

Table 6.1 shows that more women than men are likely to be getting certain benefits – in particular, those related to caring, longer life expectancy and poverty. More than twice as many women as men receive Carer's Allowance for looking after a person with a disability. The contributory and means-tested versions of Employment and Support Allowance and Jobseeker's Allowance are not distinguished – but if they were, the data would show more men claiming the contributory versions (Bennett and Sutherland, 2011). More Income Support claimants are women because of the lone-parent population in particular. More women also claim Bereavement Allowance, Attendance Allowance (a cost-related disability benefit for older people) and State Pension, in part because women tend to outlive men. Although not shown here, Child Benefit is also paid overwhelmingly to women, as it is (unusually) paid to the mother by default.

Table 6.2 shows that far more single women (lone parents) claim Child Tax Credit, by itself or with Working Tax Credit. The low numbers on Working Tax Credit only partly reflect low take-up among people without children. In some 80 per cent of in-work families in receipt of Child Tax Credit, this is paid to a woman.

Women and welfare reform

The 1980s and 1990s saw various cuts in benefit levels, and:

> ... from the late 1990s, there have been some piecemeal improvements, but by and large a continuing general decline. Changes have included tightening contribution conditions and behavioural conditionality, the abolition of some benefits and dependants' additions, and cuts in survivors' benefits – a pincer movement in which women are more likely to have been caught. (Bennett and Sutherland, 2011, summary)

Lewis and Bennett (2004) warned against policies that assumed a financial independence that did not yet exist for many women. But derived rights, which are rights gained by one individual by virtue of their relationship to another individual with rights, have been abolished for new claims (for example, dependant increases in state pensions). Other provisions have been made 'gender-neutral' but simultaneously downgraded (bereavement benefits). Increasingly, outside the state social security system, private pension schemes are shifting from defined benefit schemes with a Widow's Pension to defined contribution schemes in which this is an optional extra (Price, 2008, p 20; see also Chapter 9, this volume).

Table 6.1: Benefits receipt by gender, 2017

	Women		Men		Total[b]
Benefit[a]		%		%	
Carer's Allowance[c]	826,340	68	393,360	32	1,219,710
Employment and Support Allowance	1,137,910	48	1,241,090	52	2,378,990
Incapacity Benefit	28,390	60	19,290	40	47,680
Jobseeker's Allowance	189,490	39	295,400	61	484,880
Income Support	506,550	82	107,770	18	614,320
Bereavement Allowance	51,850	74	17,930	26	69,780
Incapacity Benefit/Severe Disablement Allowance	52,040	65	28,320	35	80,360
Disability Living Allowance[d]	1,170,070	48	1,262,300	52	2,432,370
State Pension	7,229,140	56	5,652,890	44	12,882,040
Attendance Allowance[e]	1,033,880	65	546,860	35	1,580,740
Pension Credit	1,165,050	63	687,580	37	1,852,630
Widow's Allowance	20,520	100	0	0	20,520
Universal Credit[f]	264,429	43	345,411	57	609,896
Total	**13,704,049**	**56**	**10,617,491**	**44**	**24,321,596**

Notes:

[a] All data has been sourced from DWP benefits statistical summaries, Quarterly benefits summary: August 2017 (supporting data tables), unless otherwise stated.

[b] Total figures are taken from the DWP official data and may not sum to total due to rounding and unknown or missing data.

[c] This 'all entitled cases' figure includes 410,000 claimants who were entitled to Carer's Allowance but who were not in receipt of payment, for example, because they were in hospital. These individuals are still officially counted by the DWP as claimants.

[d] As in [c], this figure includes claimants who were entitled to DLA, but were not in receipt of payment.

[e] This figure includes 140,000 claimants who were entitled to Attendance Allowance, but were not in receipt of payment.

[f] Source: Data tables: Universal Credit, monthly experimental official statistics to 14 September 2017, Table 3.1, People on Universal Credit by month, gender, age, duration, employment, conditionality regime and job centre district, May 2013 to September 2017.

Initial data research by Cathy Wells; main research for Tables 6.1 and 6.2: Rita Griffiths

Table 6.2: Child and Working Tax Credit receipt by gender, 2017

	Women	%	Men	%	Total
Child Tax Credit (CTC) and Working Tax Credit (WTC)[a]					
Single claimants out of work, CTC only	782,700	94	50,900	6	833,600
Single in work, WTC and CTC	972,800	95	48,800	5	1,021,600
Single in work, CTC only	126,900	89	16,100	11	143,000
Single in work, WTC only	166,700	55	138,100	45	304,800
Total single people on tax credits	2,049,100	89	253,900	11	2,303,000
Joint claims by payee, working couples with children[b]					
CTC and WTC	534,400	75	180,600	25	715,000
CTC only	556,600	85	96,500	15	653,100
Total working couples with children	1,091,000	80	277,100	20	1,368,100

Notes:

[a] Source: HMRC Child and Working Tax Credit statistics, April 2017, Table 3.1: Recipient families by ages and gender of adults.

[b] Source: HMRC Child and Working Tax Credit statistics, April 2017, Table 7.1 In-work families with children.

Initial data research by Cathy Wells; main research for Tables 6.1 and 6.2: Rita Griffiths

Developments under recent Labour governments (1997-2010) have been described as largely aimed at tackling poverty (Annesley et al, 2010), rather than taking a holistic gender perspective, but they had a positive impact for many women, because women are more likely to live in poverty (Pascall, 2012). This is particularly the case for BME women (Hall et al, 2017), as noted above. Labour's policies extended rights for women – including during maternity – as well as introducing paid paternity and unpaid parental leave. Periods of caring were recognised as a form of contribution for gaining rights to earnings–related state pension. Higher benefits for families eased pressures on lone parents and women in couples. Labour also introduced means-tested tax credits, including Child Tax Credit and Working Tax Credit from 2003, increasing the amount for most 'main carers'.

Labour did not increase benefit levels as much in its later years in power, even before the crisis in 2008/09. But it was the Conservative/Liberal Democrat coalition in government from May 2010 that – after briefly protecting benefits – introduced significant 'austerity measures'. These included cuts to benefits/tax credits and restructuring of provision.

Cuts to benefits and tax credits

Social security cuts affected families with young children especially, so women of working age found their incomes disproportionately affected, in part because they were usually the people receiving benefits for children (Bennett, 2015). BME women suffered particularly, given the greater likelihood that they are living in households with dependent children, especially large families (Hall et al, 2017). This emphasis continued under the Conservative government from 2015. There was a range of cuts to Housing Benefit and Council Tax Benefit; several additional payments for young children introduced by Labour were abolished, as was the family element of tax credits; from April 2017, the numbers of children counted for Child Tax Credit and Housing Benefit claims were restricted, with only limited exceptions; and other reductions were made in tax credits and Universal Credit (see below). Significant savings came from uprating many benefits/tax credits by less than inflation and by freezes (for example, for four years from 2016).

In addition to cuts in the incomes that women receive themselves, in low-income families they often manage the daily budgeting, and so are more likely to bear the costs when there is not enough to go around (WBG, 2005). Thus, whoever's income is directly affected by cuts, women often bear the brunt.

Pensioners, however, were largely protected from cuts in benefits. The 'triple lock' meant that pensions were increased by price rises (now measured differently, by the Consumer Price Index [CPI] rather than the Retail Price Index [RPI]), earnings increases or 2.5 per cent, whichever produced the highest amount. Most Housing Benefit cuts applied solely to non-pensioners, and when Council Tax Benefit was decentralised, with a 10 per cent cut, the government said that pensioners must be protected. But the Women's Budget Group has argued that single pensioners, more often women, have been hit hard by cut-backs in social care funding.

Restructuring of social security

'Welfare reform' – restructuring social security – did not start in 2010 with the coalition government. Indeed, change has been almost constant since the 1980s (Millar, 2009), with one or more Bills virtually every year. But, as well as the cuts described, there has also been significant restructuring since 2010. This has resulted in reduced access to, and amounts of, non-means-tested benefits, giving individuals of working age an income in their own right when not in work. Employment and Support Allowance for claimants not in the more disabled 'support group' was limited to 12 months, and then cut to the level of Jobseeker's Allowance for the same group. Gender issues have not been prominent in debates. Bennett and Sutherland (2011) point out, however, that women losing access to a non-means-tested benefit, while fewer in number than men, lose a higher proportion of their income; they are also less likely to be compensated via a means-tested alternative, as their partner is more likely to have earnings disqualifying them. They argue that back-tracking on ensuring an independent income for individuals not only runs counter to gender equality goals, but also fails to reflect the increasing expectation that all should be self-sufficient in providing for their own financial security.

In reforms in April 2017, bereavement benefits were 'modernised' in line with an 'adult worker' model (Daly, 2011). They now resemble an extended lump sum payment more than an earnings replacement benefit, and are no longer paid to parents until their children grow up (House of Commons Work and Pensions Committee, 2016). (They are also tax-free, are ignored for means-tested benefits and are not removed on marriage.) The argument was that with more women in employment – and a benefit that is now also paid to widowers – there was no further need for such a long-term benefit. Carer's Allowance, on the other hand, has escaped relatively unscathed, perhaps reflecting the 'deserving' image of informal carers for disabled/elderly people, and the reluctance to be seen to undermine them in the face of cuts to social care.

The state pension was increased, and became single-tier from April 2016 (with no additional earnings-related element, unless it had been earned before that date). Pension age was raised for both sexes, but especially for women, with a 1950s cohort experiencing the steepest rises. The pressure group WASPI (Women Against State Pension Inequality) was formed as a result. The new pension still relies on a long contributions record (with credits for time spent caring). It will benefit women who were less likely to gain an adequate basic pension because it is higher. However, earnings-related provision on top is now obtainable only through occupational or personal private pensions. These are less likely to redistribute towards lower-paid people or to cover interruptions to employment for caring, as the state equivalent did. Many commentators fail to consider the distributive impact overall of this change, across public and private sectors, although this is particularly important in relation to UK pension provision because of the important role of private pensions.

Over time, joint claiming for means-tested benefits/tax credits has increased, with both partners in couples responsible for meeting conditions. This started under Labour, initially with young couples without children having to claim means-tested Jobseeker's Allowance jointly. Research into Labour's measures to help claimants' partners (largely women) into work found that the dynamics of couple relationships overlaid all other factors in how both individuals approached employment (Coleman and Seeds, 2007; Bennett, 2009). Yet arguably, the implications of this finding were not fully integrated into policy thinking on 'welfare to work' strategies.

Benefit conditionality is not new. But another important development is the ratcheting up of conditionality over time (Watts et al, 2014). Lone parents in particular have seen repeated changes (reductions in the age of the youngest child at which they reach the stage where they must engage with employment). But caring responsibilities are not always fully recognised, and easements (modifications in conditionality) are not always implemented for those affected (Ariss et al, 2015).

Child Benefit contributes to the costs of a child. It is equivalent to a tax allowance, balancing taxation between those with and those without children. But the 2010–15 coalition government introduced a high income charge. Now, anyone claiming Child Benefit when they and/or their partner earns above a certain amount must give up the claim, or the higher earner has to suffer a tax claw-back. This has caused significant losses among higher-income households, but only for those with children (De Agostini et al, 2014). And for some, this move now links one partner's tax situation to the Child Benefit claim, compromising the individual taxation introduced in 1990.

Some powers over social security have been devolved to the smaller nations, in particular Scotland (Simpson, 2017). Scotland has used its new powers to reverse or mitigate some benefits/tax credits cuts (O'Hagan, 2016). Northern Ireland has done the same, although in somewhat different ways. The Scottish government is consulting on introducing a new Maternity and Early Years Allowance, and is committed to equalising the rate of Carer's and Jobseeker's Allowance. It has introduced a Social Security Bill, which sets out principles on which social security benefits should be based. (And see below, on Universal Credit.)

Cumulative gender impact assessment of welfare reforms

Governments have regularly carried out equality impact assessments of individual 'welfare reforms' – although a previous prime minister described these as unnecessary (Cameron, 2012). But the Fawcett Society took the coalition government to court in 2010 because there was no overall equality impact assessment of the measures included in the 'Emergency' Budget, many of them detrimental to women. Cumulative assessment is essential to capture the gendered effects of cuts and restructuring. A House of Commons Library briefing (Cracknell and Keen, 2016) outlines ways to estimate the impact of benefits/tax changes on gendered households (single-adult households, divided by sex) and on individual incomes by gender. This analysis shows the bulk of changes in social security and direct taxation hit women's incomes (Bennett, 2015) – for example, as of the 2016 Autumn Statement, over 86 per cent of net savings from 2010–20 had come from women (see also De Henau, 2017).

The implications of this analysis are contested. Full Facts (cited in Cracknell and Keen, 2016) argues that the effects are an 'artefact of … demographics', and does not mean that women are being deliberately targeted. And the government challenges the inclusion/exclusion of certain measures, arguing that the increased economic security due to sound public finances should be taken into account. This might be more convincing if researchers had not found that, taking account of inflation, savings from coalition benefits/tax credits cuts were used not for deficit reduction but for paying for direct tax changes – including real increases in personal tax allowances. Because of their higher incomes, men tend to benefit more from direct tax cuts (Hall et al, 2017) – especially as personal allowances rise above the level of many low-paid women's annual pay, meaning that they no longer benefit from increases. So these moves transferred income from the poorest (and some of the very richest) to those in the richer half of society (De Agostini et al, 2014).

The government also argued that such analysis does not recognise that couples are likely to share their resources. This point recurs in an assessment of the cumulative impact of cuts for the Equality and Human Rights Commission (Reed and Portes, 2014; a further analysis is currently being conducted). However, as the Women's Budget Group argues, there is no need to go inside the 'black box' of the family to investigate sharing of resources when finding out whether more savings are coming from women's pockets or men's wallets. Decisions do have to be made about whether to allocate incomes to those receiving them solely as 'conduits' for others (see, for example, Avram et al, 2016). So Cracknell and Keen (2016), for example, count Child Benefit as the woman's income. This is not the same as arguing that mothers benefit directly. No investigation of intra-household allocation is required; the point is that women are losing income they receive themselves, over which they are therefore likely to have more control (Hills et al, 2010).

Analysis has also demonstrated that benefit cuts and tax changes since 2010 have had a greater impact on BME women. For example, Hall et al (2017), reporting on analysis by Landman Economics for the Women's Budget Group, find that Asian women in the poorest third of households will lose on average 19 per cent of their income by 2020 compared to a situation in which the policies in place in May 2010 had continued to 2020; for Black women in the poorest households, this loss is on average 14 per cent of their income. Both of these figures are higher than the equivalent averages for White women.

Gender implications of new and potential policy measures

Even the analyses above, although cumulative, tend to focus on the direct impact of changes on women and men's incomes. But too few analyses, official or unofficial, examine not just the relative resources of women and men resulting from changes but also other gendered implications. These include how these incomes are labelled and for what purpose they are paid; their potential impact on individuals' security and autonomy; and how changes may affect gender roles, relationships and inequalities within the home and outside. These implications should be examined both at the point of change and over the longer term. This is what is attempted below, in carrying out gender analysis of one new measure (Universal Credit) and another that has been widely discussed (universal basic income).

Universal Credit

Universal Credit, a major structural reform, is described as 'new' because it is being introduced gradually, with full roll-out by 2021/22 (see Chapter 3, this volume). It replaces six means-tested benefits and tax credits, and is paid to people in or out of work. Universal Credit is not universal in the sense of being non-means-tested. Instead, it is a 'super means-tested benefit', with 'universal' here meaning 'comprehensive'. The coalition government's impact assessment (DWP, 2012) claimed that it 'is gender neutral. Where men and women are in the same circumstances they are treated equally....' But this is to fundamentally misunderstand gender analysis, given that many women and men are precisely not in the same circumstances (Bennett, 2012).

Universal Credit is not a 'credit' in practice, as it is paid in arrears. It is paid as one monthly payment into a single account. If couples cannot agree about which account, the benefit is paid to the 'responsible carer' in the case of those with children; for those without children, it will be paid to the person with the main responsibility for paying the bills. In addition, for all claimants, there can be personal budgeting support and exceptional (temporary) arrangements for those identified as finding it hard to cope or facing domestic violence and so on. In justifying payment into one account as similar to choosing where to pay your wage (DWP, 2011), the government fudged the difference between individual wages and a couple having several different streams of income. Under current arrangements, different benefits and tax credits are also paid to different individuals within couples. Under Universal Credit, most of these arrangements no longer exist. In particular, no element for children is payable to the 'main carer' as before. This move may therefore deprive some individuals of any income, unless they have Child Benefit or other non-means-tested benefits of their own (WBG, 2011). And it fails to match how low-income families control their budget day to day – often managed by the mother. In addition, changes of circumstances (except pay) will be applied on a whole-monthly basis, whenever they occur. This will make budgeting on a low income harder, with a loss of flexibility in dealing with changes (Millar and Bennett, 2017).

Universal Credit involves joint claims for couples and extended conditionality that will particularly affect partners, largely women (Millar and Bennett, 2017). And regulations on 'easements' – modifications of conditionality for lone parents, extended to partners in couples with caring responsibilities – are replaced by (weaker) guidance. In couples, parents who are not the 'responsible carer' are denied any recognition that caring responsibilities may affect their claim. If one partner refuses to sign their claimant commitment (CPAG, 2017), the claim cannot proceed. And a partner's action, or inaction, could – as now – result in a sanction (reduction in benefit) affecting the whole family.

There has been concern about incentives for (potential) 'second earners', often women. In comparison to tax credits, incentives to earn, or earn more, worsen for many under Universal Credit. This is so despite the requirement, subject to personalised conditionality rules, to get more hours and/or higher pay to reach the earnings threshold (which is joint for couples). Policy here is thus pulling in two different directions. The government argued that a higher income for the main breadwinner under Universal Credit would increase the family's work/life choices; but this treats choice as an unproblematic, non-gendered concept, and ignores the possibility that the 'second earner' may be a main earner in future.

The Scottish government is altering Universal Credit in several ways, as allowed under its devolved powers. It will pay it more frequently, and pay the housing element direct to the landlord. It also undertook to split payments between the partners in a couple (Engender, with others, 2016) not just when there is domestic violence, as in the rest of the UK, but as a default arrangement.

Universal basic income

There is increasing discussion in the UK and elsewhere about a universal basic income (Hirsch, 2015; House of Commons Work and Pensions Committee, 2017; see also Chapter 14, this volume). Unlike Universal Credit, this could claim to be truly universal, being non-means-tested as well as non-contributory and non-taxable. It would be paid to each individual, perhaps with a residence test. It is included here to discuss its gender implications, taking into account, as before, resources, roles and relationships.

Paying universal basic income to individuals gives an independent income not based on a partner's presence, resources or actions. This is particularly important for women. Some people have also argued that it would recognise and value unpaid caring work. For example, Zelleke (2011, p 39) sees it as 'socialising the cost of supporting care', as carers have an income financed by the whole community. This seems more arguable. A universal basic income would be paid to everyone, caring or not; it is therefore hard to see it as a reward for or recognition of unpaid caring.

In addition, there are concerns about how to provide an individual income in ways that do not prejudice economic independence in the longer term for women in particular (Bennett, 2005). Zelleke (2011) suggests that a universal basic income would allow low-paid workers to choose to stay at home and take care of their children. Lister (1999) discussed the dilemmas inherent in considering the relationship of citizenship and paid work, and paying a low 'cash for care' state benefit with no right of return to work appears more likely to lead to longer-term labour market exit by women (Lewis, 2009). So 'second earners', and female parents in particular, who receive universal basic income might withdraw from the labour market or reduce their hours (Forget, 2011; Gray, 2017). This does not therefore seem to be the way to achieve the more equal sharing of paid work, caring and the costs of caring between women and men that many believe is fundamental to gender equality goals.

Conclusion

As Bennett and Sutherland (2011) argued, most 'welfare reform' debates focus on simplification, work incentives and/or benefit levels, without considering the unit of assessment (individual/family) or eligibility criteria – how people qualify for benefits. But these two key issues have crucial implications for the resources, roles and relationships of women and men, now and in the longer term. In addition, when assessing redistribution in relation to gender, we should include the implications of any policy measures for private and informal as well as state provision.

Three principles could take reforms in a positive direction: financial autonomy and economic independence for women and men; sharing care more equally between the sexes, and between parents/carers and society; and sharing the costs of caring more equally. But, as Bennett (2005, p v) also concluded, when advancing these principles, benefits/tax credits reforms 'can only ever be one element of a broader and more comprehensive strategy to combat gender inequalities'.

Overview

Different forms of social security benefits/tax credits have different, gendered, implications for women and men in terms of access and amount.

Austerity measures and structural 'welfare reforms' since 2010 have disproportionately reduced women's incomes, because women are more likely to have lower incomes and to receive benefits for others, particularly children; these two factors are not unconnected.

A gender impact assessment should consider not only the direct effects of policy measures on women and men's relative resources, but also how these may affect gender roles and relationships between women and men, now and in the longer term.

Seeing the main goal of social security as addressing household need at one point in time, rather than ensuring individual security over a lifetime, is unlikely to provide a helpful framework for future policy to improve gender equality.

Questions for discussion

1. How might we better value caring while simultaneously trying to avoid solidifying the current gendered division of labour between women and men?
2. Is it important to pay benefits for the costs of children to the person defined as the 'main carer'?
3. When determining social security entitlement for an individual, what are the arguments for and against taking a partner's presence, actions and resources into account?

Key reading

Bennett, F. (2015) 'The impact of austerity on women', in L. Foster, A. Brunton, C. Deeming and T. Haux (eds) *In defence of welfare 2*, Social Policy Association, pp 59-61 (www.social-policy.org.uk/what-we-do/publications/in-defence-of-welfare-2/).

Cracknell, R. and Keen, R. (2016) *Estimating the gender impact of tax and benefits changes*, Briefing Paper no SN06758, London: House of Commons Library (http://researchbriefings.parliament.uk/ResearchBriefing/Summary/SN06758#fullreport).

Pascall, G. (2012) *Gender equality in the welfare state?*, Bristol: Policy Press.

Website resources

www.equalityhumanrights.com/en
  Equality and Human Rights Commission

www.fawcettsociety.org.uk
  Fawcett Society

http://wbg.org.uk/analysis/publications/universal-credit
  Women's Budget Group (including gender analysis of Universal Credit)

References

Adam, S. and Brewer, M. (2010) *Couple penalties and premiums in the UK tax and benefit system*, IFS Briefing Note (BN102), London: Institute for Fiscal Studies (www.ifs.org.uk/bns/bn102.pdf).

Annesley, C., Gains, F. and Rummery, K. (2010) 'Engendering politics and policy: The legacy of New Labour', *Policy & Politics*, vol 38, no 3, pp 389-406.

Ariss, A., Firmin, C., Meacher, M., Starmer, K. and Urwin, R. (2015) *Where's the benefit? An independent inquiry into women and Jobseeker's Allowance*, London: Fawcett Society (www.fawcettsociety.org.uk/blog/wheres-benefit-independent-inquiry-women-jobseekers-allowance).

Avram, S., Popva, D. and Rastragina, O. (2016) *Accounting for gender differences in the distributional effect of tax and benefit policy changes*, Euromod Working Paper Series EM 7/16, Colchester: Institute of Social and Economic Research, University of Essex.

Bennett, F. (2005) *Gender and benefits*, EOC Working Paper Series no 30, Manchester: Equal Opportunities Commission.

Bennett, F. (2009) *Gender and social inclusion*, Oxford: Oxfam GB.

Bennett, F. (2012) 'Universal credit: Overview and gender implications', in M. Kilkey, G. Ramia and K. Farnsworth (eds) *Social Policy Review 24: Analysis and debate in social policy 2012*, Bristol: Policy Press, pp 15-34.

Bennett, F. (2015) 'The impact of austerity on women', in L. Foster, A. Brunton, C. Deeming and T. Haux (eds) *In defence of welfare 2*, Social Policy Association, pp 59-61 (www.social-policy.org.uk/what-we-do/publications/in-defence-of-welfare-2/).

Bennett, F. and Sung, S. (2013) 'Gender implications of UK welfare reform and government equality duties: Evidence from qualitative studies', *Oñati Socio-legal Series*, vol 3, no 7, pp 1202-21 (http://opo.iisj.net/index.php/osls/article/viewFile/244/345).

Bennett, F. and Sutherland, H. (2011) *The importance of independent income: Understanding the role of non-means-tested earnings replacement benefits*, Working Paper 2011-09, Colchester: University of Essex (www.iser.essex.ac.uk/files/iser_working_papers/2011-09.pdf).

Browne, J. (2011) 'How could the government perform a gender impact assessment of tax and benefit changes?', *Observations*, London: Institute for Fiscal Studies (www.ifs.org.uk/publications/5611).

Cameron, D. (2012) 'Cameron "calls time" on Labour's equality impact assessments', Speech, Confederation of British Industry Conference, 19 November, BBC News (www.bbc.co.uk/news/uk-politics-20400747).

Coleman, N. and Seeds, K. (2007) *Work focused interviews for partners and Enhanced New Deal for Partners evaluation: Synthesis of findings*, DWP Research Report 417, Leeds: Corporate Document Services.

CPAG (Child Poverty Action Group) (2017) *Welfare benefits and tax credits handbook*, London: CPAG.

Cracknell, R. and Keen, R. (2016) *Estimating the gender impact of tax and benefits changes*, Briefing Paper no SN06758, London: House of Commons Library (http://researchbriefings.parliament.uk/ResearchBriefing/Summary/SN06758#fullreport).

Daly, M. (2011) 'What adult worker model? A critical look at recent social policy reform in Europe from a gender and family perspective', *Social Politics*, vol 18, no 1, pp 1-23.

Daly, M. and Rake, K. (2003) *Gender and the welfare state*, Cambridge: Polity Press, in association with Blackwell Publishing Ltd.

De Agostini, P., Hills, J. and Sutherland, H. (2014) *Were we really all in it together? The distributional effects of the UK Coalition government's tax-benefit policy changes,* Working Paper 10, Social Policy in a Cold Climate, London: Centre for Analysis of Social Exclusion, London School of Economics (http://sticerd.lse.ac.uk/dps/case/spcc/wp10.pdf).

De Henau, J. (2017) *Gender impact of social security spending cuts,* London: Women's Budget Group (https://wbg.org.uk/wp-content/uploads/2017/03/WBG_briefing_Soc-Security_pre_Budget.pdf).

DWP (Department for Work and Pensions) (2011) *Welfare Reform Bill Universal Credit: Equality impact assessment,* London: DWP.

DWP (2012) *Welfare Reform Act 2012: Impact assessments* (www.gov.uk/government/collections/welfare-reform-act-2012-impact-assessments).

EEC (European Economic Community) (1979) *Council Directive 79/7 EEC of 19 December 1978 on the progressive implementation of the principle of equal treatment for men and women in matters of social security* (http://eur-lex.europa.eu/legal-content/EN/TXT/?uri=CELEX%3A31979L0007).

Engender (with others) (2016) *Securing women's futures: Using Scotland's new social security powers to close the gender equality gap* (www.engender.org.uk/content/publications/Securing-Womens-Futures---using-Scotlands-new-social-security-powers-to-close-the-gender-equality-gap.pdf).

Forget, E. (2011) 'The town with no poverty: The health effects of a Canadian guaranteed annual income field experiment', *Canadian Public Policy/Analyse de Politiques,* vol 37, no 3, pp 283–305.

Gray, A. (2017) *Behavioural effects of a Citizen's Income on wages: Job security and labour supply,* Citizen's Income Trust (http://basicincome.org/news/2017/04/behavioural-effects-citizens-income-wages-job-security-labour-supply/).

Griffiths, R. (2017) 'No love on the dole: The influence of the UK means-tested welfare system on partnering and family structure', *Journal of Social Policy,* vol 46, no 3, pp 543–61.

Hall, S.-M., McIntosh, K., Neitzert, E., Pottinger, L., Sandhu, K., Stephenson, M.-A., Reed, H. and Taylor, L. (2017) *Intersecting inequalities: The impact of austerity on Black and Minority Ethnic Women in the UK,* London: Women's Budget Group and Runnymede Trust with RECLAIM and Coventry Women's Voices.

Hills, J., Brewer, M., Jenkins, S.P., Lister, R., Lupton, R., Machin, S., et al (2010) *An anatomy of economic inequality in the UK: Report of the National Equality Panel,* CASEreport60, London: Centre for Analysis of Social Exclusion, London School of Economics and Political Science.

Hirsch, D. (2012) *Does the tax and benefit system create a 'couple penalty'?,* York: Joseph Rowntree Foundation (www.jrf.org.uk/report/does-tax-and-benefit-system-create-couple-penalty).

Hirsch, D. (2015) *Could a 'citizen's income' work?,* York: Joseph Rowntree Foundation.

House of Commons Work and Pensions Committee (2016) *Support for the bereaved, Ninth report of session 2015-16*, HC551, London: The Stationery Office (www.publications.parliament.uk/pa/cm201516/cmselect/cmworpen/551/551.pdf).

House of Commons Work and Pensions Committee (2017) *Citizen's Income, Eleventh report of session 2016-17*, HC793, London: The Stationery Office (www.publications.parliament.uk/pa/cm201617/cmselect/cmworpen/793/79303.htm).

Land, H. and Rose, H. (1985) 'Compulsory altruism for some or an altruistic society for all?', in P. Bean, J. Ferris and D. Whynes (eds) *In defence of welfare*, London: Tavistock, pp 74-99.

Lewis, J. (2009) *Work-family balance, gender and policy*, Cheltenham: Edward Elgar.

Lewis, J. and Bennett, F. (2004) 'Introduction' to special issue on individualisation, *Social Policy and Society*, vol 3, no 1, pp 43-6.

Lister, R. (1999) 'Reforming welfare around the work ethic: New gendered and ethical perspectives on work and care', *Policy & Politics*, vol 27, no 2, pp 233-46.

Millar, J. (ed) (2009) *Understanding social security: Issues for policy and practice*, Bristol: Policy Press.

Millar, J. and Bennett, F. (2017) 'Universal credit: Assumptions, contradictions and virtual reality', *Social Policy and Society*, vol 16, no 2, pp 169-82.

O'Hagan, A. (2016) 'Redefining welfare in Scotland – with or without women?', *Critical Social Policy*, vol 36, no 4, pp 649-71.

Pascall, G. (2012) *Gender equality in the welfare state?*, Bristol: Policy Press.

Price, D. (2008) *Measuring the poverty of older people: A critical review*, Report of an ESRC Public Sector Placement Fellowship June 2007-January 2008, London: King's College London.

Reed, H. and Portes, J. (2014) *Cumulative impact assessment: A research report by Landman Economics and the NIESR for the Equality and Human Rights Commission*, Research Report 94, Manchester: EHRC (www.equalityhumanrights.com/sites/default/files/research-report-94-cumulative-impact-assessment.pdf).

Roantree, B. and Shaw, J. (2014) *The case for taking a life-cycle perspective: Inequality, redistribution, and tax and benefit reforms*, Report (R92), London: Institute for Fiscal Studies (www.ifs.org.uk/comms/r92.pdf).

Simpson, M. (2017) 'The social Union after the coalition: Devolution, divergence and convergence', *Journal of Social Policy*, vol 46, no 2, pp 251-68.

Watts, B., Fitzpatrick, S., Bramley, G. and Watkins, D. with ESRC-funded project research team (2014) *Welfare sanctions and conditionality in the UK*, York: Joseph Rowntree Foundation.

WBG (Women's Budget Group) (2005) *Women's and children's poverty: Making the links*, London: WBG (http://policy-practice.oxfam.org.uk/publications/womens-and-childrens -poverty-making-the-links-112550).

WBG (2011) *Welfare Reform Bill 2011 – Universal Credit payment issues*, London: WBG.

WBG (2016) *Gender impact of the Autumn Financial Statement: Briefing from the Women's Budget Group*, London: WBG (https://wbg.org.uk/wp-content/uploads/2016/12/AFS2016_Briefing_WBG.pdf).

Zelleke, A. (2011) 'Feminist political theory and the argument for an unconditional basic income', *Policy & Politics*, vol 39, no 1, pp 27-42.

7

Social security and the 'management' of migration

Emma Carmel and Bożena Sojka

Summary

This chapter discusses the complex, and often controversial, relationship between social security and migration. It explores how the tension between desiring exclusion of immigrants from society, while encouraging their inclusion in the labour force, is regulated by contemporary social security. On the one hand, migrants may have entitlements and access to social security that shapes their socioeconomic position and life chances as they move to and from the UK. In this case, migrants are a specific social group, just like other social groups, whose characteristics and biographies shape their social security access and rights (Sainsbury, 2012). On the other hand, social security rules and regulations also intersect with immigration policy and law. In this case, social security also acts as an extended form of immigration control and policing (Crowley, 2001).

The chapter discusses the relationship between migration and social security in three dimensions:

- political/ethical questions;
- conceptual challenges;
- policy practice.

It also explores the implications of this relationship for the generation of complex hierarchies of belonging and social citizenship for particular groups of migrants.

Introduction

The presence of migrants in a society tests the limits of social citizenship and of what it means to belong. This is one of the reasons why questions of migrants' rights and access to social security can be so controversial. Our ideas about 'migrants' and 'migration' rest on underlying assumptions of what it means to be a 'member' of society. In turn, these ideas require us to answer the questions: when does an outsider (the migrant 'stranger') become an insider ('member' of society)? When do 'They' become 'Us'? What, if any, are reasonable conditions to establish whether someone should be recognised as 'Us'? These questions are often controversial and the answers contested, and the UK is no exception.

The UK has long been a country of both emigration and immigration, and it is no stranger to anti-immigration movements. For well over 100 years, anti-immigration politics have contested who settles in the UK, from where, for how long, in what numbers, and with what rights to stay, work and make a claim on social resources (including social security). This anti-immigration politics has ranged from anti-Semitic opposition to the settlement of refugees from Russia and Eastern Europe in the early 20th century, to racist political rhetoric about threats to nationhood from post-colonial migration in the 1960s and 1970s, to fears of cultural and economic threat from East European migrants in the 2000s (Holmes, 1991; Gilroy, 2002). Furthermore, both migration and social security policies have long been shaped by racialised assumptions about national membership (Hall, 1997; Modood, 2005). Embodied in regulations, such assumptions have worked to marginalise and exclude both migrant minority ethnic groups, but have also shaped how migrant communities settled in the UK over time (Craig, 2007; Phillimore et al, 2017). And yet, over this same period, migration, immigration and settlement have not only continued, but have often also been facilitated and encouraged by policies to increase migration and immigration. Both in relation to rights, and in relation to migration controls, there are three areas of contention that shape our understanding of how social security and migration are linked together.

- *Political and ethical questions:* Should welfare states limit access to social security on the basis of residence, integration and employment? Should preferred migrant workers have preferential access to social security? Is this 'fair'?
- *Conceptual challenges:* What defines a migrant and their rights? Are there any circumstances when a migrant can 'belong'? How? When? Why?
- *Policy practice 'on the ground':* What sort of conditions of skill, education, income and language can be applied to (im)migrants before they enter a country? How long does a 17-year-old need to have spent in the UK in order to access financial support for their post-compulsory education? What kinds of protection should

a woman have, when her immigration status depends on her being a wife, but she experiences domestic violence?

This chapter has three main sections. The first examines how migration and migrants' social security have been linked together, and problematised, in political discourse. The second explores how underlying concepts of citizenship, belonging and rights directly shape how social security policy has been developed in relation to migrants. The third explores how migrants' social security is organised in practice, and with what implications for migrants' rights and belonging in the UK.

Political questions and debates

Immediately after the Second World War, adopting a strategy similar to other European states, inward migration from former British colonies was encouraged to access cheap sources of labour, and to support postwar economic recovery. Economic difficulties in the 1970s–1990s led to restrictions on entry for migrant employment, but with special arrangements for healthcare workers who were in short supply. The main pathways to entry and settlement were for family reasons, and refugee status. Labour demand increased again in the late 1990s–early 2000s, especially the perceived need for both 'skilled' and seasonal migration, and was encouraged by the state. Typically for an economically developed state of the Global North, the UK has had a strongly utilitarian approach to migration – encouraging 'economically useful' migrants to come to the UK, but being less willing to endorse their acceptance as members of (an increasingly diverse) society (Vertovec, 2007).

The 2004 and 2007 enlargements of the European Union (EU) resulted in rapid increases in the number of migrant workers from new member states. In 2004 there were 167,000 residents of the UK from EU8 countries, but by 2008 this number had grown to 701,000 (ONS, 2015). (EU8 is shorthand for the eight Central and Eastern European member states that joined the EU in 2004. Romania and Bulgaria, which joined in 2007, are referred to as the EU2. Those countries that were member states before 2004 [of which the UK was one] are the EU15.) The Office for National Statistics (ONS, 2015) estimates that at the end of 2015, one in eight people in the UK were born abroad (13.3 per cent, or 8.6 million). The largest group of settled non-British residents are those with Polish citizenship (916,000, of whom 108,000 were born in the UK), followed by India (362,000), Republic of Ireland (332,000), Romania (233,000), Portugal (219,000) and Italy (192,000). Overall, there has been a shift in countries of origin from post-colonial, Commonwealth migration, to migration from EU member states.

Early in the 2000s, increased migration from the EU was welcomed in political discourse that managed to denigrate existing minority ethnic communities in racist terms, while also positioning EU migrants from Eastern Europe as a cheap, useful resource to fill labour market shortages (McDowell, 2008; Paul, 2015). The main political charges brought against migrants stem from 'welfare chauvinism', a political discourse evident in a number of European welfare states (Kremer, 2016). Welfare chauvinism is especially found where entitlement to social security is through residence or need (means-tested), rather than by contribution (Kvist, 2004). This normative position on social security is expressed in arguments that immigration happens because of 'benefit tourism' or 'social tourism'. These arguments suggest that an (implicitly generous) welfare system (in our case, the UK) needs to be protected against migrants who come there in order to claim benefits. An important context to the economic dimension of these arguments is the age distribution of the non-national population. The UK Census showed that for most EU (non-UK) nationals, the percentage of 15- to 64-year-olds varies from 80 per cent to over 90 per cent (European Union Committee, 2017, Figure 6). In keeping with this age profile, in the year ending June 2016, the majority of EU nationals moving to the UK reported doing so in order to work (72 per cent). Of those coming to work, 57 per cent reported they had a definite job to go to, while 43 per cent arrived looking for work. The most common reason given by non-EU nationals for moving to the UK was to study (47 per cent).

The differences in these figures between EU and non-EU migrants inevitably reflect the restrictions on non-EU nationals' access to employment in the UK. Most non-EU migrants are granted entry and residence for only highly skilled or very specialist employment, and cannot claim social security due to their visa terms and conditions.

So, despite 'benefit tourism' arguments, it should come as no surprise that migrants are considerably less likely than nationals to claim social security benefits, even if the evidence is fragmented and data sources incommensurate (see Box 7.1). This finding also conforms to international evidence showing that migrants tend to have less access to social security than non-migrants (Morissens and Sainsbury, 2005; Koopmans, 2010) and are more likely to be in employment than the equivalent national population.

On the basis of the (admittedly unsatisfactory) empirical evidence on the high percentage of migrants coming to the UK to work or study, the proportionately high numbers who are employed and close to proportional percentages claiming in-work benefits, it is more plausible to argue that most migrants choose the UK for the ease of finding employment in the UK's flexible – and precarious – labour market, as well as for classic migration reasons such as familiarity with the language and existing social networks.

Despite the lack of evidence for social security being a 'magnet' for so-called 'benefit tourists', of course these ideas continue to influence political discourse and policy-making. One of the reasons for this is that these arguments touch on underlying concerns around belonging and citizenship. We now look at these in more detail.

Box 7.1: 'Benefit tourism': problematic evidence and counter-argument

Immigration numbers: Unlike most European countries, the UK does not have a system of national registration of residents. There are no records of how many EU citizens are resident in the UK. Non-EU nationals are recorded through their visa registration.

NINo registrations: The Department for Work and Pensions (DWP) records nationality at registration for National Insurance numbers (NINos). This data shows a dip in registrations in 2011, and in the immediate post-referendum period. It also reveals significant regional variations, reflecting the diversity of the UK's labour market and types of employment available to different categories of migrant. However, NINo registration includes school leavers with non-UK citizenship and does not provide data on numbers leaving the labour market, or the UK, and then returning; it does not account for those who become naturalised citizens or permanent residents later.

Relative employment rates, benefit claimants and expenditure: Immediately prior to the 2016 referendum, the Labour Force Survey showed that people born outside the UK comprised *17.6 per cent of the working-age population.* Despite this,

- Between 2010 and 2016, the *number* of jobseekers who were non-UK nationals at NINo registration decreased, although non-UK nationals as a *percentage* of all jobseekers grew from around 7 per cent to around 13 per cent.
- However, between 2010 and 2016, only 7.4 per cent of working-age individuals receiving key out-of-work benefits had been non-UK nationals at NINo registration. This implies that non-UK jobseekers were not claiming out-of-work benefits.
- In 2016, only 3 per cent of DWP total expenditure on out-of-work benefits was on European Economic Area (EEA)-led claims (£886 million, of £32.7 billion).
- In 2016, 16 per cent of DWP total expenditure on in-work benefits was on EEA-led claims (£814 million of £4.9 billion).

Differences in income and benefit levels between the UK and countries of origin: It is possible to argue that the differences in benefit levels between the UK and EU8 make the UK an 'attractive destination' for EU8 migrants. There are three counter-arguments to this:

- EU8 migrants' entitlement to social security is highly restricted.
- Benefit levels are not directly comparable, as they also need to account for differences in living costs.
- The UK does not have high benefit levels in comparison to other north-western European countries, so the choice to come to the UK in particular cannot be explained as 'benefit tourism'.

Sources: DWP (2016a); Keen and Apostolova (2017)

Conceptual challenges: linking migration, social security and 'welfare'

A key aspect of defining 'who is a migrant' is their mobility. In our case, we are interested in those who have moved their settled place of residence from one country to another, at least once. In UK law, it is only after five (or in some cases ten) years' (legal) residence that someone has the chance to acquire the status of what is called 'permanent resident'. This makes five years the key regulatory marker between those who are outsiders or strangers, and those who 'belong'. Furthermore, it is only following naturalisation as a citizen that someone acquires the same political rights as other citizens, and an unequivocal right to equal treatment.

Such definitions establish key legal criteria around which an individual's social security rights are established. However, while these criteria establish 'broad brush' rights based on someone's migration status, social security rules also apply in ways that not only affect whether a migrant receives a benefit, but also, in turn, affect the legality of their migration status. A migrant can, without experiencing a major life event or change, find themselves in a new legal category, as government policy or legal definitions change (see Carmel and Kan, 2018). Box 7.2 shows the different definitions of 'residence' that might be at play in defining whether someone is a migrant in the UK, and what their legal social security entitlements are. It is this type of policy complexity that has provoked some of the trickier challenges of post-Brexit policy planning, especially as we lack data on the circumstances of current resident EU nationals.

So, while all benefit claimants are subject to conditionality, for migrants, such conditionality is interwoven with their citizenship, migration and residence status in complex and overlapping hierarchies of belonging (Morris, 2002; Carmel and Paul, 2013). Most migrants cannot access *means-tested* social security benefits when residing in the UK. To do so would violate the legal conditions of their entry and residence. For family and labour migrants, these conditions usually require them or their immigration 'sponsor' to show that they can be supported financially without recourse to social security. Yet migrants who are regularly and legally employed may earn entitlements to social security through their *contributions to insurance-based benefits* such as pensions, sickness insurance and contributions-based Jobseeker's Allowance. One of the central questions for migrants is what happens to those contributions if they return to their country of origin, or move on to a third country. This issue is dealt with under international agreements on *social security portability* (see Chapter 8, this volume), but even where these agreements exist, the very process of moving from one place to another can entail significant loss of entitlements for migrants (see, for example, Meyer et al, 2013).

In both these examples, social security regulations act as an internal 'border', demarcating both who belongs (that is, not those who are temporary), and who is more legally and socially privileged as a migrant because they are able to access social security as they move (that is, those in regular employment) (Carmel et al, 2016; Shutes, 2016; Shutes and Walker, 2017).

Box 7.2: Definitions of key rights of residence for migrants in the UK

- *Right to reside (legal residency)* is a right to live in the UK. Terms and conditions, which depend on the legal status of the migrant and/or their entry/residence visa, also affect rights to work and claim benefits. A person who has no 'right to reside' can be deported. It is possible to lose the right to reside by claiming benefits, as 'self-sufficiency' is a normal requirement for legal residency.
- *Ordinarily resident* where the UK is someone's main home. This was historically adequate to secure access to the NHS.
- *Habitually resident* applies where a person has an intention to settle, and their centre of life is in the UK. Originally a test to determine which EU member state would be liable to pay benefits for an entitled EU worker and their family, habitual residence has been increasingly narrowly interpreted to restrict those entitlements. An EU citizen must have both a right to reside and be habitually resident to claim social security benefits (see Box 7.3).
- *Indefinite leave to remain* (legal 'right to settle') applies to non-EU nationals, from a number of immigration categories, where a person has been granted 'leave to remain', has kept to the terms of their UK visa and has been continuously resident in the UK for 10 years (with no single absence of more than 6 months, and total absence of no more than 18 months). Refugees and those with humanitarian protection can apply after five years' continuous legal residence.
- *Permanent resident* applies where an EU citizen has been legally resident in the UK for five years, with an absence of no more than 12 months, and they can apply for 'permanent resident' status (see Table 7.1). Permanent residence status needs to be renewed every five years, and is also a necessary step in the process of naturalisation. Permanent residents are entitled to equal treatment to nationals in respective of employment and social rights, including access to social security.

Migrants in low-skill precarious employment, or working via agencies or as self-employed, may not be making contributions to social security, so the migrant workers do not earn their social security entitlements. National citizen workers can face the same conditions, but migrants can find it especially hard to contest these practices, because they lack knowledge, language skills and fear being reported for immigration offences. Employers can also under-declare the amount of work done by the migrant, or the work itself might be illegal or a result of modern slavery (Wilkinson and Craig, 2011). In these circumstances, migrants' social rights are not directly affected by the social security regulations, but rather by the intersection of these regulations with the UK's precarious and flexible labour market and the vulnerability of migrants to exploitation.

Social security regulations have been tightened for EU workers in precarious and low-paid employment (see below). These regulatory changes imply changes in defining the categories of 'who belongs' or who has access to social citizenship. There is an elision between the emblematic 'non'-citizen (the marginalised and precarious migrant) and the 'failed' citizen (the marginalised and precarious 'benefit scrounger'; see Anderson, 2013), even 'desirable' migrants are subject to highly conditional, and gendered, assumptions about membership (Kofman, 2013). These contrast with an emblematic 'Us' (for example, the coalition and Conservative governments' 'hard-working families'), a distinction that also disguises the degree of shared economic and social conditions of exploitation and vulnerability faced by migrant and non-migrant alike.

Policy in practice

In policy, these already overlapping, complex and contested concepts of residence, migration and social rights are translated into similarly complex categories of legal status. These directly affect migrants' access to, and experience of, social security. Contemporary UK immigration policy has a myriad of entry categories, including, as a limited list of examples, wealthy 'investor' migrants; skilled workers in shortage occupations; family members of current migrants, residents or citizens (each treated differently, and also dependant on the family relationship and income); workers sent by their employer on temporary postings; au pairs and domestic staff; students; and refugees and asylum-seekers. For the UK, the distinction between EU and non-EU nationals has been critical, and is likely to remain important post-Brexit. Each category brings with it a specific immigration status, but this can change over time with extended residence, or changes in circumstances, contributing to what the Supreme Court has described as an unworkably complex immigration system (House of Lords, 2016; Kennedy, 2017). Also, assumptions about alleged 'benefit tourism' or 'social tourism' can also generate policy practices by staff, that (may) constitute unlawful racial/ethnic discrimination, such as demands for additional documentation to establish eligibility. Here we focus on the main categories of migrant, and examine their social security rights and entitlements in practice (see Box 7.3).

> **Box 7.3: Key categorisations of migrant status relevant for social security entitlements**
>
> - *EU citizens:* a national of an EU member state 'exercising their Treaty rights' to move and work in another member state, or an EU national family member of someone who is exercising their Treaty Rights.
> - *EEA nationals:* citizen of a member state of the EEA (for example, Norway or Switzerland), entitled to similar rights of free movement to EU nationals.
> - *'Third country nationals' (TCNs):* also referred to as foreign nationals, non-EU or non-EEA foreign nationals or overseas migrants.
> - *Asylum-seeker:* person who has applied for protection and legal residence as a refugee, under international law, and awaits a decision as to whether or not they are going to be recognised as a refugee.
> - *Refugee:* person whose application for asylum was successful.
> - *Humanitarian protection:* person whose application for asylum did not meet the specific conditions for refugee status but who are still considered in need of protection.
> - *Discretionary leave to remain:* person whose application for asylum was unsuccessful, but whom it is not considered (for other legal reasons or personal circumstances) possible to deport.

EU and EEA nationals

The rights of EU citizens are laid down in Directive 2004/38 and Article 21 of the Treaty for the European Union, and the interpretation and elaboration of these in UK law, policy and guidelines. Social security rights are further shaped by Regulation 883/2004 on the coordination of social security between member states. EU citizens who legally reside in another member state and are employed, self-employed, self-sufficient or who are a family member of an EU citizen who is, are entitled to equal treatment to nationals. Consequently, EU nationals may access some social security in the UK, such as Child Benefit and tax credits. In practice, entitlements are conditioned by legal category of residence, employment status (whether they are considered to be a 'worker', or a 'retained worker' if unemployed), and, of course, contributions. EU nationals may not access non-contributory benefits during their first three months' residence. All EU citizens and their family members are entitled to live in the UK for longer than three months providing they can demonstrate they are not an 'unreasonable burden' on the UK's social assistance system, and that they have comprehensive health insurance. This secures their 'right to reside' (see Box 7.1) and is required if later applications for permanent residence are to be successful. EU nationals who are 'workers' have a 'right to reside' for at least six months.

These legal definitions have their origins in EU law, but have been translated into, and interwoven with, social security regulations and guidelines for DWP decision-makers, with profound effects on the rights of those nationals. Key definitions are 'habitual residence', 'genuine and effective work' and 'genuine prospect of work' (see Box 7.4). In 2014/15 the UK government introduced several measures to limit EU citizens' access to social welfare, using welfare chauvinist assumptions. Policies were designed to 'discourage people, who have no established connection or who have broken their connection with the UK, from migrating here without a firm offer of employment or imminent prospect of work' (DWP, 2014, p 1). The measures included three months' waiting period on arrival prior to claiming income-based Jobseeker's Allowance; requirement for jobseekers to provide robust evidence to have a 'genuine prospect of finding work' to carry on to receive Jobseeker's Allowance, Housing Benefit, Child Benefit and Child Tax Credit after six months; withdrawal of Housing Benefit for jobseekers; introduction of higher minimum earnings thresholds for 'genuine and effective work'; and finally, EU nationals who are unable to pass the Habitual Residence Test would not be entitled to Universal Credit (in areas where this benefit was introduced).

So, EU nationals who are employed or self-employed and whose work is considered genuine and effective are considered to have the legal status of 'worker'. As such, they are entitled to equal treatment with nationals in employment, and can access social benefits after the first three months' residence. Someone who becomes unemployed from such 'genuine and effective work' can 'retain' their worker status for up to six months, and therefore continue to be entitled to equal treatment with nationals, as long as they are also considered 'habitually resident' in the UK. At six months, such 'habitually resident' 'retained workers' must have a 'genuine prospect of work' in order to continue to have this status (DWP, 2015; Kennedy, 2017).

In all three of these tests, it has become difficult for those in precarious and low-paid employment to meet these conditions, as they each impose definitions of work and pay that are above the norm for migrants in low-skill and insecure work (see Box 7.4). Yet the consequences of losing the status of worker are profound for migrants. They lose access to out-of-work benefits, but also housing assistance, healthcare, and in some cases, the right to stay in the UK.

Third country nationals (TCNs)

Most migrants from outside the EEA have limited right to remain and are subject to immigration control as well as to the condition that they have 'no recourse to public funds' during their stay in the UK. A person with limited leave to remain is considered a person subject to immigration control (PSIC) and not entitled to most social security benefits and tax credits.

Box 7.4: Testing belonging in practice? The role of social security guidelines for EU nationals

Habitual Residence Test (HRT)
- This applies to all people, including British nationals, who have recently arrived in the UK and who claim means-tested social security benefits, or housing assistance.
- Individuals who do not meet the HRT are ineligible for benefit.
- The HRT includes questions about:
  - home, including payment of bills
  - residence and schooling of children
  - residence and visits of other family members
  - place, duration, type and income from (previous) employment
  - property ownership abroad
  - frequency and duration of visits abroad.

Genuine Prospect of Work Test (GPoW)
- EU citizens who become unemployed while residing in the UK can normally stay in the UK for up to six months while looking for a new job and (after the first three months' residence) claim benefits.
- After six months, they must have a GPoW in order to continue to be considered 'workers' and be entitled to benefits as EU workers.
- Policy changes since 2014 mean that GPoW usually means an actual job offer, usually full-time regular employment above minimum wage levels.
- If the EU migrant loses the status of a 'worker', they can lose their right to benefit, and
  - Without benefit entitlement, EU migrants without co-resident children will lose their right to reside (see Box 7.2), as they are considered an 'unreasonable burden' on the welfare system.

Genuine and effective work (GEW)
- The term used by the European Court of Justice to determine whether someone is 'exercising their Treaty Rights' to move between member states and thus qualifies as a 'worker'.
- GEW is distinguished from work that is 'marginal and ancillary'. If work is 'marginal and ancillary', the EU citizen is not a 'worker' and can only stay more than three months in another member state if they have comprehensive sickness insurance and are not an 'unreasonable burden' on the welfare system.
- The European Court of Justice also ruled that it is up to member states to determine their definition of GEW.

- In the UK (as with some other member states), GEW is interpreted strictly. DWP decision-maker guidelines make it difficult for EU nationals working in the 'gig economy', in agency work and on zero-hours contracts to show that their work conforms to these requirements.

These examples show how social security regulations are deployed to shape immigration control 'under the radar', especially for those in lower-paid and insecure employment.

Source: Authors' own research; O'Brien (2016); DWP (2016b)

The Welfare Reform Act 2012 limited access to contribution-based benefits such as Jobseeker's Allowance, Statutory Maternity Pay, Statutory Paternity Pay or Statutory Sick Pay to those TCNs currently employed in the UK. However, TCNs who work may still not be allowed to claim benefits if they are not also considered to be habitually resident. The Habitual Residence Test (HRT) established residency of recently arrived individuals who wish to claim benefits (including British returnees). Immigrants who entered the UK under sponsorship (typically, a family member guarantees to provide requisite financial support) are able to claim means-tested benefits if they reside in the UK for at least five years or if their sponsor has died.

Post-Brexit, with the likely insertion of new EU national residents into existing migration schemes offering temporary residence specifically attached to employment, family relationships or a sponsor, there will be many more people who fall into this migrant status, with few to no social security rights. Alternatively, the adoption of new labour migration schemes especially for EU citizens would continue to privilege their status in comparison to TCNs. This would also enable them to, for example, participate in the coordination of social security (social security portability; see Chapter 8, this volume) in the EU. If this continues to be the case, EU nationals would still have relatively privileged access to some important employment-related benefits, such as statutory maternity pay. They would also have the ability to generate social security entitlements by combining contributions from the UK and employment in other EU member states.

Asylum-seekers

An asylum-seeker is a person who has applied for asylum under the 1951 International Convention on the Status of Refugees. A person remains an asylum-seeker for as long as his or her application or an appeal against refusal of his or her application is pending. Asylum-seekers' social rights are established by individual states, and their legal status determines their rights and entitlements to residency, work and access to welfare. Asylum-seekers have a right to reside while their application is considered.

Following a ban on employment for asylum-seekers in 2002, from 2005 asylum-seekers who had waited for over 12 months for a decision on their asylum claim, or who had been refused asylum but invoked new evidence, or are not perceived as responsible for the delay in decision-making, could apply for permission to work. This only permits employment listed in the UK's official shortage occupation list and expires once the asylum claim is finalised. Asylum-seekers who are not granted protection immediately lose all rights and are liable for detention and deportation. They may apply for short-term support on a payment card (not cash) known as 'Section 4' while they are awaiting departure and if they can provide reasons why their departure from the UK is delayed. In 2017, the Supreme Court ruled that the government cannot require asylum-seekers to appeal a judgment from outside the UK (that is, they should not be deported if appealing a decision), but they can still be detained.

Asylum-seekers are detached from welfare provisions linked with employment as they are not allowed to work. They are also not entitled to non-contributory social security benefits such as income-based Jobseeker's Allowance, Income Support and Housing Benefit. Asylum-seekers and their families who are considered 'destitute' may be provided with accommodation and/or basic financial support from the Home Office and organised by local authorities while awaiting a decision on their case. Accommodation is provided on a no-choice basis and is arranged by a policy to disperse asylum-seekers across the country. Refusal to use this accommodation can result in the withdrawal of benefits.

In the case of asylum-seekers, it is the definition of 'destitution' in practice that is the key legal marker of whether a person can access social security. Destitution is defined very narrowly, and is framed against a repetition of assumptions about 'benefit tourism', a key objective of assessments being 'to make best use of taxpayers money and to minimise incentives for economic migration' (Home Office, 2017, section 1). The guidelines to decision-makers make frequent claims of expectation of applicants lying and providing misleading information: this is financial support expressed as an extension of immigration control (Home Office, 2017), perhaps reflecting its location in the Home Office, rather than the DWP. *All* assets and income, including that held overseas, down to the last penny, and all jewellery over a total value of £1,000 are included in calculations. Immigration officials are expected to judge the likelihood of whether an applicant could sell their assets, and sometimes, estimate how much it might be worth, even if abroad. Children, and families with children, are subject to different discretionary criteria, according to statutory duties under the Every Child Matters framework (Home Office, 2017, section 2). The cash payment itself is extremely small at half the allowance for a single person on Jobseeker's Allowance (over-25s) (DWP, 2016b; Home Office, 2017).

Refugees and subsidiary protection

If an application for asylum is successful, a migrant can claim social security benefits on the same basis as nationals, although they may still face barriers in understanding the system and accessing their entitlements, due to discrimination, as well as language and cultural barriers.

Table 7.1 summarises the key points in respect of rights to residence, work and social security benefits. As it shows, family members are treated in different ways for each group. This is further complicated for families with mixed immigration status, where one family member may have entitlements that could be jeopardised – or enhanced – by the status of another family member and *their* entitlements. Three observations might be made, however. First, that the complexity and constraints in practice mean that access to social security, even for pre-Brexit 'free movers', has always been conditional. Second, that the formal status of refugee, or humanitarian protection, although rarely granted, acts as a gateway of deservingness through which migrants move beyond their status as migrants and into an equivalence (in social security regulation) with UK nationals. Third, that before this gateway can be breached, for those seeking asylum, UK social security is not provided as security (against contingency) or even as support (to meet concrete need). Rather, it is wielded as a weapon against the abstract conception of the imagined 'benefit tourist'. The consequences of this approach for individuals, in terms of poverty, need and deprivation, are, however, far from abstract.

Conclusion

In our introduction to this chapter we referred to three significant dimensions that shape our understanding and experience of migration on the one hand, and of social security on the other.

We have seen how *ethical and political questions* about social security for migrants shed light on conditions for social security more generally. For example, the special status of children as dependants and vulnerable is contingent on assumptions about treatment of children, what is a family and what responsibilities different family members should have. Furthermore, the 'marking out' of exclusion/inclusion of migrants is always partly achieved through the conditionality of social security, framed against a political assumption about who migrants are and what they do. This has implications for the wider study of migration, as it shows us that (im)migration policy is not just achieved by rules on entry, stay and employment in immigration law. Rather, we should conceptualise social security rules themselves as a fundamental part of organising, policing and (sometimes) protecting preferred/non-preferred migrants – determining 'who belongs'.

Table 7.1: Social security rights and migration in the UK, by category of migrant

Entry status	Rights of residence	Right to work	Right to social security	Family members
EU nationals	**Yes** if person is 'exercising their Treaty rights' or an EU national and family member of someone who is: - employed - self-employed - registered as a jobseeker (up to six months)	Yes	Yes. Conditional	Close relatives of EU nationals with the right to reside who also have the right to reside (that is): - spouse or civil partner - children and grandchildren under 21 - dependent parents or grandparents Non-EEA relatives require a visa
Third country nationals	**Yes** with appropriate visa	**Yes** Work visa required	**Limited and highly conditional**	Close relatives of permanent residents can stay for six months or more as: - partner - parent - when they come to look after a child - when they come to be looked after by family - with a 'family of settled person visa'
Asylum-seekers	**Yes** while application is processed	**No**	**Extremely limited** - Basic accommodation and support only if destitute	**No**, until a decision on asylum application is made
Refugees and subsidiary protection	Yes - Refugees and humanitarian protection: five years, then application for indefinite leave to remain - Discretionary leave – variable, up to three years	**Yes** Varies for discretionary leave	**Yes. Rights-based** Access all welfare rights as UK citizens	Partner or children can apply to join them in the UK: - if they were separated when as a refugee they were forced to leave their country or - if the refugee has asylum and five years' humanitarian protection but not British citizenship

133

Furthermore, we have seen that the ways in which migration is *conceptualised* changes over time, and this profoundly affects the social security treatment of migrants. Being a 'migrant' is not a fixed status with a single and clear sociological, political, policy or legal definition. Rather, the word 'migrant' (and other labels, too) are used to describe *and create* diverse social categories that change over time according to economic circumstances, political preferences and social understandings. Nonetheless, these temporary social categories are purposefully deployed in policy and law to mark out hierarchies of belonging – who belongs and under what conditions – at any one time. This has implications for the wider study of social security, as we can see that other forms of social categorisation and their policy definitions will play similar roles in reproducing ideas about who belongs in society and on what terms.

Finally, the study of migration and social security also draws attention to the importance of *policy practice* and the 'operational dimension' of social security governance (Carmel and Papadopoulos, 2003). Because the social security rights of migrants are entangled with the immensely complex (im)migration laws in the UK, this highlights the importance of understanding policy as not just what is written on paper, but on how policy is done in practice.

Brexit processes may attempt to guarantee the rights of existing EU citizens, but in practice, these rights were already conditional and not always clear pre-Brexit. Available options for replacing free movement will likely make the UK's unworkable and unwieldy immigration law more opaque, and further reduce entitlement to social security for migrant workers and their families in the UK.

Overview

We emphasise the importance of challenging common-sense understandings of what migration is and who is a migrant when studying migrants' social security.

Conceptual questions of citizenship and belonging, as well as political and ethical questions of fairness, desert and obligation, are especially heightened when we examine migrants and immigrants' social security rights, entitlements and access to benefits.

The social security rights of migrants are entangled with the immensely complex immigration laws in the UK, and this draws attention to the complex hierarchies of belonging and privilege that are attached to different categories of migrant status in the UK, with those seeking asylum being the most vulnerable.

Questions for discussion

1. As the UK exits from the EU, what conditions, if any, would you attach to EU nationals' rights to stay, work and claim social security in the UK? And in the future?
2. Should migrants who apply for refugee status ('asylum-seeker') be permitted to work in the UK while they are waiting for their case to be decided? On what political, ethical, social and/or economic grounds do you justify your answer?
3. What, if anything, makes refugees (rather than other migrants) especially deserving of social protection and support?

Key reading

Carmel, E. and Paul, R. (2013) 'Complex stratification. Governing migrant rights in the European Union', *Regions and Cohesion*, vol 3, no 3, pp 56-85.

Morris, L. (2002) *Managing migration: Civic stratification and migrants' rights*, London: Routledge.

Sirriyeh, A. (2015) '"All you need is love and £18,600": Class and the new UK family migration rules', *Critical Social Policy*, vol 35, no 2, pp 228-47.

Website resources

https://migrantsrights.org.uk
   Migrants' Rights Network (MRN)

www.gov.uk/government/publications/safeguarding-the-position-of-eu-citizens-in-the-uk-and-uk-nationals-in-the-eu
   Government paper on post-Brexit rights for EU citizens

https://theconversation.com/home-office-leak-an-expert-reviews-the-proposed-brexit-immigration-system-83584
   The Conversation

https://theconversation.com/hard-evidence-does-benefits-tourism-exist-22279
   Evidence on 'benefit tourism'

www.gov.uk/government/uploads/system/uploads/attachment_data/file/607212/Fees_table_April_2017.pdf
   Inequalities in access to the UK labour market and social security before entry and during stay: visa, document and naturalisation fees 2017

References

Anderson, B. (2013) *Us and them? The dangerous politics of immigration control*, Oxford: Oxford University Press.

Carmel, E. and Kan, H. (2018) 'Knowledge and expertise in European migration governance: Politics, power and practices', in S. Bonjour (ed) *Handbook on the governance of migration in Europe*, London: Routledge.

Carmel, E. and Papadopoulos, T. (2003) 'The new governance of social security in the UK', in J. Millar (ed) *Understanding social security* (1st edn), Bristol: Policy Press.

Carmel, E. and Paul, R. (2013) 'Complex stratification: Understanding European Union governance of migrant rights', *Regions and Cohesion*, vol 3, pp 56-85.

Carmel, E., Sojka, B. and Papiez, K. (2016) *Free to move, right to work, entitled to claim? Governing social security portability in the European Union*, Welfare State Futures, TRANSWEL Working Papers, WSF: Berlin (https://welfarestatefutures. files.wordpress.com/2017/05/wsf-working-paper-transwel-1-december-2016-webfinal.pdf).

Craig, G. (2007) '"Cunning, unprincipled, loathsome": The racist tail wags the welfare dog', *Journal of Social Policy*, vol 36, no 4, pp 605-23.

Crowley, J. (2001) 'Differential free movement and the sociology of the "internal border"', in E. Guild and C. Harlow (eds) *Implementing Amsterdam*, Oxford: Hart, pp 13-33.

DWP (Department for Work and Pensions) (2014) *The removal of Housing Benefit from EEA jobseekers*, Impact Assessment, 27 February, Leeds: DWP, p 1.

DWP (2015) 'Decision-maker guidelines. Decision-making and appeals: Extending GPOW assessments to stock EEA nationals', Memo 2/15. Leeds: DWP.

DWP (2016a) *National Insurance numbers allocated to adult overseas nationals*, London: DWP.

DWP (2016b) 'Proposed benefit and pension rates 2017 to 2018', in *Pensions*, London: The Stationery Office.

Gilroy, P. (2002) *There ain't no black in the Union Jack: The cltural politics of race and nation*, London: Routledge.

Hall, S. (1997) 'The local and the global: Globalization and ethnicity', *Cultural Politics*, vol 11, pp 173-87.

Holmes, C. (1991) *A tolerant country? Immigrants, refugees and minorities in Britain*, London: Faber & Faber.

Home Office (2017) *Assessing destitution*, London: Home Office.

House of Lords (2016) *Brexit: Acquired rights, European Union Committee, 10th Report of Session 2016-17*, London: House of Lords.

House of Lords European Union Committee (2017) *Brexit: UK-EU free movement of people, 14th Report of Session, HL Paper 121*, London: House of Lords.

Keen, R. and Apostolova, V. (2017) *Statistics on migrants and benefits*, House of Commons Briefing Paper, CBP 7445, London: House of Commons Library.

Kennedy, S. (2017) 'Measures to limit obstacles in accessing welfare are made at the national level and are designed to protect welfare provision migrants' access to benefits', Commons Library Standard Note, House of Commons.

Kofman, E. (2013) 'Gendered labour migrations in Europe and emblematic migratory figures', *Journal of Ethnic and Migration Studies*, vol 39, pp 579-600.

Koopmans, R. (2010) 'Trade-offs between equality and difference: Immigrant integration, multiculturalism and the welfare state in cross-national perspective', *Journal of Ethnic & Migration Studies*, vol 36, pp 1-27.

Kremer, M. (2016) 'Earned citizenship: Labour migrants' views on the welfare state', *Journal of Social Policy*, vol 45, pp 395-415.

Kvist, J. (2004) 'Does EU enlargement create a race to the bottom? Strategic interaction among EU member states in social policy', *Journal of European Social Policy*, vol 14, pp 301-18.

McDowell, L. (2008) 'Old and new European economic migrants: Whiteness and managed migration policies', *Journal of Ethnic and Migration Studies*, vol 35, pp 19-36.

Meyer, T., Bridgen, P. and Andow, C. (2013) 'Free movement? The impact of legislation, benefit generosity and wages on the pensions of European migrants', *Population, Space and Place*, vol 19, p 6.

Modood, T. (2005) *Multicultural politics: Racism, ethnicity, and Muslims in Britain*, Minneapolis, MN: University of Minnesota Press.

Morissens, A. and Sainsbury, D. (2005) 'Migrants' social rights, ethnicity and welfare regimes', *Journal of Social Policy*, vol 34, pp 1-22.

Morris, L. (2002) *Managing migration: Civic stratification and migrants' rights*, London: Routledge.

O'Brien, C.R. (2016) 'Civis capitalist sum: Class as the new guiding principle of EU free movement rights', *Common Market Law Review*, vol 53, pp 1-42.

ONS (Office for National Statistics) (2015) *Population by country of birth and nationality*, August, London: ONS.

Paul, R. (2015) *The political economy of border-drawing: Arranging legality in European labour migration policies*, Oxford and New York: Berghahn.

Phillimore, J., Humphris, R. and Khan, K. (2017) 'Reciprocity for new migrant integration: Resource conservation, investment and exchange', *Journal of Ethnic and Migration Studies* (www.tandfonline.com/doi/full/10.1080/136918 3X.2017.1341709).

Sainsbury, D. (2012) *Welfare states and immigrant rights: The politics of inclusion and exclusion*, Oxford: Oxford University Press.

Shutes, I. (2016) 'Work-related conditionality and the access to social benefits of national citizens, EU and non-EU citizens', *Journal of Social Policy*, vol 45, pp 691-707.

Shutes, I. and Walker, S. (2017) 'Gender and free movement: EU migrant women's access to residence and social rights in the UK', *Journal of Ethnic and Migration Studies*.

Vertovec, S. (2007) 'Super-diversity and its implications', *Ethnic and Racial Studies*, vol 30, no 6, pp 1024-54.

Wilkinson, M. and Craig, G. (2011) 'Wilful negligence: Migration policy, migrants' work and the absence of social protection in the UK', in E. Carmel, A. Cerami and T. Papadopoulos (eds) *Migration and welfare in the new Europe*, Bristol: Policy Press, pp 177–96.

Part Two
Issues in policy and practice

8

Social security in a global context

Nicola Yeates

Summary

Social security is a cornerstone of the international commitment to human rights. Initiatives to improve coverage and take-up of social security benefits and to reduce poverty and inequality have had some successes, but many millions of people worldwide lack access to social security rights. A more robust and coherent approach to international social security coordination is needed to facilitate countries in improving social security standards and the quality of systems of benefits provision and delivery. This chapter explores the global dimensions of social security policy, provision and administration, and relates them to the UK. It comprises four main sections:

- The first reviews the global applicability of the term 'social security' and reflects on how statutory social security operates within broader welfare systems internationally.
- The second contextualises the UK social security system in relation to the variety of systems worldwide, in 'developed' and 'developing' countries.
- The third provides a brief overview of the history of inter-governmental collaboration and policy on social security, and identifies different kinds of organisations involved.
- The fourth discusses the significance of international social security agreements in contemporary social security policy-making.

Introduction

In the UK 'social security' predominantly refers to the system of cash benefits administered mainly by central government. Equating social security with state-administered cash benefits is not, however, the international norm. As the International Labour Organization (ILO) notes, 'in many countries a sharp distinction is commonly drawn between social security on the one hand, and poverty alleviation measures on the other' (ILO, 2000, p 29). Thus, in the US, 'social security' refers only to social insurance retirement and survivors' and disability benefits, while social assistance payments are referred to as 'welfare'. In France and many Latin American countries, 'social security' refers to social insurance benefits, including healthcare benefits, and excludes some social assistance benefits delivered at local level. In the Republic of Ireland, the term 'social welfare' is used in preference to 'social security', and while these terms are broadly synonymous, social welfare benefits do not include some disability, sickness and maternity benefits that are referred to as 'health-related' payments and administered by regional health boards. The ILO includes public spending on healthcare in addition to benefits (in cash and in kind) in its social security expenditure data because healthcare and social security are integrated in most countries.

The term 'social protection' captures the idea that income security derives from a combination of market, informal and public arrangements. Social protection refers to non-statutory income maintenance schemes, formal and informal, in addition to statutory schemes. This term draws attention to the broad range of arrangements and institutions to which individuals and households turn in order to satisfy their income needs. Thus, the strict identification of social security with government activity risks losing sight of private market-based arrangements and non-statutory providers, such as employers (occupational pensions and sick and maternity pay) and commercial agencies (personal pensions, private savings, private unemployment and care insurance). Also, in many countries worldwide, family members are also expected to support one another financially (Midgley and Kaseke, 1996), so a focus on statutory systems alone risks obscuring the significance of culturally determined obligations and practices of mutual financial support emanating from informal family, kin, neighbourhood and community ties.

International remittances sent from overseas migrants back home are an example of informal arrangements. These are a significant source of essential income for a large share of the world's population. In 2015, worldwide remittance flows exceeded US$600 billion. This is a conservative estimate; the true size of remittances, including unrecorded flows through formal and informal channels, is known to be significantly larger. Of that amount, developing countries are estimated to receive about US$440 billion, which is nearly three times the amount of official development assistance received by them (The World Bank, 2016).

Remittances are a vital source of household income and are particularly important for people living in countries without a comprehensive statutory system of social security or who cannot afford to buy income maintenance products from commercial companies. The UK is one of the top 10 countries that send remittances abroad, and among the top 30 countries worldwide that receive remittances (The World Bank, 2016). In short, migrant remittances play a significant part in household financial security worldwide, in rich as well as poorer countries (Owusu-Sekyere, 2013).

Beyond remittances, informal arrangements also include charitable donations arising from religious norms such as alms-giving in Christianity and *zakât* in Islam. *Zakât* is a form of alms-giving for people of the Muslim faith who are required to give 2.5 per cent of their wealth for the benefit of the poor in the Muslim community. These funds are collected and distributed by *zakât* agencies (see www.submission.org/zakat.html and www.zpub.com/aaa/zakat.html). Informal arrangements also include cooperative associations or mutual benefit societies, such as funeral, credit and informal savings societies providing assistance in cash and in kind (Midgley, 1997). Informal or 'traditional' systems often operate at a local level without any state recognition or support, although in some countries statutory and informal systems have been integrated as a means of supporting informal systems and/or extending statutory coverage (Midgley and Kaseke, 1996). Such arrangements exist in both 'developed' and 'developing' countries, although they are particularly significant in countries that do not have comprehensive statutory social security systems.

The provision of cash benefits to individual claimants is only one way in which governments around the world pursue the goal of income maintenance. Other ways of doing so include directly subsidising the prices of housing, food, transport and energy. These subsidies provide substantial indirect wage subsidies, although subsidising prices is not equivalent to direct wage subsidies. Such wage subsidies may complement limited cash benefits systems or substitute for them entirely. Finally, employment is a key source of financial security. Where lifetime employment is guaranteed, there is no need for the state to provide unemployment benefits. This has been the case for many public sector workers and civil servants around the world. The introduction of employment flexibility pursuant to public sector reforms has withdrawn guaranteed lifetime employment and in turn led to the extension of unemployment benefits for these groups.

Social security principles and systems around the world

The establishment of global social security principles can be considered one of the foremost achievements of international politics in the 20th century. Access to social security was identified as a human right under the United Nations (UN) 1948 Universal Declaration of Human Rights (see Box 8.1) and reiterated by the International Covenant on Economic, Social and Cultural Rights (1966), which 'recognises the right of everyone to social security, including social insurance' (Article 9).

Despite seven decades of international consensus that social security is a fundamental social right, income security does not exist in practice for most of the world's population. In recognition of the yawning gap between policy intentions and the lived reality for billions of people worldwide, the UN's Sustainable Development Goals include income security as a major goal of social development to be achieved by 2030. Target 3 of Goal 1, *End poverty in all its forms everywhere* (see Box 8.2), most directly highlights the crucial significance of social security in ending poverty. The UN Sustainable Development Goals also link social protection to wider development issues. Social protection is not just about combating (or preventing) poverty; it plays a key role in ensuring wider socioeconomic security, equality and human development for all of the population.

Box 8.1: Social security and the 1948 Universal Declaration of Human Rights

Everyone, as a member of society, has the right to social security and is entitled to realization ... of the economic, social and cultural rights indispensable for his [sic] dignity and the free development of his personality. (Article 22)

Everyone who works has the right to just and favourable remuneration ensuring for himself and his [sic] family an existence worthy of human dignity, and supplemented, if necessary by other means of social protection. (Article 23.3)

Everyone has the right to a standard of living adequate for the health and wellbeing of himself and of his [sic] family, including ... the right to security in the event of unemployment, sickness, disability, widowhood, old age or other lack of livelihood in circumstances beyond his control. (Article 25.1)

Motherhood and childhood are entitled to special care and assistance. All children, whether born in or out of wedlock, shall enjoy the same social protection. (Article 25.2)

Two key aspects of security systems internationally are coverage and expenditure. Below, we look at each in turn.

Coverage

Social security is now an established feature of advanced industrialised (OECD) countries, where statutory coverage of people and social groups is almost complete. However, from a global perspective, the high level of coverage in countries like the UK and other European states is the exception to the rule. At the turn of the millennium, 'more than half of the world's population (workers and their dependants) [were] excluded from any type of statutory social security protection' (van Ginneken, 1999, p 1). The situation has not substantially improved since that time. Between 70 and 80 per cent of the world's population have no access to meaningful cash benefits beyond the limited possibilities of families, kinship groups or communities to secure their standard of living. The vast majority of people live in a state of severe 'social insecurity', 20 per cent of whom live in poverty (Cichon and Hagemejer, 2007, pp 174–5). The most recent global data available shows that only 27 per cent of the world's population enjoy full coverage of social security, whereas 73 per cent are covered partially or not at all (ILO, 2014).

The principal reasons for exclusion from social security are the absence of statutory schemes and inadequate administrative and delivery systems. The number of countries with statutory schemes grew from 57 countries in 1940 to 172 by 1995 (Dixon, 1999, p 2), and to 192 countries in 2014. Still, 27 countries and territories around the world do not have any known statutory social security scheme, affecting about 120 million people (author's calculations based on ILO

Box 8.2: UN Sustainable Development Goal 1: targets

Goal 1 targets, by 2030:

- Eradicate extreme poverty for all people everywhere, currently measured as people living on less than US$1.25 a day.
- Reduce by at least half the proportion of men, women and children of all ages living in poverty in all its dimensions, according to national definitions.
- Implement nationally appropriate social protection systems and measures for all, including sets of basic social security guarantees, and achieve substantial coverage of the poor and the vulnerable.
- Ensure that all men and women, in particular the poor and the vulnerable, have equal rights to economic resources, as well as access to basic services, ownership and control over land and other forms of property, inheritance, natural resources, appropriate new technology and financial services, including microfinance.
- Build the resilience of the poor and those in vulnerable situations and reduce their exposure and vulnerability to climate-related extreme events and other economic, social and environmental shocks and disasters.
- Ensure significant mobilisation of resources from a variety of sources, including through enhanced development cooperation, in order to provide adequate and predictable means for developing countries, in particular, least developed countries, to implement programmes and policies to end poverty in all its dimensions.
- Create sound policy frameworks at national, regional and international levels, based on pro-poor and gender-sensitive development strategies, to support accelerated investment in poverty eradication actions

Source: www.un.org/sustainabledevelopment/sustainable-development-goals

[2014] data, Table B2). Many of these are in low-income countries. However, the wealth of a country is insufficient to explain the existence of social security systems. Nor can it fully explain why some countries have better-designed systems than others. The United Arab Emirates (UAE), among one of the richest countries in the world, makes only limited legal provision for maternity and unemployment.

Furthermore, where statutory schemes do exist, the coverage of social risks or groups is not always comprehensive. Programmes in respect of old age, disability/invalidity, death, sickness and maternity are most widespread, while those in respect of unemployment, family and children are most frequently absent (Dixon, 1999; ILO, 2014). Fewer than one in ten (8 per cent) of the 172 countries and territories in Dixon's study had programmes for all of the following contingencies: old age, disability, death (including survivors' benefits), sickness, maternity, unemployment, family and children. More recent data (ILO, 2014, Table B2) show improvements since the 1990s. Forty per cent of the 182 countries for which data was available had programmes for all of the contingencies covered by Dixon's (1999) study (these data also include employment injury, which was not included in Dixon's study). Of these, 67 per cent ($n=48$) were in countries in Europe and 18 per cent ($n=13$) were in Asia; the remaining few were spread across Latin America and the Caribbean ($n=5$), Africa ($n=3$) and Oceania ($n=2$). By 2012, most countries had social security schemes covering all or most areas, albeit in many cases only for a minority of their populations. This was the case in most European countries, large parts of the Americas, and increasingly also in Asia, the Pacific and North Africa. Significant progress has also been made in the Middle East and Sub-Saharan Africa (ILO, 2014, p 4).

Those most likely to be excluded from statutory schemes are workers in cottage and small-scale industries and small shops, urban informal workers, agricultural workers, domestic workers and home workers. Even people formally covered by operating schemes may not receive benefits they have contributed to, either because they have not been able to make enough contributions or because they have exhausted their benefit entitlement. Women feature disproportionately among those without access to social security benefits and consequently also among those living in poverty. They are often unable to claim their rights and entitlements due to, for example, limited intra-household decision-making and bargaining power, unpaid work and care responsibilities that generate 'time poverty', and limited power and 'voice' within communities (Goldblatt and Lamarche, 2014; Newton, 2017). In some parts of the world, statutory schemes have collapsed or been made inoperative due to war, natural disasters or severe economic dislocation.

The absence of comprehensive statutory social security for workers in the informal economy in particular raises broader questions about the design of social security systems. An effective social security system requires widespread and sustained participation in it; thus, social insurance schemes require a large proportion of the workforce with a regular job whose earnings can be monitored and on which mandatory contributions can be collected. Unfortunately, this condition does not apply to hundreds of millions of workers worldwide whose employment and earnings are irregular or unregulated. The majority of non-covered and poor workers in developing countries are employed in the informal economy, and many of them are unable or unwilling to contribute a high percentage of their incomes to financing social security benefits that do not meet their priority needs of immediate survival, healthcare and education. Exclusion from statutory social security schemes is also attributable to legal restrictions, weaknesses in law enforcement and inadequate administrative systems. More generally, effective statutory schemes require a strong public infrastructure and sophisticated managerial and administrative capacities in order for taxes to be collected, entitlements to be calculated and benefits to be delivered (van Ginneken, 1999, 2007).

Expenditure

There is great variance in expenditure and financing of social security systems globally. Worldwide, public social protection expenditure (including health expenditure) averaged at 8.6 per cent of Gross Domestic Product (GDP) in 2010/11, having risen from 5.8 per cent in 1990. Social security expenditure here covers expenditure on pensions, employment injury, sickness, family, housing and social assistance benefits in cash and in kind, including administrative expenditure. This top-level figure obscures sharp regional disparities. Social security expenditure is highest in Western Europe, Eastern Europe and North America, followed by Latin America and the Caribbean. Africa tops the regions spending the least, followed by Asia-Pacific and the Middle East. There are also strong intraregional differences. North Africa spends more than Sub-Saharan Africa; Western Europe spends more than Central and Eastern Europe. Within Western Europe, the UK spends less than the average – 23.5 per cent compared with 26.7 per cent (ILO, 2014, Table B2).

Comparing states' public social protection expenditure *excluding* health expenditure, in around 2010/11 six countries exceeded 20 per cent (Austria, Belgium, Denmark, France, Italy and Sweden) while just four countries spent less than 10 per cent (Albania, Brunei Darussalam, Kosovo and Turkey). UK spending sits just above the European average (16.35 per cent compared with 15.47 per cent), and is the 16th highest spender among 43 European states. It spends proportionately less on social security compared with Cyprus, Germany, Greece, Hungary, Ireland, Luxembourg, Portugal, Serbia, Slovenia and Spain. Many of the below-average spenders are states in the Baltic, South-East Europe, Eastern Europe and the former USSR, but it is notable that this group also contain Scandinavian/ Nordic states (Finland and Iceland) (ILO, 2014, Table B12).

Of course, social security expenditure and legal coverage in themselves tell us little about the effectiveness or efficiency of social security policy in actually achieving its goals in practice, and in ensuring that people receive the benefits they are due and on time. Benefit non-take-up is a major problem internationally. A study of non-take-up in 16 European Union (EU) member states that vary considerably in terms of social security and welfare state design suggested that in each of the member states identified, there is at least one type of benefit for which over one-third of people who are entitled to it do not receive it (Eurofoundation, 2015). Non-take-up is an issue for a broad range of benefits and populations, and is not restricted to means-tested benefits (Eurofoundation, 2015, p 9). Walker's study of the ways that the design of social security systems and policies may deter or encourage claims helps shed some light on this problem of non-take-up. Examining the experiences of Norway, Uganda, the UK, India, China, South Korea and Pakistan, the study concluded that:

> People in poverty are repeatedly exposed to shaming by the attitudes and behaviour of the people they meet, by the tenor of public debate that either dismisses them or labels them as lazy and in their dealings with public agencies, including benefit systems. Public policies on social protection would be demonstrably more successful if, instead of stigmatising people for being poor, they treated them with respect and sought actively to promote their dignity. (Walker, 2014, Summary; see also Chase and Bantebya-Kyomuhendo, 2014)

International collaboration in social security

There is a long history of inter-governmental cooperation on social security issues (see Walker, 2005, pp 292-9). The early part of the 20th century saw the foundation of the International Labour Organization (ILO) as an affiliated agency of the League of Nations (1919). Building on the work of the ILO, the establishment of the International Social Security Association (ISSA) in 1927 brought together governmental organisations involved in social security, and gave further substance to international cooperation in that policy arena by providing a forum for policy dialogue among governmental organisations involved in social security administration throughout the world. While this began as an inter-governmental body, it has, over time, come to include non-governmental bodies, such as Provident Funds and Trust Funds, operating non-traditional social security schemes (Yeates, 2007).

The ILO has acquired particular expertise in social security, and is the key UN agency to promote policies that give substance to the formal (but often unrealised) right to social security, as set out in the UN Universal Declaration of Human Rights (see Box 8.1). It advocates guaranteed minimum standards worldwide, and plays an important role in social standard-setting (Otting, 1994). One issue the ILO faces is whether its 'flagship' convention – the Social Security (Minimum Standards) Convention (No 102), which has played an instrumental role in defining the parameters of the right to social security – is still adequate to guarantee universal social security coverage worldwide, or whether it needs to be complemented by a new instrument that is able to address the challenges faced by developing countries in a globalised world (Kulke, 2007). Cichon and Hagemejer (2007) highlight the need for a new international instrument stipulating universal access to a clearly defined 'social floor' as part of a formal endorsement of basic social security rights. The idea of a 'social floor' conveys the idea of nationally defined sets of basic social security guarantees that should ensure, as a minimum, that over the life cycle, everyone in need has access to essential healthcare and to basic income security. Together, these secure effective access to goods and services defined as necessary at national level. The ILO Social Protection Floor is consistent with the ILO's historic approach to social security in defining clear minimum standards, maximising social security coverage and locating it as a key social institution to realise human rights, labour equity and social development (Deacon, 2012; Orenstein and Deacon, 2014).

The World Health Organization (WHO), another UN agency, also has a mandate in social security through its involvement in health-related aspects of social security schemes. Other inter-governmental organisations involved in this field are international financial institutions, notably, The World Bank and the International Monetary Fund (IMF). Both of these organisations' policies bear on social security through their lending policies and packages that have required governments to cut back on social expenditure. The World Bank is particularly notable for the ways in which it advocates residual social provision for the poorest (Orenstein and Deacon, 2014). Social security matters are also part of the mandate of the Organisation for Economic Co-operation and Development (OECD), a policy forum of the world's 29 richest countries. It favours 'flexible' labour market and social security systems, and argues that, in an era of globalisation and rapid socioeconomic changes, states need to spend more – not less – on social security provision. In addition, the World Trade Organization's General Agreement on Trade in Services (GATS) covers financial services which, some argue, potentially undermines national statutory systems of social security insofar as these are seen to fall outside a general exemption that otherwise 'protects' services 'supplied in the exercise of governmental authority' from the requirement that governments facilitate the cross-border provision of financial services (GATS Article I.3c) (Yeates, 2005).

Regional groupings of nations have also developed a mandate on social security issues. Most prominent among these is the EU, but other regional formations in Africa, Asia and South America already have or are considering developing social and labour regulation. Outside the EU, only Mercosur (Southern Cone

Common Market) countries have gone as far as a supranational law on the mutual recognition of social security rights in the region (Yeates, 2014). Transregional associations of governments are also becoming involved in these matters: in 2007, the Ibero-American Summit on Social Cohesion pledged international cooperation among governments in Latin America, Spain and Portugal to allow migrant workers to transfer social security benefits between their nations as part of a policy agenda to develop publicly funded universal social protection systems (this was realised in the Ibero-American Agreement 2007). Alongside these inter-governmental organisations we see a range of development institutions such as regional development banks. For example, the Inter-American Development Bank has been instrumental in promoting the uptake of conditional cash transfer (CCT) programmes by governments across South America (Teichman, 2007). These programmes are also promoted by The World Bank, UN social agencies and European overseas aid agencies. They make the receipt of cash benefits conditional on benefit recipients' children attending primary education and receiving basic healthcare. CCT programmes are popular but they are controversial. This is because they undermine the principle of entitlements, as of a right, to social security (Devereux, 2009).

These institutions are not only a debating forum on social security; some of them have specific powers and responsibilities for policy development, and also attempt to shape global and domestic policy debates and reforms. They do this in a range of ways, including sponsoring research, reports and conferences, providing information, auditing compliance with international standards, and adding authority to critics when domestic policies are judged to fall short of international standards. However, policy implementation and enforcement is a weak area for international governmental organisations because they have no recourse to international law enforcement, and effectively depend on the cooperation of national and local officials and politicians to enact international social law. The ILO, for example, has no powers to enforce national compliance, and relies on moral persuasion and 'leverage' to achieve its objectives. The World Bank is in the same position, but has been able to exert its policy preferences through its financial lending programmes, which require recipient governments to undertake certain reforms as a condition of the loan (for further details, see Yeates, 2014).

Social security in a mobile world: international cooperation agreements

Because most countries have built their social security provision through entitlements for their own nationals, high and increasing cross-border labour mobility means that many people who migrate and live abroad either temporarily or in the long term have restricted access to social security benefits. One way in which governments have responded to this issue is by forging international reciprocal agreements that aim to tie more closely together the social security systems of participating countries. Most international agreements on social security are made on a bilateral basis, between two participating countries. Such agreements set out arrangements for social security for the nationals of the two member states party to the agreement, and are specifically tailored to those countries' circumstances. A smaller but growing number of international social security agreements are negotiated among groupings of countries. Known as multilateral agreements, many involve in the range of 10–30 states. Many countries are party to both bilateral and multilateral agreements.

Bilateral agreements

Bilateral agreements set up coordination rules for persons moving between two countries. Traditionally, these were aimed at protecting a country's citizens working abroad. Increasingly, however, they are used as a way of attracting businesses and labour from outside the signatory states (known as 'third' countries). In the EU case, the majority of agreements concluded by member states on a bilateral basis with non-EU countries contain rules on applicable legislation, equal treatment and pensions. Pension provisions protect migrants' acquired rights when they leave the national territory and allow payment of the pension in the other territory, while in some cases, provision is made for aggregating insurance, employment or residence periods. The applicable legislation rules generally include 'posting' provisions. These enable workers who fulfil certain conditions to remain subject to the social security legislation of the sending country, and exempt them from paying social security contributions in their country of work. The principle of equal treatment guarantees migrant workers the same treatment as nationals of the country in which they work (CEC, 2012, p 3).

The UK, for example, has reciprocal agreements with nearly 20 other states worldwide to protect the social security rights of UK nationals and nationals of the country of origin (see www.gov.uk/national-insurance-if-you-go-abroad). People moving from the UK to work for an employer in a country that has entered into a bilateral social security agreement with the UK government will usually pay social security contributions in that country instead of UK National Insurance (unless they are sent there temporarily by their UK employer or are self-employed, in which case they will continue to pay social security contributions to the UK). Bilateral agreements can include specific rules about where contributions are paid, who is covered and how benefits are uprated and paid. Thus, for most of the 20 or so countries with which the UK has a bilateral social security agreement, UK nationals who live in one of them and receive a UK state pension will receive an increase in their pension every year the same as their equivalents living in the UK. In the absence of a bilateral agreement, nationals are treated by their host country as a foreign national, and their rights to social security will depend on what provision it has made for foreign nationals within its social security system. Because healthcare tends to be integrated into social security systems internationally, nationals living abroad find their entitlements to social security benefits and healthcare are both affected. The need for intensive healthcare especially in older age is one key reason why some UK nationals return home to the UK after a period of living overseas. With a bilateral agreement in place, they are facilitated in doing so, and their rights built up overseas are 'ported' back to the UK.

Bilateral agreements are the cornerstone of international social security provision and coordination, and offer several advantages. Compared with multilateral agreements, bilateral agreements are easier and quicker to negotiate and conclude, involving, as they do, only two countries. They allow governments more control and regulatory discretion. The balance of power between negotiating parties is a consideration: the stronger party can exercise power over its negotiating counterpart, and by entering into an agreement with just one other government, governments can bypass multi-state political blocs and alliances that emerge in multilateral negotiations. Compared with multilateral arrangements that need the agreement of all states and tend to err towards stipulating only minimum standards, bilateral agreements have the potential to raise social standards much more rapidly, as the two negotiating parties can go further in their agreement than that which may be possible in multilateral agreements (Yeates et al, 2010).

The disadvantages of international social security coordination involving bilateral agreements with selected countries of their choice are that they tend to produce fragmented and non-transparent results. Not only is there is an incomplete network of agreements, but the agreements in place tend to have different content from country to country (CEC, 2012). This is because bilateral agreements are negotiated one at a time and reflect the particular interests of the two negotiating parties. The accumulation of so many bilateral agreements create fragmented, variable and complex arrangements that discriminate between different nationals and signatory countries. That bilateral agreements are negotiated by member states in isolation from one another, and without reference to what other countries are doing, creates a problem. In the EU, for example, certain countries may be pinpointed by the EU's main trading partners to conclude agreements, while other countries are left out. Some EU trading partners may not be covered by bilateral agreements with any EU member states at all. Moreover, there is no mechanism for coordinating EU member states' individual approaches or for solving common problems they all face (CEC, 2012, p 3). The country-tailored nature of bilateral agreements means that there is an overall lack of consistency and transparency in what social security rights people have. As the European Commission argues,

> Migrants and businesses based in third countries not only deal with fragmented social security systems when moving between EU countries, but are also confronted with distinctive national bilateral agreements when moving into and out of the EU. (CEC, 2012, p 3)

This situation can adversely impact the people concerned, as they may lose acquired social security rights otherwise available for those people moving out of, or back into, the EU. This is just as likely to affect migrant EU citizens as migrants into the EU from 'third countries' (CEC, 2012, p 3).

Multilateral agreements

Although the social security rights of persons moving into and out of EU countries are still dealt with predominantly under national rules (through bilateral agreements), multilateral social security agreements, signed by three or more governments, are becoming more common. Across Europe, the Caribbean and Latin America, Africa and the Gulf regions, coordinated multilateral approaches to international social security coordination are becoming increasingly popular. Multilateral agreements offer advantages over bilateral agreements in that they allow for a common approach to be taken, and for countries to coordinate social standards and rules among them at one time. Also, they tend to have the principle of equal treatment inscribed into them, and are more likely to include provision for workers (and their families) and cover multiple branches of social security (for example, old age, invalidity, maternity, unemployment and employment injury). However, multilateral agreements face challenges of administrative complexity and 'weight', economic challenges and political resistance by signatory states, all of which can hinder the speed with which they can be put in place and the scope of their success.

A key policy issue that governments have been trying to address bilaterally and multilaterally is how to secure the social security rights of people when they cross international state borders. An intrinsic aspect of this is moving beyond the principle of non-discrimination based on national origin to practice. Whether it concerns third country nationals or citizens, there are major challenges in deciding on what basis entitlements should be accorded, and what kinds of policy and administrative systems are capable of delivering benefits to entitled people in a timely way. For example, the social security agreement in the Gulf region – the Gulf Cooperation Council's Unified Law – has been unable to overcome the difficulty of coverage for third country nationals, who comprise the majority of the migrant workforce of the Gulf region. The failure of member states to ratify international social security agreements that otherwise aim to improve access to social benefits is also an ongoing challenge in the Caribbean and Latin American regions.

The EU experience is also one of difficulty in exporting benefits to non-EU countries. For some 25 years since the 1986 Single European Market came into existence granting free movement of labour, it was not possible for non-EU nationals, when moving to a third state, to 'export' their benefits. This meant that non-EU nationals who had made mandatory social insurance contributions were unable to 'port' their accrued entitlements to benefits and pensions when returning to their home country. It is only since December 2011, when Regulation 1231/10 came into effect, that non-EU nationals working in member states of the EU were entitled to the same treatment as EU nationals, thereby ensuring that non-EU workers would be able to receive their pensions when moving back to their home country under the same conditions and at the same rates as nationals of the member state concerned. Even with this legal guarantee, there is no certainty that it will extend effective coverage. Governments may still restrict the scope of this right. They can do this by, for example, applying restrictions to workers with contracts of less than six months' duration; by restricting family benefits for non-EU citizens admitted to follow a course of study; and by restricting access to public services, such as public housing, to overseas workers currently in employment. Post-Brexit, the UK will probably become a 'third country' as far as the EU is concerned, with a consequent reduction in rights, unless some special arrangements are made for the future.

Conclusion

The ideal of a comprehensive system of social security that ensures everyone receives a decent level of income as a means of fulfilling their right to full social participation while also respecting their human dignity remains one that enjoys a great deal of support internationally. All too often, however, there is a yawning gap between this ideal and what happens in practice. Looking at social security from an international perspective, beyond the UK and even Europe, highlights the vast differences in the ways that countries address various social risks and meet additional costs faced by people with 'special' needs. All too evident are the vast disparities in the quality of social protection between and within countries around the world. Particular challenges face lower-income ('developing') countries, which often depend on international aid for development resources, and are obliged to take account of donors' policy preferences when developing social security policy.

Here we can appreciate the significance of the social protection approaches of bilateral and multilateral agencies in shaping national policies. Global policy initiatives such as the ILO's Social Protection Floor and the UN Sustainable Development Goals in promoting global social policy goals are also critically important for the ways in which they aspire to poverty elimination, the reduction of gender and other social inequalities, the attainment of social equity and the institutionalisation of comprehensive systems of social provision. How this is done in practice are major global and national policy challenges. The formulation of strategies to raise social protection standards raises 'classic' policy dilemmas that all countries, irrespective of their development context, need to address. The enunciation of social security strategies to promote social inclusion and social equity will necessarily need to consider how the rights of internationally mobile populations are protected. Much more investment and advocacy is needed to comprehensively address these multiple global challenges to social security.

Overview

Despite the international establishment of a right to social security, more than half a century ago this right remains far from realised for the majority of the world's population.

There is a long history of inter-governmental collaboration in social security and other social policy fields, dating back to the early 20th century. International organisations of different kinds are integral to social security policy-making across the world, but they lack powers of enforcement.

A concern with minimum social and labour standards and extending statutory social security coverage has been a key priority of the ILO and its partners. The World Bank is more concerned with residualised systems of social security targeting only the poorest people.

International social security agreements are a key element of national and regional strategies to extend legal and effective coverage for citizens moving to another country to live or to work. There remain many obstacles to their effectiveness in practice.

The EU has begun to develop an external dimension to its social security policy. Its policy in this area is guided by the principle of equality (non-discrimination on the grounds of national origin) and aims to benefit EU citizens as well as third country migrants.

Questions for discussion

1. How does the UK social security system compare with other countries in terms of expenditure, design, coverage and outcomes?
2. What are the key challenges facing policy-makers in negotiating and enforcing international social security agreements?

3. What challenges to social security arise from the movement of people, services and capital across international state borders?

Key reading

Every few years the ILO produces a comprehensive overview of social protection policy in international perspective – check the ILO website for the most recent report.

Mitchell Orenstein and Bob Deacon (2014) provide a summary overview of some key developments and issues in social security and pensions as a global policy issue addressed by international organisations.

Students interested in the origins of the Social Protection Floor can follow up with Bob Deacon's (2012) study.

Otherwise, the most up-to-date sources about contemporary developments in social security issues internationally are generally found online, by checking the ILO and International Social Security Association's websites.

Website resources

www.fra.europa.eu
  European Fundamental Rights Agency

www.homeoffice.gov.uk
  Home Office

www.ilo.org/public/english/index.htm
  International Labour Organization

www.social-protection.org/gimi/gess/ShowTheme.do?tid=1321
  ILO Social Protection Floor portal

www.imf.org/external/index.htm
  International Monetary Fund

http://socialprotection.org/institutions/ international-social-security-association-issa
  International Social Security Association

www.un.org/sustainabledevelopment
  UN Sustainable Development Goals

www.worldbank.org/en/topic/socialprotection
  The World Bank, Social protection

References

CEC (Commission of the European Communities) (2012) *The external dimension of EU social security coordination*, COM(2012) 153 final.

Chase, E. and Bantebya-Kyomuhendo, G. (2014) *Poverty and shame: Global experiences*, Oxford: Oxford University Press.

Cichon, M. and Hagemejer, K. (2007) 'Changing the development policy paradigm: Investing in a social security floor for all', *International Social Security Review*, vol 60, pp 2-3, pp 169-96.

Deacon, B. (2012) *Global social policy in the making: The foundations of the social protection floor*, Bristol: Policy Press.

Dixon, J. (1999) *Social security in global perspective*, Westport, CT: Praeger.

Eurofoundation (2015) *Access to social benefits: Reducing non-take-up*, Luxembourg: Publications Office of the European Union (www.eurofound.europa.eu/publications/report/2015/social-policies/access-to-social-benefits-reducing-non-take-up).

Devereux, S. (2009) *Cash transfers: To condition or not to condition?*, Sussex: Institute of Development Studies (www.eldis.org/document/A50543).

Goldblatt, B. and Lamarche, L. (2014) *Women's rights to social security and social protection*, Basingstoke: Palgrave.

ILO (International Labour Organization) (2000) *World labour report 2000: Income security and social protection in a changing world*, Geneva: ILO.

ILO (2014) *World social protection report 2014/15: Building economic recovery, inclusive development and social justice*, Geneva: ILO.

Kulke, U. (2007) 'The present and future role of ILO standards in realizing the right to social security', *International Social Security Review*, vol 60, no 2-3, pp 119-41.

Midgley, J. (1997) *Social welfare in global context*, London: Sage.

Midgley, J. and Kaseke, E. (1996) 'Challenges to social security in developing countries', in J. Midgley and M.B. Tracy (eds) *Challenges to social security: An international exploration*, Westport, CT: Auburn House, pp 103-22.

Newton, J. (2017) 'Social protection and the transformative agenda: A focus on rights and gender', *Global Cooperation Newsletter*, International Council on Social Welfare, March, pp 9-15.

Orenstein, M. and Deacon, B. (2014) 'Global pensions and social protection policy', in N. Yeates (ed) *Understanding global social policy* (2nd edn), Bristol: Policy Press, pp 187-208.

Otting, A. (1994) 'The International Labour Organization and its standard-setting activity in the area of social security', *Journal of European Social Policy*, vol 4, no 1, pp 51-7.

Owusu-Sekyere, F. (2013) 'Critical linkages: Transnational living and prospects for private senders of money from Britain to Ghana and Nigeria', PhD thesis, Milton Keynes: The Open University.

Teichman, J. (2007) 'Multilateral lending institutions and transnational policy networks in Mexico and Chile', *Global Governance*, vol 13, pp 557-73.

van Ginneken, W. (1999) *Social security for the excluded majority: Case studies of developing countries*, Geneva: ILO.

van Ginneken, W. (2007) 'Extending social security coverage: Concepts, global trends and policy issues', *International Social Security Review*, vol 60, nos 2-3, pp 39-57.

Walker, R. (2005) *Social security and welfare: Concepts and comparisons*, Maidenhead: Open University Press.

Walker, R. (2014) *The shame of poverty*, Oxford: Oxford University Press.

World Bank, The (2016) *Migration and remittances factbook 2016*, Washington, DC: The World Bank (www.worldbank.org/en/research/brief/migration-and-remittances).

Yeates, N. (2005) 'The General Agreement on Trade in Services (GATS): What's in it for social security?', *International Social Security Review*, vol 58, no 1, pp 3-22.

Yeates, N. (2007) 'The global and supra-national dimensions of the welfare mix', in M. Powell (ed) *Understanding the mixed economy of welfare*, Bristol: Policy Press, pp 199-219.

Yeates, N. (2014) *Global poverty reduction: What can regional organisations do?*, PRARI Policy Brief No 3, Milton Keynes: The Open University (www.open.ac.uk/socialsciences/prari/files/policy_brief_3_en.pdf).

Yeates, N., Macovei, M. and Langenhove, L. (2010) 'The evolving context of world-regional social policy', in B. Deacon, M. Macovei, L. van Langenhove and N. Yeates (eds) *World-regional social policy and governance: New research and policy agendas in Africa, Asia, Europe and Latin America*, London: Routledge, pp 191-212.

9

Who benefits and who pays?

Kevin Farnsworth and Zoë Irving

Summary

How is social security funded? Who does it benefit? What is social security for? Each of these questions highlights the complexity and often conflicting aims and outcomes that are inherent in providing 'social security' in its wider conceptualisation as a system of redistribution operating in the political, economic and social spheres. This chapter:

- examines the mixed economy of financial support that is channelled through the tax and social security system, not just to individuals and households, but also to companies and corporations;
- emphasises the importance of the economy in examining the distributional consequences of the relationship between the state, private sector and social security;
- outlines key features in patterns of distribution at the micro level between individuals and households, and considers these at the macro level in the context of the function of social security.

Introduction

To address the three questions identified above, this chapter seeks to broaden the consideration of social security while drawing on well-established theoretical and empirical traditions. One of the key early analysts of social policy, Richard Titmuss, recognised the important distinction between the different ways of funding and providing public services, and the implications that flow from this. He mapped out what would come to be known as the 'mixed economy of welfare' or welfare pluralism, and this remains a significant analytical framework in informing an understanding of patterns of redistribution. According to Titmuss' (1958) 'social division of welfare' (see also Alcock et al, 2001), welfare provision consists of social welfare (provided by the state in the form of direct benefits and services), fiscal welfare (also provided by the state, but in the form of tax breaks to purchase 'welfare'-related services) and occupational welfare (provided by employers). Other authors have extended the analysis to the private for-profit sector, the voluntary and charitable sectors, and the family (see Powell, 2007). In this framework, aside from the housing-related benefits paid via local authorities, social security provision covers unemployment, in-work, sickness and disability, maternity and child-related benefits, plus pensions and tax breaks for contributions to private pension plans provided by the state. Employers also provide occupational pensions and a range of other 'above-statutory' benefits, meaning that such provision is more generous or more comprehensive than the minimum required by workplace regulations. In addition, the private sector operates as a provider of insurance services and an increasing number of state-funded employment-focused programmes for people in receipt of out-of-work benefits (see Chapter 12, this volume).

The major contribution of the 'social division of welfare' approach is that it extends the analysis of who or what *provides* various benefits and services within the welfare mix, yet, as indicated below, this approach remains too narrow in focus to capture the full scope of social security as a policy domain. One disadvantage of the mixed economy approach is that while the state sits alongside citizens and the private sector as major providers of welfare, citizens are invariably identified as the only real beneficiaries of this provision, albeit 'unequal' beneficiaries (see also Goodin and Le Grand, 1987). A second weakness is the rather limited engagement with the question of power and policy outcomes (Mann, 1989, 1991). Adrian Sinfield (1978, pp 129-56) identifies these gaps in the conclusion to his critique of Titmuss' *Social division of welfare*, where he argues strongly for a move *beyond* the divisions that lie between occupational, social and fiscal welfare and towards an analysis of the economic, political and social divisions *within* welfare. These divisions shape the ways in which different forms of welfare are delivered unequally to recipients. From a different position, Rein and Rainwater (1986) later advocated for a more holistic analysis of a 'welfare society' as opposed to the 'welfare state' that would enable a more meaningful discussion of how various actors and institutions contributed to the total delivery of welfare. The actions of others, the distribution of welfare and the distribution of power all play a part in shaping the overall welfare mix (Mann, 2009).

A political economy approach

In understanding the welfare mix as it applies to social security while taking into account the interplay of different political and economic interests, a political economy perspective, wherein the economy 'has a special weight in explaining and properly understanding polity and politics' (Gough, 2011, p 50), is especially useful. Political economy approaches draw attention to the importance of *economic growth and production* to the funding, aims and delivery of social policies (Iversen,

2005) and *economic output*, which has an important influence on the aggregate volume of employment, levels of consumption, wages, national incomes, tax revenues and the spending capacity of government.

The interaction of politics (the governance of distribution) with economics depends on how governments respond to perceived and imagined social, economic and political risks, and here, political traditions and political institutions are important. Governments can, and do, respond differently to market risks such as recession, for example, by boosting either/or a combination of help and protection for citizens (social welfare) and/or for private businesses. Support for private businesses is understood here as 'corporate welfare' (Farnsworth, 2012), and includes a range of provisions such as subsidies, financial inducements and tax incentives given either directly to individual companies or to support particular industrial sectors (for example, the motor industry). These forms of support demonstrably contribute to the aims and functions of the wider social security system.

Widening the scope of social security analysis to account for its economic dimensions also requires recognition of the significance and impact of regulation on the terms and conditions of work. In particular, wage levels, health and safety provision and contractual job security can all have important implications for the demands placed on state provisions for income maintenance and social protection. For example, increases in the National Minimum Wage could be used to reduce the costs of in-work benefits such as tax credits. Higher minimum wages, which may be desired by interests representing workers (trades unions), would increase the consumption power of recipients, with positive knock-on effects for businesses (for example, in retail). On the other hand, such a move could also impose higher costs on businesses that rely on low-wage labour, and also increase the public sector wage bill, as the wages of the lowest-paid working for local authorities and the NHS, for instance, are increased. The presence or absence of the regulation of job security also has an impact on usage of state provision. For example, permitting the use of zero-hours contracts by employers might increase workforce flexibility, company competitiveness and profits, but it can also lead to higher costs for the state (and citizens, through their tax obligations), as those such contracts, whose incomes from employment are insecure and intermittent, will have greater recourse to either in-work or unemployment benefits.

These simple examples demonstrate that to understand the social security system, a more nuanced consideration of the complex ways in which a whole range of public and social policies and non-state provision (including, among other things, wages, taxation, private and occupational welfare) cohere and collide to shape and reshape the overall welfare mix. To establish a more comprehensive overview of social security, it is important to determine who funds it, who (or what) benefits from it, and what the benefits are.

Who pays?

In the UK context, it is often assumed that social security is funded through the National Insurance system that emerged in the 20th century, as a means to guarantee the social rights of citizenship. This is certainly the arrangement that William Beveridge, architect of the present system, envisaged in the early 1940s when his *Report on social insurance and allied services* (1942) was released. The principle of social insurance, that a pooling of general risk and resources presents the most efficient method of covering a working population's potential claims against income loss, made sense in terms of actuarial calculations when the system was in its infancy in the 1940s. At this time, security in employment and the value of wages relative to living costs, combined with a male breadwinner model of working and caring, and a lower proportion of insured retirees, placed far less pressure on insurance claims. In the contemporary context, expenditure on insurance-based benefits (pensions, statutory sickness benefits, statutory maternity pay and contributory-based Jobseeker's Allowance) is greater than the amount raised in National Insurance contributions. When added to its means-tested elements (for example, basic pension and minimum income guarantee, and the non-contributory assistance benefits for unemployment, sickness and disability benefits, Housing Benefit, Council Tax Benefit and tax credits, and their new formulation in Universal Credit from 2017), the public social security budget is more than double the total of National Insurance contributions. Taken together, the various means-tested and insurance-based elements of the state social security system account for the largest single chunk of public expenditure. National Insurance contributions (paid by employers and employees) raised £118 billion in 2015/16 against total social security expenditure of £217 billion (IFS, 2015).

Clearly, social security provision is heavily reliant on other sources of revenue in addition to the National Insurance fund. Figure 9.1 compares the amount of National Insurance contributions with the revenue collected by the government via key taxes on employment income, consumption (Value Added Tax, VAT) and on business (Corporation Tax). Not all of the tax revenue represented is directed to the funding of social security, of course, and identifying how revenue is translated into spending is complicated by the availability of data and differences in terminology. From 2013/14, a summary of the relative shares of Income Tax directed towards different areas of public spending as defined by government have been included on 'Annual Tax Summary' statements sent to individual taxpayers. However, even in these official statements the government uses different sources of data to separate pensions from total 'social protection' spending, which has itself been renamed as 'welfare' (for an explanation of categories, see www.gov. uk/government/publications/how-public-spending-was-calculated-in-your-tax-summary/how-public-spending-was-calculated-in-your-tax-summary).

Nevertheless, as can be seen from Figure 9.1, taxation of individual employment and consumption represents a far greater source of revenue than that of business. This suggests that since the enacting of the social security legislation of the 1940s, responsibility for meeting the developing shortfall in funding for social security has predominantly fallen on those who use it rather than *all* those who benefit from it.

Figure 9.1: The four major sources of UK tax in the UK, 2015

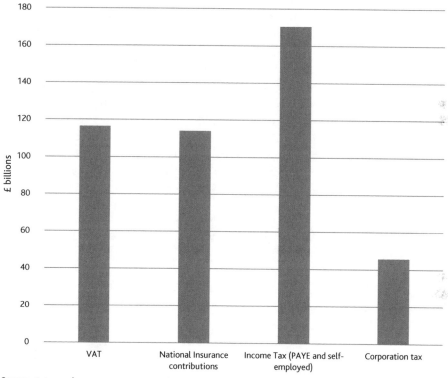

Source: stats.oecd.org

As discussed in Chapter 1, this volume, National Insurance was originally envisioned as a social insurance that would be funded by the three stakeholders – employees, *employers* and central government – in order to insure the risks encountered by employees. The contribution of private business through employers' National Insurance contributions is supplemented by company sickness benefits, and many companies also have their own schemes to provide maternity and pensions contributions through what is commonly referred to as 'occupational welfare'. Titmuss (1958) used this term to draw attention to the importance of workplace provision to overall levels of welfare received by different groups in society. Occupational welfare consists of statutory and non-statutory provision. Non-statutory provision, as the name suggests, is voluntary, provided to employees as part of their overall rewards from employment. This last point is important because, although occupational welfare is often viewed as 'philanthropy', it is perhaps more accurate to view it as part of the overall wage provided to employees, funded as much by employees and taxpayers as by employers. The key reason for this is that certain forms of occupational provision can be offset against tax obligations.

Leaving aside the role of private business in funding social security provisions and focusing on those who make direct claims on state social security, Figure 9.2 shows the effects of the tax and benefit system on income quintiles (total population divided into fifths according to income). Cash benefits and benefits in-kind (services) are shown as positive amounts; taxes as negative amounts in pounds per year. This shows higher net gains from the tax and benefit system for those on the lowest incomes, although it is the second quintile rather than the lowest that has the higher net position. Figure 9.3 focuses only on tax data, but this time looks at the tax burden as a percentage of pre-tax incomes. This reveals some progressivity in the UK tax system – where those on lowest incomes pay least tax as a percentage of income – but it also demonstrates how much more progressive income taxes are compared to the rest.

Figure 9.2: Taxes and benefits by quintile groups, 2016 (£ per year)

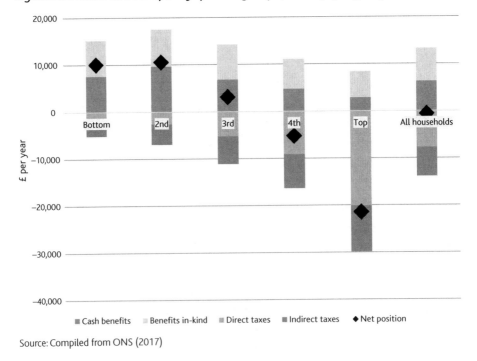

Source: Compiled from ONS (2017)

Figure 9.3: Taxes paid as a percentage of income by income quintile, 2015

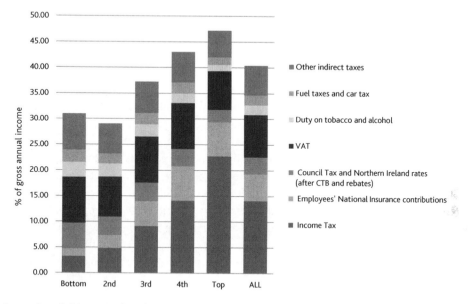

Source: Compiled from ONS (2017)

Figure 9.3 clearly illustrates the differences between progressive forms of taxation (Income Tax), regressive forms of tax (VAT, duties on cigarettes and alcohol) and flatter taxes (which include employees' National Insurance contributions). In fact, employees' National Insurance contributions are progressive between the first and fourth quintile, but regressive if we take into account those on the highest incomes. The reason for this, as noted above, is that National Insurance contributions were originally introduced specifically to pool the general risk of income loss (through unemployment and ill health and old age) rather than as a tool for vertical redistribution from rich to poor. However, the link between National Insurance contributions and insurance-based benefits has been steadily weakened over time: Gordon Brown as Chancellor in 2002 linked an increase in National Insurance contributions to a boost to the NHS budget, and the 2010-15 coalition government cut employers' National Insurance contributions (by £2,000 originally, subsequently increased to £3,000) in order to increase employment incentives for small businesses and to assist businesses struggling in the aftermath of the 2008 global economic crisis.

Thus the question of 'who pays' is highly complex, because even where it appears that one stakeholder (for example, employers) makes an equal or greater contribution, or that "those with the broadest shoulders should bear the heaviest burden" (to quote Chancellor George Osborne in his 2010 Emergency Budget speech) through progressive income taxation, other fiscal measures can counteract the progressive effects. The importance of these contributions is reduced where they are offset by the availability of tax exemptions and allowances, or by other regressive forms of revenue-raising such as consumption taxes. The question of 'who benefits' is no less complex, as the following section shows.

Who benefits? The micro level

In this section the focus is on individuals and households, and the significance of social security in supporting incomes. Figure 9.4 provides an assessment of the annual value of state benefits across the five income quintiles. This indicates that for those in the two lower income quintiles, state benefits represent the greatest share of net income. However, it also reveals that different benefits are distributed unevenly across the quintiles. Not surprisingly, the Basic State Pension is the most important benefit across all income groups, and the only important benefit, in monetary terms, for the richest fifth of the population. However, this data is skewed somewhat by the fact that it presents the value of benefits as a *percentage of net incomes*; it follows that the higher the income, the less valuable in terms of overall income the benefit will be.

Figure 9.4: Value of state benefits (cash and in-kind) per household, 2015

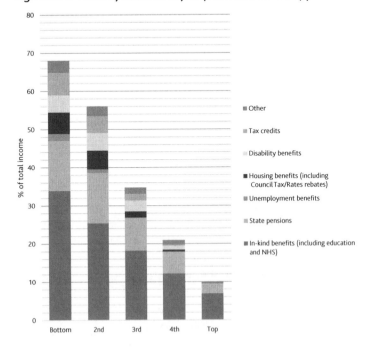

Source: Compiled from ONS (2017)

To address this issue, Table 9.1 sets out the distribution of social security benefits in terms of their monetary value to each quintile in 2015. Rather than simply list all benefits, Table 9.1 presents the most important benefits (by financial value) for each quintile group. Here the state pension is again shown to be the most significant benefit across all income groups. However, the table also illustrates that the value of pension claims for the lowest and highest quintiles are lowest. This is because the poorest are less likely to have built up entitlements to the state pension (especially the State Earnings-Related Pension Scheme [SERPS]/ additional pension element; see Chapter 5, this volume), and those on the highest incomes are more likely to have opted out of the additional pension element and invested in private pensions. It is in the second-most important, and subsequent, benefits that we find more variance. Tax credits and housing benefits (both paid to people who are working but who qualify for benefits because their incomes are low) are important for the lowest three quintiles, with child benefits and statutory maternity pay being more important for the richer quintiles.

Regarding the total value of the top 10 benefits claimed by each quintile group, there is again a familiar pattern: in monetary terms, most benefits are provided to the second quintile, least to the richest quintile. However, due to a raft of measures introduced since 2010, including the roll-out of Universal Credit in 2017, the distribution of benefits is set to change further. For the time being, the value of pensions will continue to increase because of the introduction in 2011 of the Basic State Pension guarantee (sometimes referred to as the 'triple lock'), which increases pensions in line with inflation, average earnings or by 2.5 per cent, whichever is the higher (see Chapter 5, this volume). Other benefits, in contrast, were devalued in a range of austerity measures from 2010, and will be frozen in value from 2015 until 2020. As a percentage of net income, households with the lowest incomes experienced the largest reductions as a result of tax and benefit reforms introduced between 2010-15 (Browne and Elming, 2015), while the Institute for Fiscal Studies projects that child poverty will increase from 18 per cent in 2015/16 to 24 per cent in 2020 (Browne and Hood, 2016). Changes to housing benefits will also have most impact on the poorest, and so the value, as a proportion of income, of most of the benefits identified in Figure 9.4 and Table 9.1 will reduce, while the relative value of pension income will remain stable.

Adding occupational benefits into the mix reveals a different distributional pattern of benefit emerging, with those on middle and higher incomes extracting the most. The quality of occupational welfare provision, such as the amount and scope of benefits that can be received, often increases with the length of employment and seniority within an organisation. In that it allows employers to provide distinct and cost-effective methods of rewarding staff, occupational welfare also helps to informally tie employees to their current employer – giving up a job may be easier for employees to contemplate than giving up a company house or a pension plan. In this respect, employers have relied on occupational

Table 9.1: Top 10 benefits by income quintile group, with average worth per year (£), 2015

	Bottom	2nd	3rd	4th	Top
1	State pension £2,809	State pension £3,950	State pension £3,362	State pension £2,971	State pension £2,009
2	Tax credits £1,320	Housing Benefit £1,397	Tax credits £723	Child Benefit £333	Statutory maternity pay/ Allowance £214
3	Housing Benefit £1,161	Tax credits £1,372	Housing Benefit £579	Disability Living Allowance £231	Child Benefit £152
4	Employment and Support Allowance £517	Disability Living Allowance £626	Disability Living Allowance £475	Housing Benefit £218	Disability Living Allowance £140
5	Child Benefit £498	Child Benefit £536	Child Benefit £475	Statutory maternity pay/ Allowance £195	Student Support £111
6	Income Support £261	Employment and Support Allowance £403	Employment and Support Allowance £312	Tax credits £162	Council Tax/ rates benefits £64
7	Disability Living Allowance £260	Income Support £219	Personal Independence Payment £122	Student Support £105	Housing Benefit £40
8	Student Support £159	Student Support £217	Attendance Allowance £122	Employment and Support Allowance £95	Carer's Allowance £29
9	Jobseeker's Allowance £143	Pension Credit £194	Pension Credit £113	Council Tax/ rates benefits £90	Personal Independence Payment £20
10	Pension Credit £119	Carer's Allowance £184	Council Tax/ rates benefits £110	Pension Credit £85	Attendance Allowance £20
Total value	£7,247	£9,098	£6,393	£4,485	£2,799

Note: The five most important benefits are shaded darkest to lightest in descending order based on the distribution for the bottom quintile to distinguish their significance across the groups. Income quintile calculations include benefit values.

Source: Compiled from ONS (2017) database

welfare to help retain existing workers, control demands for higher pay or to try to attract new workers (Papadakis and Taylor-Gooby, 1987, p 106). Occupational welfare can therefore be used to retain employees in whom the employer has invested heavily, or can be used to attract skilled workers to the company (in whom other employers have invested). It is arguable that the 'company loyalty' effects of occupational welfare help to prevent free-loader problems, where companies entice skilled employees, trained at the expense of other companies, with financial and non-financial incentives.

From the perspective of wider government aims for economic policy, state regulations can manage the attractiveness of occupational welfare to employers through provision in the tax system. Occupational welfare allows employers to pay their staff in more tax-efficient ways. By pooling risks or purchasing services on behalf of employees, employers can provide a range of non-wage benefits that may operate in a similar way to state social security provision. Some forms of occupational provision are also tax-exempt, increasing further the value of workplace benefits, but this time at the expense of taxpayers more generally. However, because occupational benefits are seldom distributed evenly within the workplace (more senior workers tend to extract more occupational benefits than more junior workers, and men tend to extract more benefits than women), they also represent a taxpayer-subsidised award to relatively privileged employees.

In order to indicate the value of occupational welfare to employees, Figure 9.5 reveals the breakdown of different components of *non-labour* costs in the UK. This presents the proportion spent by employers on the various components that make up the total pay of workers, other than direct remuneration. Employers' social security contributions such as National Insurance are captured in 'statutory social contributions'. Employers' imputed social contributions include the costs of above-statutory provision for payments such as sickness benefits and maternity provision and 'payments for days not worked' includes paid holidays (including official 'bank holidays'). All of these areas, with the exception of vocational training, perform key social security functions for those in work.

In addition to occupational welfare, there are other forms of provision that operate in similar or identical ways to benefits that are traditionally regarded as constituting 'social security'. In some cases changes in one form of state intervention will directly impact eligibility for another (known as 'negative-sum trade-offs'). This range of provision includes state-backed finance, for example, student loans, support for mortgage interest payments, Individual Savings Accounts (ISAs) (which are tax-free to an upper limit in any financial year), and the 'Help to Save' scheme available from 2018 for those in receipt of Working Tax Credit or Universal Credit, and also tax-free allowances such as personal tax allowances and tax exemptions for childcare and pensions. The Fabian Society has estimated that tax changes since 2010 in particular will mean that, by 2020, the top 20 per cent of income earners will extract as much in tax allowances than is paid in welfare benefits for the poorest 20 per cent (Harrop, 2016).

Figure 9.5: Shares of non-labour costs in the UK by type of payment, 2014

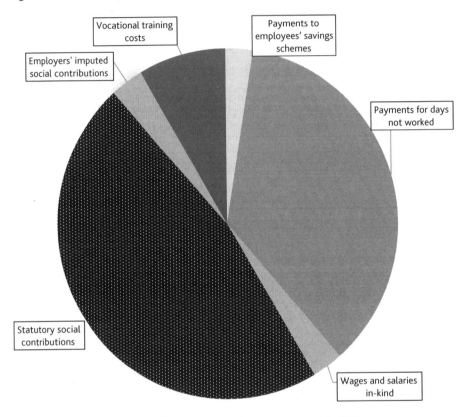

Source: Compiled from data released by the Eurostat Labour Costs Survey data, 2014

As the analysis is extended beyond individual recipients of what is popularly understood as social security provision, it becomes increasingly apparent that the benefits of social security are enjoyed much more widely than is depicted in the restricted debate on low-income or non-working citizens. As well as benefiting their direct recipients, for example, maternity and sickness benefits, tax credits and housing benefits also bring key benefits to employers. These public provisions enable employers to cover the contingency of 'surplus' or 'unproductive' labour while employees are on leave or working less than full time; for example, unemployment benefits maintain unemployed people during economic slowdowns so that they are in a position to take up employment when the economy recovers. In-work benefits in particular, such as tax credits and housing benefits, while meeting some needs for income maintenance, also contribute directly to the profits of private businesses. As Whitfield (2001, p 144) puts it, such provisions 'appear to support the working poor but they are de facto wage and income subsidies to employers.' Tax credits support low-paid workers, but also incentivise employers to continue to pay low wages, safe in the knowledge that low pay will be supplemented by the government and ultimately taxpayers (Citizens UK, 2016). Thus, while they might provide some employees with greater flexibility to work part time, reduce poverty traps and increase the incomes of those on the lowest incomes, they may also serve to dampen wage rates at the bottom end of the labour market and lock individuals into low-paying employment.

The existence of wage subsidies in the social security system has a long and hotly debated history dating back to the Speenhamland system established in Berkshire, England, in 1795 (Polanyi, 2001; Grover, 2015; see also Chapter 3, this volume). State support for low-wage employment has increased dramatically this century. By 2010-11, almost one-fifth of Housing Benefit claimants were in work and, as Figure 9.6 illustrates, 50 per cent of the incomes of the lowest-paid 10 per cent of workers were made up of tax credits and housing benefits. For the next decile, the figure is almost 40 per cent. Insofar as these benefits are necessary to support government-approved living standards, they can also be viewed as effective wage subsidies that ultimately support the profits of employers paying wages on which it is insufficient to live (Dean, 2012; Farnsworth, 2015; Citizens UK, 2016).

This is not to suggest that provision of these subsidies should be removed, but the sustainability and efficacy of the shift to long-term wage subsidy is questionable, particularly in the context of the current economic climate where wage levels in general are not increasing and there is consequently less prospect of increased Income Tax revenue. Measures such as substantial increases to the minimum wage (as occurred in 2015 when it was increased by 3 per cent for adults) and the introduction of the National Living Wage for those aged 25 and above in 2016 may reduce reliance on tax credits for some workers, but may also have an impact on commercial viability for some businesses, or consequential increases in prices as businesses pass on increased labour costs to consumers. Wider reductions in the value of tax credits and housing benefits as austerity measures are extended to in-work benefits, on the other hand, will almost certainly result in increased poverty for recipients (see Chapter 3, this volume). Thus the balance to be struck between facilitating the benefits of social security for employees, employers and society more generally is interlaced by wider concerns about how the economy should be managed, in addition to distributional concerns of achieving social justice through fair shares from the state social security system. The final section of this chapter considers these challenges in the context of their political foundations.

Figure 9.6: The share of in-work benefits in the total income of the lowest five income deciles, 2010

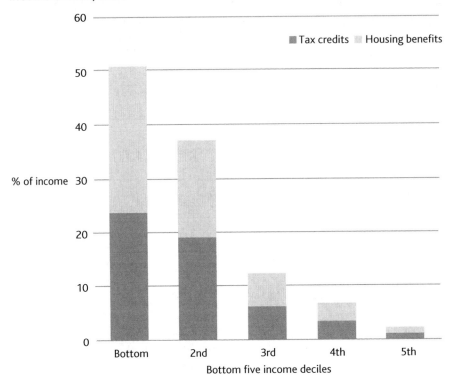

Source: Based on ONS data for 2010 (the latest available) from http://statistics.dwp.gov.uk/asd/asd1/hb_ctb/hbctb_release_aug12.xls

What is social security for? The macro level

The third and final question examined in this chapter asks, *what is social security for?* This is a big philosophical question addressed throughout this book, and one that exposes the underpinnings of social security systems and their perceived benefits to society. Answers to this question vary depending on political complexion and the way in which the interests of particular economic and/or social groups are privileged. The provision of social security encompasses both economic and social functions, as well as political aims that rest on beliefs about the fairness of economic obligations and rewards. As the previous sections of this chapter have shown, social security is used in wider strategies of economic management to manipulate and dis/incentivise labour market and company behaviour, and broadly, it is expected that the benefits of this will accrue to society as a whole, through economic growth and competitiveness. Social security is also a form of societal protection because, in macro-economic terms, it is counter-cyclical. This means that in times of economic contraction, which are expected within the theoretical business cycle, unemployment and other state benefits automatically increase to protect both the livelihoods and future employability of newly unemployed people, as well as their capacity as consumers. This is known as the 'automatic stabiliser' effect, and is expected to reduce both the length and depth of economic downturns.

Alongside economic management, social security also benefits society in its function as a 'social stabiliser', where the availability of cash transfers in respect of unemployment, sickness and old age, for example, acts as a palliative to prevent social unrest in the event of economic decline, and to maintain the legitimacy of governments. From this perspective, social security helps to legitimate capitalism by making the individual losses within the market system more tolerable. While this may benefit society in terms of social stability, it also highlights the function of social security as a method of social control which, in the contemporary context, is evidenced in more punitive approaches to the conditions of eligibility and increasing stigma experienced by those making claims (see Chapter 11, this volume).

On the right of the political spectrum some would argue that these eligibility control measures are necessary to maintain work incentives, and that state social security benefits should only be available to those unable (rather than 'unwilling') to sell their labour due to incapacity through illness, disability or old (or young) age. Others on the left would contend that social security should operate as a check on the commodifying effects of capitalism, whereby people are reduced only to the value of their labour power as this, in itself is a societal disbenefit, because the distribution of market rewards has no foundation in ideas of 'fairness'.

A number of commentators have drawn attention to the decommodifying potential of social security in providing independence to citizens in the face of social and economic challenges. Esping-Andersen (1990, p 21) explores decommodification as a marker of differentiation (and progress) among different welfare states. In his analysis, rights to state provision that represent an alternative means to maintaining a livelihood other than paid work imply a positive 'loosening of the pure commodity status' of citizens, and a welcome lessening of individuals' reliance on market forces to meet their welfare needs. Although decommodification applies to welfare domains beyond social security, cash benefits are a core element. The suggestion is that the more generous social security is, and the fewer conditions placed on recipients of it, the greater the decommodifying potential of individual welfare states. On both grounds, in comparison to other advanced economies, the UK system has become more commodifying over time. However, since the financial crisis in 2008, advanced economies have all been required to revisit their political and economic visions regarding the role of social security, in its state, occupational and corporate forms, and many have chosen to align provision more closely with economic rather than social goals.

In the decade since 2007 when the disruption in the global economy began, the redistributive aims of social security have experienced their greatest challenges since the systems were first established in the 1940s, and as far back as the late 19th century in some cases.

As the earlier sections of this chapter set out, redistribution through social security is complex and certainly does not represent a straightforward set of transfers from rich to poor. The welfare economist Nicholas Barr (2001, p 2) has suggested that in redistributive terms, 'it might be argued that the piggy-bank aspect' – which effectively operates as a form of enforced savings that redistributes income over a person's lifetime – 'is *the* key function of the welfare state' rather than its 'Robin Hood' function of redistributing income from rich to poor. Again, this analysis goes beyond the domain of social security alone, but the benefits of social, occupational, fiscal and corporate welfare all contribute to the smoothing of risks across society and the life course. What Barr's (2001) statement also points to is the operation of obligations and rewards, since it implies that, generally, citizens make claims on the welfare state that are commensurate with their contributions to it. However, as observed in one international assessment:

> There are significant differences across countries in the extent to which social policy goals are pursued through the tax system or in the role of private provision within national social protection systems. These differences point to substantial variance in the re-distributional nature of social systems. Some private social programmes may generate a more limited redistribution of resources than public ones, and tax advantages towards private pension and health plans are more likely than not to benefit the relatively well-to-do. (Adema and Ladaique, 2009, p 14)

Hence, the overall welfare of citizens depends on the provision and distribution, as well as redistribution, of taxation, tax exemptions, public provision and workplace provision. To return to a point raised earlier, social security is about much more than state benefits.

Conclusion

This chapter has presented an examination of the benefits of social security that takes account of the variety of channels through which 'social security' is provided. Both the 'social division of welfare' and 'mixed economy' approaches to understanding welfare provision are useful in identifying and incorporating elements and actors engaged in social security provision that are neglected in the popular focus on state benefits. However, these approaches also have weaknesses in that they do not necessarily recognise the structural influences and constraints imposed by economics and politics, and they also do not convey the more indirect channels linked to conditions of employment and wider economic policy through which social security can be provided. Political economy approaches are better able to account for these dimensions and to make links between the micro-level relationships of contributions and benefits and the macro-level analysis of the purpose of social security in the national economy.

The funding of social security has long since ceased to be a state-organised system of social insurance. In the contemporary context, the sources of funding are broader, and the interaction between the tax and benefit system, and between the obligations, contributions and benefits attributed to individual citizens and private businesses, is both complex and contradictory. In terms of 'who pays?', there is no clear evidence that social security, in its broader conceptualisation, necessarily leads to vertical redistribution from rich to poor, or that corporations support citizens. Similarly, when the question of 'who benefits?' is considered at the micro level it is clear that some elements of state social security provision, particularly in-work benefits, are more beneficial to those on lower incomes. However, it is also apparent that these forms of provision also extend significant benefits to businesses by protecting low wage bills. Employees, especially those more senior and those whose skills are in demand, benefit from the provisions of occupational welfare, but so do the businesses that employ them.

Finally, in considering what social security is for, the chapter has addressed the wider societal benefits that social security brings. Social security fulfils an important function in encouraging economic growth, and in maintaining both economic and social stability, but there are costs associated with these functions. Economic stability in particular, through meeting the extra demands made on state provision during times of recession, requires political (and financial) commitment to the cushioning effects of unemployment provisions. The quality and generosity of this commitment is mediated by the extent to which decommodification forms part of accepted national welfare settlements between the key stakeholders – the state, employees and businesses. Existing settlements have been under considerable strain since the 2008 financial crisis, and this has brought the purpose of social security into sharp relief for policy-makers. From the perspective adopted in this chapter it is clear that a more comprehensive understanding of the 'whole economy of welfare' that accounts for contributions and benefits beyond the traditional channels is required if fair and effective distributive outcomes in social security are to be achieved.

Overview

This chapter provides an analysis of the beneficiaries and contributors to the social security system and the complexity in attempting to draw distinctions between them. The discussion demonstrates that the interactions between citizens, the state and the market require a broader conceptualisation of 'who pays' and 'who benefits' from social security.

Changes in the economy, in patterns of employment and the conditions under which it is undertaken have entwined the redistributive outcomes of the contemporary social security system with the system of taxation and forms of occupational and corporate welfare. These outcomes provide benefits for companies, employees, direct claimants and the state.

Social security plays an important economic function in ensuring stability for national economies in periods of economic downturn, protecting the incomes of those who lose their employment and ensuring that levels of consumption are maintained. Countries differ in the extent to which this purpose of social security is recognised and interpreted in policy aims.

Without a fuller understanding of the 'whole economy' of social security it is unlikely that the societal benefits of redistribution will be either transparent or achieved.

Questions for discussion

1. In what ways can the 'mixed economy' approach enable a more comprehensive understanding of the benefits of social security to individuals and society?
2. Why is it so difficult to determine the relative contributions of employers and employees to the general funding of social security provision?
3. How does the state subsidise wages through social security, and what are the benefits of wage subsidies to governments, employers and employees?

Key reading

Farnsworth, K. (2012) *Social versus corporate welfare: Competing needs and interests within the welfare state*, London: Palgrave.

Powell, M. (ed) (2007) *Understanding the mixed economy of welfare*, Bristol: Policy Press.

Sinfield, A. (1978) 'Analyses in the social division of welfare', *Journal of Social Policy*, vol 7, no 2, pp 129-56.

Website resources

www.corporate-welfare-watch.org.uk
  Corporate Welfare Watch

http://fiscalwelfare.eu
  Fiscal Welfare

www.ifs.org.uk
  Institute for Fiscal Studies

www.jrf.org.uk
  Joseph Rowntree Foundation

www.gov.uk/government/organisations/low-pay-commission
  Low Pay Commission

References

Adema, W. and Ladaique, M. (2009) *How expensive is the welfare state? Gross and net indicators in the OECD Social Expenditure Database (SOCX)*, OECD Social, Employment and Migration Working Papers, No 92, Paris: OECD Publishing (http://dx.doi.org/10.1787/220615515052).

Alcock, P., Glennerster, H., Oakley, A. and Sinfield, A. (eds) (2001) *Welfare and wellbeing, Richard Titmuss's contribution to social policy*, Bristol: Policy Press.

Barr, N. (2001) *The welfare state as piggy bank: Information, risk, uncertainty and the role of the state*, Oxford: Oxford University Press.

Beveridge W. (1942) *Social insurance and allied services* (Beveridge Report), London: HMSO.

Browne, J. and Hood, A. (2016) *Living standards, poverty and inequality in the UK: 2015-16 to 2020-21*, London: Institute for Fiscal Studies.

Browne, J. and Elming, W. (2015) *The effect of the coalition's tax and benefit changes on household incomes and work incentives*, IFS Briefing Note (BN159), London: Institute for Fiscal Studies.

Citizens UK (2016) *The public subsidy to low wage employers*, London: Citizens UK.

Dean, H. (2012) 'Welcome relief or indecent subsidy? The implications of wage top-up schemes', *Policy & Politics*, vol 40, no 3, pp 305-21.

Esping-Andersen, G. (1990) *The three worlds of welfare capitalism*, Cambridge: Polity.

Farnsworth, K. (2012) *Social versus corporate welfare: Competing needs and interests within the welfare state*, London: Palgrave.

Farnsworth, K. (2015) *The British corporate welfare state*, SPERI Paper No 24, Sheffield: SPERI.

Goodin, R. and Le Grand, J. (1987) *Not only the poor: The middle classes and the welfare state*, London: Allen & Unwin.

Gough, I. (2011) 'From financial crisis to fiscal crisis', in K. Farnsworth and Z. Irving (eds) *Social policy in challenging times: Economic crisis and welfare systems*, Bristol: Policy Press, pp 49-64.

Grover, C. (2015) 'Social security policy and low wages in austere times', in Z. Irving, M. Fenger and J. Hudson (eds) *Social policy review 27*, Bristol: Policy Press, pp 33-54.

Harrop, A. (2016) *For us all: Redesigning social security for the 2020s*, London: Fabian Society.

IFS (Institute for Fiscal Studies) (2015) *Social security spending*, London: IFS (www.ifs.org.uk/tools_and_resources/fiscal_facts/public_spending_survey/social_security).

Iversen, T. (2005) *Capitalism, democracy and welfare*, Cambridge: Cambridge University Press.

Mann, K. (1989) *Growing fringes: Hypothesis on the development of occupational welfare*, Leeds: Armley Publications.

Mann, K. (1991) 'The social division of welfare: a class struggle perspective', in N. Manning (ed) *Social policy review 1990-91*, Harlow: Longman & Social Policy Association, pp 243-61.

Mann, K. (2009) 'Remembering and rethinking the social divisions of welfare: 50 years on', *Journal of Social Policy*, vol 38, no 1, pp 1-18.

Papadakis, E. and Taylor-Gooby, P. (1987) *The private provision of public welfare: State, market and community*, Brighton: Harvester Wheatsheaf.

Polanyi, K. (2001 [1944]) *The great transformation: The political and economic origins of our time*, Boston, MA: Beacon Press.

Powell, M. (ed) (2007) *Understanding the mixed economy of welfare*, Bristol: Policy Press.

Rein, M. and Rainwater, L. (1986) 'The public/private mix: The institutions of social protection', in M. Rein and L. Rainwater (eds) *Public/private interplay in social protection: A comparative study*, New York: M.E. Sharpe, pp 3-24.

Sinfield, A. (1978) 'Analyses in the social division of welfare', *Journal of Social Policy*, vol 7, no 2, pp 129-56.

Titmuss, R. (1958) *Essays on the welfare state*, London: George Allen & Unwin.

Whitfield, D. (2001) *Public services or corporate welfare: Rethinking the nation state in the global economy*, London: Pluto Press.

10

Public attitudes to 'welfare'

John Hudson

Summary

In a democratic society like the UK, it might be presumed that major shifts in social security policy reflect the 'will of the people', policy frameworks altering in response to changing public attitudes. In practice, however, the link between the two is somewhat fuzzy, public attitudes being only one part of a complex mix of influences on policy.

This chapter examines public attitudes to 'welfare' in the UK. It outlines:

- the broad patterns of support for social security in the UK;
- shifts in public attitudes over time;
- how public attitudes feed into the policy-making process;
- the complexities we face in understanding attitudes to 'welfare'.

Introduction

This chapter unpacks key debates around attitudes to 'welfare', first, summarising what we know about contemporary attitudes, before moving on to explore how attitudes have shifted over time and then, to explore wider questions about the ways in which public attitudes have shaped social security policy in the UK. Much of the literature in this field refers to 'public attitudes to welfare', but it should be acknowledged at the outset that the term 'welfare' is itself contentious and seen by some to encapsulate a particular set of values about social security (Hudson et al, 2016a). Lister (2011), for instance, argues it is an American import that has 'besmirched' debate, being used in political discourse to displace the broader notion of social security by tying cash transfers to the notion of 'welfare dependency'. We share the concerns about the language, but because 'welfare' is increasingly the term that politicians and commentators use in public debate it is also a term that those surveying public attitudes often use too. This chapter therefore follows the convention of placing 'welfare' in inverted commas to reflect that the term captures popular and political understandings of social security, but that it is a loaded and contested term.

Contemporary attitudes to 'welfare'

With much of the political discourse surrounding social security pejorative in nature it is often presumed that public attitudes to 'welfare' must be similarly hostile. Jensen (2014; see also Jensen and Tyler, 2015) has powerfully argued that a negative political and media discourse has fuelled support for welfare reform and retrenchment. She dubs this a 'new welfare commonsense' which 'functions by cleaving the body politic into two: those that put in and those that take out, those who get "something for nothing" (welfare without work) and those that get "nothing for something" (work without welfare)' (Jensen, 2014, para 2.5).

In the UK we are fortunate to have robust time series data capturing public attitudes to 'welfare' because this has been a key focus of the British Social Attitudes (BSA) survey since the early 1980s. Figure 10.1 draws on BSA data from 2015 (the most recent available), which suggests that public attitudes reflect this stereotypical division of 'deserving' and 'undeserving' groups. In particular, attitudes towards unemployed people are noticeably 'harder' than attitudes to other groups covered by the survey. For instance, 45 per cent of respondents said they would like to see less government spending on benefits for unemployed people, but just 7 per cent favoured reductions in spending on benefits for retired people and only 2 per cent on benefits for people who care for those who are sick or disabled (Clery, 2016, p 5). When probed on the detail of how benefits for the unemployed should be designed, harsh views can again be detected: when asked if someone in receipt of unemployment benefits should take a job that may be unsuitable for some reason or remain on benefits while looking for an alternative job, 88 per cent agreed a minimum wage job should be taken, 82 per cent agreed a short-term contract role should be taken and 83 per cent agreed a job the person was not interested in should be taken (Clery, 2016, p 10). Moreover, 60 per cent agreed that unemployment benefits should be available only for a limited time rather than for as long as it takes to find a job, which Clery (2016, p 8) noted was tighter than anything that had been proposed by the Cameron governments or its predecessors.

A similar distinction between attitudes towards different groups can be found in questions about in-work benefits which top up the wages of low-income households: while 55 per cent of respondents feel the government should top up the wages of a couple with children (compared to 29 per cent saying they should look after themselves) and 66 per cent do so for lone-parent households (compared to 21 per cent saying they should look after themselves), just 25 per cent agree that the government should top the wages of a couple *without* children, with 61 per cent saying they should look after themselves (Clery, 2016, p 7).

Figure 10.1: Percentage of BSA respondents* who would like to see more/less government spending on benefits for

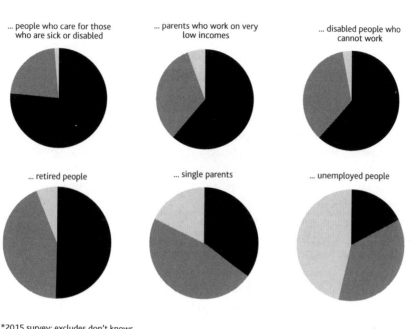

Note: *2015 survey; excludes don't knows.

Source: BSA survey

However, as these figures suggest, public attitudes to 'welfare' are nuanced, supportive of some interventions and less so of others. Indeed, it should be stressed that much of the BSA data underlines – spending on benefits for unemployed people aside – that more people support *increases* in benefits spending than favour reductions, often overwhelmingly so. As Figure 10.1 shows, this is particularly so for benefits for people who care for those who are sick or disabled, parents who work on very low incomes, and people with disabilities who cannot work (Clery, 2016, p 5; NatCen Social Research, 2017), where a clear majority of respondents favour increased spending and only a tiny minority favour cuts in spending.

A number of conclusions might be drawn from contemporary BSA data. The first is, as Baumberg (2014a) puts it, that 'Benefit attitudes are not simply "hard" or "soft" but complex and uneven.' A second is that there is a clear hierarchy of support that reflects 'deserving' and 'undeserving' stereotypes (Hudson et al, 2016b): support for spending on benefits for people with disabilities, low-income working families with children and retired people being higher than support for benefits for single parents, low-income working households without children and unemployed people. Finally, attitudes towards benefits for unemployed people stand apart from attitudes towards other groups, being noticeably more hostile.

A 'hardening' of attitudes to 'welfare'?

It is commonly argued, by political actors and academic researchers alike, that contemporary public attitudes to 'welfare' are 'harder' than attitudes in the past: that people are less inclined to support spending on social security, favour tougher conditions being attached to benefits and/or believe payment rates should be reduced, for example. Indeed, in 2015 the House of Commons Work and Pensions Committee announced it would review the principles of social security, in part because 'over a long period of time, voters have been withdrawing support for Britain's welfare state on the basis that they believe it is no longer fair' (House of Commons Work and Pensions Committee, 2015).

Similar claims are often echoed by academic analyses of the BSA data. For instance, Deeming (2015, p 867) argues the BSA data show a 'fundamental shift in public views on welfare provision over the past three decades' and that 'at the start of the 21st century, a distinct attitudinal shift begins to emerge.' Deeming (2015, p 867) places particular stress here on the fact that relatively few see benefits as inadequate today, and that a clear majority believe that 'out-of-work benefits are too generous and promote the dependency culture.' Some analyses suggest relative stability in attitudes in recent years mask a broader shift when a longer view is taken. For instance, Taylor-Gooby and Taylor (2015, p 93) suggest that the lack of movement in contemporary BSA data around attitudes to benefit spending should be placed in the context of 'years of a steady decline in support for spending on public services in general and on welfare in particular.' Similarly, Baumberg (2014b, p 114) notes that movements in the BSA data in recent years 'are relatively slight in comparison to the more far-reaching hardening of attitudes that came in the preceding 10 to 15 years.'

There is little doubt, as these authors argue, that at least some attitudes to welfare have hardened in the period covered by the BSA. Most notably, the proportion of respondents agreeing 'The government should spend more money on welfare benefits for the poor, even if it leads to higher taxes' has been much lower in the 2000s than it was in the 1980s and early 1990s, falling from a peak of 61 per cent in 1989 to below 50 per cent by 1995 and a low of 27 per cent in 2009, but with some signs of an upturn in the early 2010s (see Figure 10.2). Moreover, attitudes towards unemployed people seem to have qualitatively shifted over time according to the BSA data, as 'public opinion remains far more inclined to view unemployment as an individual responsibility than it was in the late 1980s and early 1990s' (Taylor-Gooby and Taylor, 2015, p 83).

Figure 10.2: The government should spend more money on welfare benefits for the poor, even if it leads to higher taxes

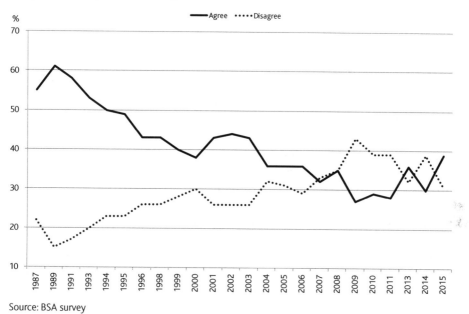

Source: BSA survey

There has been much debate over why this might be the case. Some analysts suggest there are clear links with shifts in political discourse following the end of the postwar welfare consensus and a broader move away from the solidaristic values of the postwar era. For instance, Deeming (2015, p 871) argues the BSA data 'clearly reveal a departure from societal or structural explanations for unemployment towards individualist interpretations with an emphasis on human agency', and he points to New Labour's repackaging of social security policy in the 1990s/early 2000s around a more conditional model as pivotal in shifting public opinion. Such claims resonate with much theorising in sociology about individualisation processes in 'late modern' societies (see Dawson, 2012, for an overview of these debates).

However, there are complications in examining BSA data over time that must be acknowledged, the thorniest of which is that the survey responses at each time point reflect the social, economic and political context at the moment any question is asked. For example, when asked whether the government should spend more money on benefits for the poor even if it leads to higher taxes, a respondent's answer will, we can presume, be in part affected by the level of spending, the level of taxation and the level of poverty at that moment in time, or at least their perceptions of these factors. A fall in the proportion agreeing that spending should increase may therefore reflect a belief that spending was too low in the 1980s but rose to a more reasonable level in the 2000s, rather than reflecting a 'hardening' in underlying attitudes. Curtice (2010) refers to this movement in attitudes because of changes in the underlying context as a 'thermostat' effect (so called because when someone is asked whether a room is too hot or too cold, their response is largely shaped by the temperature of the room at that point in time), and suggests it is key in explaining much of the shift in attitudes around public spending during the New Labour governments.

At the same time, however, Curtice (2010) suggests that New Labour helped foster a more 'conservative' outlook in some broader ways, arguing the BSA data show 'the public, including Labour supporters themselves, no longer ha[d] as much belief in the importance of equality and of government action to secure it as it once did.' Moreover, it is important to note that a key aspect of the thermostat effect has been that public support for spending more on benefits for unemployed people usually increases when unemployment is high: Taylor-Gooby and Taylor (2015, p 93) suggest the fact that BSA data indicate people remained 'relatively unsympathetic' to increased spending following the global financial crisis of the late 2000s is therefore particularly significant.

However, a recent strand of work undertaken by Hudson et al (2016b, c) has argued that analyses of attitudes to 'welfare' using BSA data might be misleading because the survey stretches back only to the 1980s. Their 'bounce thesis' expands the thermostat argument in a number of key ways. First, they argue that, in the absence of hard data, many presume the trend shown in Figure 10.2 must be a continuation of a pattern stretching back further in time: that is, that support for spending increases would be higher still if the BSA had operated during the 'postwar welfare consensus' years of the 1950s and 1960s (Hudson et al, 2016c). Second, having pieced historical data together from older one-off surveys and opinion polls, they argue that this is unlikely to be the case and that, contrary to expectations, it may well be that public support for boosting social spending actually rose in the 1980s as compared to the earlier decades, making it one of the moments in which public support for 'welfare' was particularly high. Third, they suggest this fits the 'thermostat' effect thesis: in the 1980s economic problems were severe and there was deep political debate about the fairness of major cuts to benefits; sympathy for those in need was likely to be high on this basis. Box 10.1 provides some examples from the historical data they assembled.

Hudson et al (2016c) do not claim that there have been no changes in public attitudes to 'welfare' over time: indeed, they note that there appear to have been important shifts around benefits for families with children, which seem to have become more popular over time. Moreover, subtle but important changes in context cannot be easily detected in survey questions; for instance, while benefits for people with disabilities appear to have been relatively well supported by public opinion for many decades, intense political debate of the finer details of programme design over the past decade or so (see Chapter 4, this volume) underlines that precisely who might be deemed by the public to fall into the 'deserving' group here may be rather different than in the past. Moreover, some analyses of the BSA data suggest that there are significant differences in some attitudes when different generations are compared with Duffy et al (2013, p 30) suggesting 'Generation Y' (those born between 1980 and 2000) are more sceptical about the fairness and efficacy of social spending than previous generations.

Box 10.1: Public attitudes in the golden age of 'welfare'

Wincott (2013, p 820) argues that orthodox histories of social policy typically invoke the notion of a 'golden age' of the welfare state in the postwar period, which is contrasted against the reformed welfare state that has existed since. He argues this 'highly stylised account' does not sit well against the evidence of what has actually happened.

Hudson et al (2016c) suggest nostalgic 'golden age' narratives often permeate discussion of public attitudes to 'welfare' too, and, echoing Wincott, suggest that the empirical reality is more complex than often assumed, fluctuating for and against higher spending during these decades (see Hudson et al, 2016b for fuller details).

Significantly, earlier surveys often uncovered pejorative attitudes to 'welfare', with 'deserving' and 'undeserving' stereotypes often informing public attitudes in the 'golden age' of welfare. For instance:

- In a 1967 survey, 73 per cent of respondents agreed that there were many people drawing the main means-tested benefit of the time 'who could really be earning enough to support themselves if they wanted to' (Wedderburn, 1967; Wiseman, 1967).
- In a poll conducted in 1968, 89 per cent agreed with 'Too many people don't bother to work because they can live well enough on the dole', and 87 per cent agreed 'Too many take advantage of benefits by taking time off work' (Klein, 1974).
- A 1977 survey similarly reported 80 per cent of respondents agreeing 'Nowadays too many people depend on welfare', and 70 per cent agreeing with that 'There's so much welfare now it's made the people of this country lazy' (Golding and Middleton, 1982).

By contrast, some sources tracking attitudes across the 1960s, 1970s and 1980s suggest a rise in support for 'welfare' in the 1980s. For example, responses in Gallup polling on the causes of poverty (see below) show public opinion moving towards *structural* rather than *individual* explanations in the 1980s.

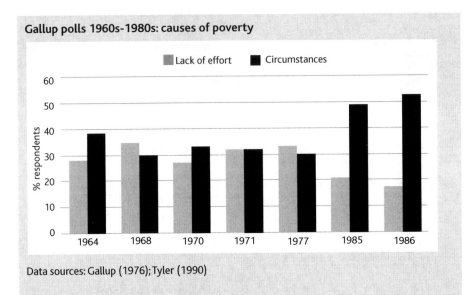

Gallup polls 1960s-1980s: causes of poverty

Data sources: Gallup (1976); Tyler (1990)

Wincott's (2013, p 820) observation that 'current efforts to defend or extend the welfare state will be undermined if they are invariably compared to a golden past, particularly one that never actually existed' seems pertinent with respect to attitudes to 'welfare' debates.

These qualifications aside, however, there are perhaps more historical continuities between past and present attitudes to 'welfare' than often suggested, raising questions about how far public attitudes shape social security policy. It may be that one reason so many people subscribe to the view that there has been a significant decline in support for 'welfare' since the postwar era is that many commentators – not unreasonably – expect broad movements in political attitudes to have arisen in response to shifting public concerns. Viewed from this perspective, both the great expansion of social policy in the 1940s-1960s during the postwar welfare consensus years and the roll-back of elements of it by the Thatcher governments from 1979-90 are explained as democratic responses to shifting public demands. The reality seems likely to be have been more complex, with movements in public opinion and social policy linked much less clearly than this.

For instance, Bradshaw and Mayhew (2004, p 12) used BSA data up to 2001 to explore whether public attitudes were in tune with the increasingly negative political rhetoric around 'welfare' from the 1980s onwards, particularly arguments that 'welfare dependency' had undermined public support for the welfare state; they concluded that, 'Although social attitudes to the welfare state and to dependency are clearly complex they are much more positive than the rhetoric of the political elite would suggest.' In other words, they found little to suggest that public attitudes had been supportive of Thatcher's 'rolling back' of the welfare state.

Equally, in a review of opinion poll data from the 1940s-1970s, Klein (1974, p 411) noted that the strong pro-welfare state political consensus of this putative 'golden age' of welfare was not always easy to detect in public attitudes data, in particular, because 'Public opinion – in contrast to elite opinion – tends to be moralistic [… based on a] distinction between the deserving and undeserving poor.' Moreover, he noted that some key surveys suggested there was little difference on 'welfare' issues between different groups of voters; instead, 'the real distinction seems to be between public and elite opinion, rather than between social classes or party supporters' (Klein, 1974, p 411). On this basis, Klein (1974, p 417) argued that a paradox could be seen at this point in time whereby 'it is precisely those who want the greatest social changes who should be most elitist in their approach.'

Public attitudes and the politics of 'welfare'

So, while histories of the welfare state often emphasise the dramatic paradigmatic shifts in the principles underpinning UK social policy as it moved towards a more expansive model of social citizenship in the 1940s and then radically back towards a more individualistic one in the 1980s, there is good reason to believe that public attitudes did not move clearly and directly in the same directions each time. Why might it be that movements in public attitudes and social policy are not always clearly in tune?

One reason is that public attitudes to 'welfare' can be difficult to read. Indeed, survey data sometimes point to seeming contradictions in public attitudes. For instance, Baumberg (2014a, b) notes that BSA data have shown both that the vast majority (some 77 per cent in 2013) agree that large numbers falsely claim benefits but that only a minority (33 per cent in 2013) agree that 'most people on the dole are fiddling'. This may partly be accounted for by the wording of questions, but it also likely reflects that many people view the social security system as having strengths and weaknesses rather than being simply 'good' or 'bad'. This fuzziness likely applies not only to specific policy instruments, but to broader underlying principles too. In a classic study of public attitudes to 'welfare' undertaken in the 1980s, Taylor-Gooby (1982, 1985; Beedle and Taylor-Gooby, 1983) suggested 'pragmatic acceptance' rather than 'positive commitment' to the welfare state captured the mood well; much the same may also be said of attitudes in the 2000s. A complex mix of abstract ideas, personal experiences and self-interest typically shape each individual's attitudes to 'welfare'.

But we can also add to this mix that most people have a limited knowledge of the details of the social security system. For instance, in a review of 46 measures across 18 datasets capturing the UK, Baumberg Geiger (2017; see also Baumberg Geiger and Meuelman, 2016) found that the British public significantly overestimate the level of spending on unemployment benefits compared to pension spending and overestimate the levels of benefits most people receive; half of respondents believed claims for out-of-work benefits had risen over the past 15 years when they had in fact fallen sharply; and, even allowing for the difficulties in measuring the level of social security fraud, the public overestimate its level against any realistic measure. Baumberg Geiger and Meuelman (2016, p 294) note there are nuances here that need to be accounted for – for example, people tend to *underestimate* benefit levels in some areas such as pensions – but they conclude that 'these nuances do not change the overall picture, in which the evidence strongly supports the assumption of widespread myths.' Hudson et al's (2016b, p 706) review of data sources covering the 1940s to early 1980s similarly noted that one of the key themes running through these sources was that 'most of the public have a rather hazy knowledge of the details of policy.'

It might be added that this limited knowledge is oftentimes accompanied by a limited interest in social security policy too. So, while – with the exception of benefits for unemployed people – most BSA respondents say they would rather see more spending on benefits and only a small proportion say they would like to see less (see Figure 10.1), it is also the case that few respondents see social security benefits as the highest priority for spending. In the 2015 survey, for instance, only around 2 per cent placed it as their highest priority and around 5 per cent in their top two priorities; by contrast, around one in four placed health in their top two priorities and around 60 per cent did so for education (NatCen Social Research, 2017). Older surveys tend to show similar patterns; indeed, one of the very first surveys of public attitudes to the welfare state, conducted in the late 1950s, concluded that 'The attitude of [respondents] towards the social services was enthusiastic rather than critical, but there is not much doubt that this attitude is governed by their enthusiasm for the health services' (PEP, 1961, p 39). Following a detailed study conducted in the early 1980s, Beedle and Taylor-Gooby (1983, p 15) pointed to 'suggestive evidence of strong ambivalence in opinions, based both on misconceptions about the system and on individual experience of it', which they concluded pointed to 'pragmatic acceptance' rather than a 'positive commitment' to welfare.

When attitudes are fuzzy, ambivalent and pragmatic, and knowledge limited, the challenges politicians and researchers face in 'reading' attitudes to 'welfare' are naturally magnified. But in also stressing the import of individual experience in shaping attitudes, Beedle and Taylor-Gooby hint at another complexity in unpacking the attitudes and policy link: that our often limited experiences and knowledge of social security mean attitudes surveys can struggle to capture underlying attitudes. For instance, one of the most controversial social security reforms of recent years was the 'Bedroom Tax' (see Chapter 1, this volume) that reduced Housing Benefit payments for claimants living in social housing judged to be under-occupied. Polling data initially suggested that the measure had public support, with a YouGov poll in the month before implementation (March 2013) finding 49 per cent in support and 38 per cent opposed, but YouGov polling following implementation of the policy soon showed a different picture, as experience of the reform and awareness of its impact spread; by July 2014, 49 per cent were opposed to the policy against 41 per cent in support (Jordan, 2014; see also Hudson et al, 2016b).

This could be taken to suggest that campaigns to boost awareness of the reality of the benefits system might shift public attitudes to 'welfare', but the literature offers a number of reasons for us to be cautious here. One is, as Baumberg Geiger and Meuelman (2016) note, that there is little evidence that the so-called 'myth-busting' approaches used by many campaigning organisations are effective in shifting attitudes, not least because people often do not accept evidence that challenges their underlying beliefs. Another reason is that when people have personal experiences of the benefits system, particularly with respect to out-of-work benefits, they do not automatically connect injustices in their own experiences with wider social injustices. Indeed, Patrick's research (2016, 2017; see also Chapter 11, this volume), in which she used qualitative longitudinal methods to capture the unfolding 'lived experiences' of 'welfare reform' over a period of three years, found the opposite was often the case.

From attitudes to values and culture

Some theorists have argued that we might usefully distinguish between *attitudes to 'welfare'*, conceptualised as being related to the present moment and so sensitive to the current context and potentially unstable over time, from more enduring and stable *societal values*, with the most enduring societal values comprising the foundation of a nation's *culture* (see Hudson et al, 2014).

This may sound a rather abstract distinction, but it becomes relevant for understanding social security when considered from a cross-national perspective. It is commonly argued in the comparative social policy literature that welfare states display 'path-dependent' trajectories (Pierson, 2004), whereby cross-national differences in social policies are said to reflect long-term, historically rooted, differences. The most prominent example is Esping-Andersen's (1990) claim that the welfare systems of rich countries fall into three distinct types – the social democratic, liberal and conservative/corporatist regimes; while his typology is well known, his argument that membership of the different regimes was, in large part, historically determined is less well known. So, for instance, Sweden being an example of his social democratic regime with strong social rights and low inequality and the US being an example of his liberal regime with weak social rights and high inequality was not seen as the outcome of current political choices in each country, but a reflection of long-term differences in the politics of social policy stretching back many decades and beyond.

Some theorists have highlighted culture as one of the factors that might explain why countries follow one path or another. Indeed, Esping-Andersen (1996, p x) observed that different regions of the world are 'quite distinct in terms of cultural and political legacies, economic development, and shared social policy traditions.' Analyses of welfare systems in East Asian countries have often stressed the role of Confucian values in driving a distinctive model of welfare in the region (see, for example, Jones, 1990; Goodman and Peng, 1996); indeed, Rieger and Liebfried (2003, p 243) go so far as to suggest that 'Confucian culture can be identified as the fundamental cause of an independent path of welfare state evolution in East Asia.'

Some commentators eschew culturally deterministic perspectives such as the 'Confucian welfare' argument on the basis that culture is rarely the decisive factor in shaping social policies (see Hudson et al, 2014). However, there is stronger support for more nuanced contributions to the debate that see culture as *one* of the factors that might interplay with other forces in shaping social policy. In Pfau-Effinger's (2005; cf 2004, pp 37-61) 'welfare culture approach', culture is seen as an important factor shaping social policy, but its influence is mediated by political actors, social structures and institutions in policy-making. Hudson et al (2014; see also Jo, 2011) tested such arguments using detailed cross-national statistical data stretching back to the early 1980s. They found some clear examples of variations in societal values being associated with variations in policies across rich countries. For instance, even after accounting for factors such as political and economic differences, countries with strongly conservative social norms were likely to have lower levels of spending on unemployment benefits than countries where these social norms were more liberal.

But comparative theorists add yet another complexity to this debate by pointing to the role policies themselves might play in the political process. While policies are usually seen as the outcome of the political process, some theorists argue that 'policy feedback loops' mean they can be inputs into the process too. As Skocpol and Amenta (1986, p 149) famously put it, 'not only does politics create social policies, social policies also create politics'; in other words, the design of social policies themselves might shape our values, perceptions and interests. In a detailed cross-national quantitative methods analysis of how governments had adapted their welfare states in the face of heightened global economic competition, Swank (2002) found that social security spending was less likely to be cut in countries where social policies were universal and well funded than in countries where they were targeted and less well funded. This, he suggested, was somewhat paradoxical in that countries with lower social spending were more likely to conclude it should to be cut to help economic competitiveness; he suggested that policy feedback loops were a key cause of this outcome, voters in countries with the more minimal and targeted system being more tolerant of spending cuts than those in countries with well-funded universal systems. In a similar cross-national quantitative methods analysis, Larsen (2006, p 143) argued that cross-national differences in the perception of the poor and unemployed in part reflect how social policies affect our outlook, his analysis suggesting in particular that the extent to which welfare state institutions divide people into 'them' and 'us' plays a key role in shaping public attitudes to welfare, selective systems being more likely to foster negative attitudes and less likely to foster positive attitudes towards the poor (cf van Oorschot, 2006).

A key conclusion to draw from these debates is that those looking to interpret attitudes data must account for the nuances and complexities underneath the headline data. Given that social policy often deals with complex normative debates about fairness, desert and social justice (van Oorschot, 2000), we should not expect to find simple and uniform patterns of public opinion. Context matters when interpreting such data. But a second key observation is that, at the macro level, the link between public attitudes and social policy design is often weaker than imagined. In part this is because policy-makers also face the difficult challenge of interpreting fuzzy information about public attitudes, but it is also because the policy-making process itself is, of course, only partially driven by public demands and societal values, which are important but rarely decisive in shaping policy decisions (cf Pfau-Effinger, 2005). This is not to say that politics, policy and public attitudes are unrelated, but that they are linked in complex ways.

Overview

It is often argued that public attitudes to 'welfare' in the UK have 'hardened' in recent decades as society has become more individualistic and the postwar political consensus around the welfare state has collapsed.

However, while political discourse around social security shifted considerably as the UK moved from a 'golden age' of welfare in the postwar period, the continuities in public attitudes to 'welfare' were probably greater than often imagined. While it is likely that some attitudes have 'hardened', public attitudes do not tend to be simply 'hard' or 'soft', but instead, are complex and uneven, sometimes contradictory, and often characterised by ambivalence or pragmatic acceptance. In practice, many people view the social security system as having strengths and weaknesses rather than being simply 'good' or 'bad'.

That movements in public attitudes to 'welfare' do not neatly match movements in policy agendas raises some interesting questions, but also underlines that public attitudes are only one factor in shaping social security policy. Moreover, attempts to trace the influence of public attitudes on social security usually point to the complex ways in which policies and attitudes are interlinked, each influencing the other rather than there being a simple one-way relationship.

Adding a temporal dimension muddies the picture further, for it raises difficult questions concerning the potential role of each nation's culture in shaping contemporary attitudes.

Nonetheless, although public attitudes are rarely decisive in shaping policy decisions, they undoubtedly play a significant role in shaping the context for political debate about social security policy.

Questions for discussion

1. How might we best characterise contemporary public attitudes to 'welfare'?
2. Have public attitudes to 'welfare' hardened over time?
3. What role should public attitudes play in shaping social security policy?

Key reading

Clery, E. (2016) 'Welfare', in E. Clery, J. Curtice and M. Phillips (eds) *British Social Attitudes 33: Britain divided? Public attitudes after seven years of austerity?*, London: NatCen Social Research.

Hudson, J. and Lunt, N., with Hamilton, C., Mackinder, S., Meers, J. and Swift, C. (2016) 'Exploring public attitudes to welfare over the Longue Durée: Re-examination of survey evidence from Beveridge, Beatlemania, Blair and beyond', *Social Policy & Administration*, vol 50, no 6, pp 691-711.

Jensen, T. (2014) 'Welfare commonsense, poverty porn and doxosophy', *Sociological Research Online*, vol 19, no 3.

Website resources

http://natcen.ac.uk/our-research/research/british-social-attitudes
British Social Attitudes survey series

www.europeansocialsurvey.org
European Social Survey

Acknowledgements

This chapter draws on a number of previous publications written with colleagues: their contribution to these works and the productive discussions we had during and since writing them have been invaluable and contributed to much of the thinking in this chapter. Particular thanks are due to Nam Jo, Antonia Keung, Neil Lunt, Ruth Patrick, Emma Wincup, Charlotte Hamilton, Sophie Mackinder, Jed Meers, Chelsea Swift, Ben Baumberg Geiger and Kayleigh Garthwaite.

References

Baumberg, B. (2014a) 'Attitudes to benefits are not as negative as they seem', *The Conversation*, 17 June.

Baumberg, B. (2014b) 'Benefits and the cost of living', in A. Park, C. Bryson and J. Curtice (eds) *British Social Attitudes 31*, London: NatCen, pp 95-122.

Baumberg Geiger, B. (2017) 'The role of knowledge and "myths" in the perceived deservingness of social security benefit claimants', in W. van Oorschot and F. Roosma (eds) *The social legitimacy of targeted welfare: Attitudes to welfare deservingness*, Cheltenham: Edward Elgar, pp 173-92.

Baumberg Geiger, B. and Meuelman, B. (2016) 'Beyond "mythbusting": How to respond to myths and perceived undeservingness in the British benefits system', *Journal of Poverty and Social Justice*, vol 24, no 3, pp 291-306.

Beedle, P. and Taylor-Gooby, P. (1983) 'Ambivalence and altruism: Public opinion about taxation and welfare', *Policy & Politics*, vol 11, pp 15-39.

Bradshaw, J. and Mayhew, E. (2004) 'Public attitudes to dependency and the welfare state', *International Journal of Market Research*, vol 46, no 1, pp 49-64.

Clery, E. (2016) 'Welfare', in E. Clery, J. Curtice and M. Phillips (eds) *British Social Attitudes 33: Britain divided? Public attitudes after seven years of austerity?*, London: NatCen Social Research, pp 23-42.

Curtice, J. (2010) 'Thermostat or weathervane? Public reactions to spending and redistribution under New Labour', in A. Park, J. Curtice, K. Thomson, M. Phillips, E. Clery and S. Butt (eds) *British Social Attitudes: 26th report*, London: Sage, pp 19-38.

Dawson, M. (2012) 'Reviewing the critique of individualization: The disembedded and embedded theses', *Acta Sociologica*, vol 55, no 4, pp 305-19.

Deeming, C. (2015) 'Foundations of the workfare state – Reflections on the political transformation of the welfare state in Britain', *Social Policy & Administration*, vol 49, no 7, pp 862-86.

Duffy, B., Hall, S., O'Leary, D. and Pope, S. (2013) *Generation strains: A Demos and Ipsos MORI report on changing attitudes to welfare*, London: Demos.

Esping-Andersen, G. (1990) *The three worlds of welfare capitalism*, Cambridge: Polity.

Esping-Andersen, G. (1996) 'After the golden age? Welfare state dilemmas in a global economy', in G. Esping-Andersen (ed) *Welfare states in transition: National adaptations in global economies*, London: Sage, pp 1-31.

Gallup, G.H. (1976) *The Gallup international public opinion polls, Great Britain, 1937-1975*, Westport, CT: Greenwood Press

Golding, P. and Middleton, S. (1982) *Images of welfare: Press and public attitudes to poverty*, Oxford: Martin Robertson.

Goodman, R. and Peng, I. (1996) 'The East Asian welfare states: Peripatetic learning, adaptive change, and nation-building', in G. Esping-Andersen (ed) *Welfare states in transition: National adaptations in global economies*, London: Sage, pp 192-224.

House of Commons Work and Pensions Committee (2015) 'Contributory welfare state investigated by Committee', Press Release, 22 December.

Hudson, J., Jo, N.-K. and Keung, A. (2014) *Culture and the politics of welfare: Exploring societal values and social choices*, Basingstoke: Palgrave.

Hudson, J., Patrick, R. and Wincup, E. (2016a) 'Introduction to themed special issue: Exploring "welfare" attitudes and experiences', *Journal of Poverty and Social Justice*, vol 24, no 3, pp 215-26.

Hudson, J. and Lunt, N., with Hamilton, C., Mackinder, S., Meers, J. and Swift, C. (2016b) 'Exploring public attitudes to welfare over the Longue Durée: Re-examination of survey evidence from Beveridge, Beatlemania, Blair and beyond', *Social Policy & Administration*, vol 50, no 6, pp 691-711.

Hudson, J. and Lunt, N., with Hamilton, C., Mackinder, S., Meers, J. and Swift, C. (2016c) 'Nostalgia narratives? Pejorative attitudes to welfare in historical perspective: survey evidence from Beveridge to the British Social Attitudes Survey', *Journal of Poverty and Social Justice*, vol 24, no 3, pp 227-43.

Jensen, T. (2014) 'Welfare commonsense, poverty porn and doxosophy', *Sociological Research Online*, vol 19, no 3.

Jensen, J. and Tyler, I. (2015) '"Benefits broods": The cultural and political crafting of anti-welfare commonsense', *Critical Social Policy*, vol 35, no 4, pp 1-22.

Jo, N.-K. (2011) 'Between the cultural foundations of welfare and welfare attitudes: The possibility of an in-between level conception of culture for the cultural analysis of welfare', *Journal of European Social Policy*, vol 21, no 1, pp 5-19.

Jones, C. (1990) 'Hong Kong, Singapore, South Korea and Taiwan: Oikonomic welfare states', *Government and Opposition*, vol 25, pp 446-62.

Jordan, W. (2014) '"Bedroom tax" as divisive as ever: Half of the public now oppose the bedroom benefit rules, up from 38% in March 2013', YouGov UK, 18 July (https://yougov.co.uk/news/2014/07/18/bedroom-tax-divisive-ever/).

Klein, R. (1974) 'The case for elitism: Public opinion and public policy', *Political Quarterly*, vol 45, pp 406-17.

Larsen, C.A. (2006) *The institutional logic of welfare attitudes: How welfare regimes influence public support*, Aldershot: Ashgate.

Lister, R. (2011) 'Our social security system must guarantee real welfare', *The Guardian*, 29 August (www.theguardian.com/commentisfree/2011/aug/28/robin-hood-poor-welfare).

NatCen Social Research (2017) *British Social Attitudes Survey, 2015* (3rd edn), UK Data Service, SN: 8116 (http://doi.org/10.5255/UKDA-SN-8116-3).

Patrick, R. (2016) 'Living with and responding to the "scrounger" narrative in the UK: Exploring everyday strategies of acceptance, resistance and deflection', *Journal of Poverty and Social Justice*, vol 24, no 4, pp 245-59.

Patrick, R. (2017) *For whose benefit? The everyday realities of welfare reform*, Bristol: Policy Press.

PEP (1961) *Family needs and the social services: A survey*, London: George Allen & Unwin.

Pfau-Effinger, B. (2004) *Development of culture, welfare states and women's employment in Europe*, Aldershot: Ashgate.

Pfau-Effinger, B. (2005) 'Culture and welfare state policies: Reflections on a complex interrelation', *Journal of Social Policy*, vol 34, no 1, pp 3-20.

Pierson, P. (2004) *Politics in time: History, institutions and social analysis*, Princeton, NJ: Princeton University Press.

Rieger, E. and Leibfried, S. (2003) *Limits to globalization: Welfare states and the world economy*, Cambridge: Polity Press, in association with Blackwell.

Skocpol, T. and Amenta, E. (1986) 'States and social policies', *Annual Review of Sociology*, vol 12, pp 131-57.

Swank, D. (2002) *Global capital, political institutions and policy change in developed welfare states*, Cambridge: Cambridge University Press.

Taylor-Gooby, P. (1982) 'Two cheers for the welfare state: Public opinion and private welfare', *Journal of Public Policy*, vol 2, pp 319-46.

Taylor-Gooby, P. (1985) *Public opinion, ideology and state welfare*, London: Routledge.

Taylor-Gooby, P. and Taylor, E. (2015) 'Benefits and welfare: Long-term trends or short term reactions?', in J. Curtice and R. Ormston (eds) *British Social Attitudes 32*, London: NatCen, pp 74-101.

Tyler, D. (1990) *British opinion polls, 1960-1988*, Reading: Research Publications.

van Oorschot, W. (2000) 'Who should get what, and why? On deservingness criteria and the conditionality of solidarity among the public', *Policy & Politics*, vol 28, no 1, pp 33-48.

van Oorschot, W. (2006) 'Making the difference in social Europe: Deservingness perceptions among citizens of European welfare states', *Journal of European Social Policy*, vol 16, no 1, pp 23-42.

Wedderburn, D. (1967) 'How adequate are our cash benefits?', *New Society*, 12 October, pp 512-16.

Wincott, D. (2013) 'The (golden) age of the welfare state: Interrogating a conventional wisdom', *Public Administration*, vol 91, pp 806-22.

Wiseman, J. (1967) 'Our survey assessed', *New Society*, 2 November, pp 625-7.

11

Everyday life on benefits

Ruth Patrick, Margaret Mbaikaize and Sue Watson

Summary

One of the functions of social security benefits is to provide a source of income to people who have no, or limited, financial resources. Despite this, there is a long history of deriding people who are receiving out-of-work benefits as being part of a problem of 'welfare dependency', with the suggestion that claimants too often choose benefits over paid work. In exploring experiences of benefits receipt, this chapter details the extent of the (mis)match between lived experiences and the dominant narrative on 'welfare'. Drawing on qualitative data, it examines experiences of 'getting by' on benefits during a period of ongoing welfare state retrenchment. It challenges the dominant narrative on 'welfare', and includes first-hand accounts from two individuals (Sue and Margaret) who have experiences of navigating the UK's social security system.

The chapter examines:

- the dominant narrative of welfare dependency;
- the lived experiences of out-of-work benefits receipt;
- the work of 'getting by';
- socially valuable forms of contribution made by out-of-work benefit claimants.

In the light of this evidence, the final section considers the meaning and experience of choice and individual agency for individuals trying to 'get by'.

Introduction

We hear a great deal from politicians and in the media about 'welfare' and the lives of those who receive it. As successive rounds of welfare reform have been rolled out since the late 1980s, there have also been important academic and think tank analyses of how individuals are affected by the changes introduced (see, for example, Hood and Oakley, 2014; Beatty, 2015).

What is frequently missing however – from both the popular narrative and the research evidence base – are the voices and experiences of those in receipt of out-of-work benefits themselves. These voices contain the 'expertise of experience' (Age UK, 2015) that comes from direct engagement with the UK's benefits system. In this chapter, such expertise is foregrounded in exploring the lived experiences of 'getting by' on benefits. The lived experiences documented here cover the period between 2011 and 2016, during which time there was substantial retrenchment in the pursuit of austerity policies and 'welfare reform' (see Chapter 1, this volume). This chapter draws on 'the lived experiences of welfare reform study' (see Box 11.1). It also features Sue and Margaret's accounts of claiming benefits. Their reflections can help us to understand 'life on benefits', and are revealing in the extent to which they challenge popular characterisations.

Box 11.1: The lived experiences of welfare reform study

This study was a piece of qualitative longitudinal research designed to develop new knowledge and understanding on experiences and responses to welfare reform. Between 2011 and 2016, repeat interviews were conducted with a small group of individuals directly affected by some of the benefit changes introduced by the 2010-15 Conservative and Liberal Democratic coalition government. Ruth spoke to 22 people (sampled to include single parents, disabled people and young jobseekers) as they anticipated, experienced and reflected on welfare reform. Repeat interviews allowed Ruth to 'walk alongside' individuals as benefit changes were implemented. This made it possible to better understand how far the policy intent mapped on to individual experiences, and to develop a rich understanding of transitions and journeys over time (Patrick, 2017). Ethical principles of anonymity and informed consent were prioritised throughout, and the names detailed in this chapter are pseudonyms, although Sue and Margaret are writing in their real names.

The research included a participatory element – what has since become known as the Dole Animators project (Dole Animators, 2013; Land and Patrick, 2014). Working with Ruth and an animator, Ellie Land, a small group of the research participants made an animated film that highlighted their experiences of welfare reform. The film has been viewed more than 14,000 times on YouTube, and the group remain active in seeking to present their own account of what 'getting by' on benefits entails. Sue and Margaret, who describe their experience in Boxes 11.3 and 11.4, are both Dole Animators, and were each involved in the research study from the outset.

The dominant narrative of welfare dependency

With the importing of the Americanisation 'welfare' to describe out-of-work benefits (Lister, 2015), the UK has also imported a narrative that views 'welfare' and the lives of those who receive it as necessarily and inevitably negative. There is a long history of deriding out-of-work social security receipt (Golding and Middleton, 1982; Dean and Taylor-Gooby, 1992). In political discourse, it is common to identify problems of 'welfare dependency' and to draw on individual high-profile case studies as examples of a wider shortcoming with the benefits system, and recipients themselves (Garthwaite, 2011; Jensen and Tyler, 2015). Divisive dichotomies are repeatedly drawn between a lauded hard-working majority and welfare dependants, with tough interventions then required to encourage but ultimately compel individuals on benefits to make the right choices. From different political perspectives, there has often seemed to be an unwillingness to challenge this dominant framing, with political parties instead competing to be seen as *the* party that will represent hard-working families (cf Gentleman, 2015).

This dominant framing is mobilised to defend ongoing cuts to the level of social security benefits and restrictions to eligibility for support. Further, the intensification and extension of welfare conditionality is justified as being necessary to enable transitions from 'welfare' into work. Measures such as the benefit cap (which sets a maximum that can be received by families with children) and restrictions in eligibility for child-related financial support for those with more than two children are described as 'fair' attempts to ensure that those on benefits have to make the same choices as those in employment (see Chapter 2, this volume). This rationalising – albeit subject to sustained critique in academic and policy circles (Hills, 2015; Jensen, 2015) – appears to be quite persuasive, with welfare reform and a tough rhetoric on 'welfare' consistently polling well in public attitudes surveys (Taylor-Gooby, 2015; Hudson et al, 2016). An analysis of changing attitudes to welfare, drawing on the British Social Attitudes (BSA) survey, found that people are commonly concerned about individuals 'fiddling the system', feeling that the benefits system too often 'discourages work and rewards the wrong people' (Duffy et al, 2013, p 5).

The political narrative is bolstered and reinforced by a media that has long been content to critique and (most often) condemn the lives of those on out-of-work benefits (Golding and Middleton, 1982; Briant et al, 2013; Tyler, 2014; Plunkett, 2015). A sub-genre of reality television shows – or 'Poverty Porn' – operates to recast poverty as light entertainment. Viewers are invited into the homes of some of Britain's poorest (and often most vulnerable) households and implicitly encouraged to judge their lives and – all too often – find them wanting.

Taken together, the political narrative and media presentation of 'welfare' constitutes a 'machine of welfare common sense' (Jensen, 2014) that sustains an inherently negative and problematic view of out-of-work benefits. This machine operates to crowd out alternative narratives, making it more difficult for divergent accounts to be heard. This is particularly problematic given the extent to which the dominant narrative fails to reflect the everyday realities and experiences of those on out-of-work benefits.

Lived experiences of out-of-work benefits receipt: hard choices and going without

While the dominant narrative frames 'welfare dependency' as providing a life of relative ease and comfort, in fact poverty and out-of-work benefits receipt are closely entwined. Inevitably, the impact and experiences of this poverty are often overshadowed by the popular characterisation and rhetoric. This persists despite growing evidence of the hardship (even destitution) that individuals on out-of-work benefits can face.

Notable here is the massive rise in foodbanks, which today feature as an everyday part of our charitable infrastructure. Between April 2016 and March 2017, the largest provider of foodbank parcels – The Trussell Trust – provided 1,182,954 three-day emergency food supplies. Of this number, 436,938 went to children (The Trussell Trust, 2017). The most extreme form of poverty – destitution – is also a visible and growing problem. Research for the Joseph Rowntree Foundation estimated that 1.25 million individuals in the UK are destitute, including 300,000 children (Fitzpatrick et al, 2016). Here, destitution is defined as being unable to afford the basic essentials required in order to eat, keep clean and stay warm and dry.

People on out-of-work benefits are particularly vulnerable to poverty (Macinnes et al, 2015), and often struggle to make ends meet. Box 11.2 highlights the gap between the levels of benefits and 'Minimum Income Standards' – what members of the public judge households need if they are to be able to afford an acceptable standard of living.

Everyone that Ruth interviewed was living in poverty at the time of their first interviews. By most definitions, they were both relatively and absolutely poor. Those who experienced persistent poverty highlighted the bleak reality they faced:

> 'You only get so much money a month just to live on and once you've paid for your bills and your food and bus fares and stuff you haven't got much money to live on. I don't ever go out.... I just stay at home on my own.' (Karen)

> 'Disgusting. I hate it. Scrimping and saving. It's horrible.' (Sophie)

Box 11.2: Minimum Income Standards and benefit levels

The Minimum Income Standard (MIS) is a consensual mechanism for measuring the income households need if they are to be able to afford a reasonable standard of living. First established in 2006, it is undertaken by the Centre for Research in Social Policy at Loughborough University.

The MIS is 'based on detailed research with groups of members of the public specifying what items need to be included in a minimum household budget' (Centre for Research in Social Policy, 2017). This approach makes it possible to capture what households need in their weekly budget, and how much they will need to earn if they are to have this income available to them.

The 2017 MIS (Padley and Hirsch, 2017) found that single people need to earn at least £17,900 before tax to achieve the Minimum Income Standard, while a couple with two children would need to earn at least £20,400 each. Benefit levels are far below the MIS. In 2017, single people could afford only 36 per cent of the budget, with a couple with two children able to afford 59 per cent.

The MIS is invaluable in providing a dynamic, consensual way of measuring what the public feel is necessary to afford a reasonable standard of living in today's UK. However, critics of this measurement argue that items within the basket of necessary goods are too generous, and are unreasonable as a 'minimum' of basic essentials (Snowden, 2014).

Managing on benefits frequently entailed hard choices as available money was often insufficient to purchase everything an individual and/or their household required. Cath had to take a break from paying her gas and electricity bills for a fortnight when she needed new underwear, while James explained:

> 'It's scary because obviously there's so much to do and you haven't got a right lot of money to do it with, so you've got to prioritise what comes first. Then sometimes it can be them shoes on her feet can last another weekend but that food in the kitchen won't, so the food comes before the shoes, you know what I mean?'

Hard choices were linked to what Karen called 'constantly juggling', a never-ending battle to stretch limited funds to meet basic needs and having to choose between competing necessities. Closely connected with having to make difficult decisions was the necessity of simply 'doing without', particularly so that children could have what they needed. Two of the single mothers in the study spoke of foregoing meals so that their children would have enough to eat, while others described having to do without basic items such as a washing machine or proper heating:

> 'I go without my meals sometimes. I have to save meals for me kids. So I'll have, like a slice of toast and they'll have a full meal. And if they don't eat something, if they haven't picked at it, I'll eat theirs….' (Chloe)

Having to make hard choices, and budgetary sacrifices or simply 'going without' are recurrent themes in other studies of people living in poverty (Beresford et al, 1999; Lister, 2004; Shildrick and MacDonald, 2013; Hickman et al, 2014; Lister et al, 2014; Pemberton et al, 2014). Cath explained what 'getting by' entailed when her money had run out:

> 'I have tea with sour milk and I do eat bread that's mouldy. But it's only, like, for two days before I get paid, so I'm all right.'

Food poverty was a recurrent theme in the interviews, with those experiencing benefit sanctions particularly likely to report being unable to afford to feed themselves. Adrian – who faced repeated sanctions during the time of the research – spoke of using foodbanks in an effort to get by, as well as sometimes stealing food and having to resort to emergency provision intended for the homeless. He explained:

> '… there's a curry run on Tuesday nights outside crown court so I go there…. Well, the problem is that's meant for the homeless, but because I'm sanctioned and I'm starving, that's where I have to go.'

Adrian was not the only person Ruth interviewed who reported shoplifting as part of his struggle to 'get by', and this form of 'survival crime' is recognised as a growing problem in the UK (Dwyer and Bright, 2016; Fitzpatrick et al, 2016).

It was common for parents to feel that poverty impacted adversely on their children, even as they tried to shield them from it. Sophie described how her poverty meant she was not always able to afford fresh food for her children, describing this as one way in which being on benefits made it more difficult to meet what she saw as her responsibilities to her children:

> 'They go on about children that are obese…. Well, the bit of benefits that you do get once you've paid out on your bills and that lot you might have 40 quid left. What else do you buy? You can't go and buy all fresh stuff and meat and stuff like that. It is more freezer stuff than 'owt, to last you.'

There was also a clear relationship between the struggle to 'get by' and the difficult choices that entailed, and a resultant exclusion whereby participants felt unable or unwilling to participate in social everyday activities due to their poverty and lack of income. As the Child Poverty Action Group (CPAG) has said: 'at its heart, poverty is about exclusion from social participation' (2001, p 29). Chloe felt unable to answer her landline telephone, as she was fearful that any phone call could be a demand for a debt that she was unable to settle. Cath explained how she had stopped going on daytrips organised by her housing association as she had to bring a packed lunch to save money, but this left her feeling excluded, given that the other tenants ate in cafes. Cath also chose not to attend various support groups and activities as she felt that the cost of a coffee in the cafes and museums where they met was prohibitive:

> 'I know I bang on about money but, with meeting in a place where a cup of tea's £1.75, I want a hundred tea bags and two pints of milk for that.'

Evidence of the exclusion of people living in poverty from many of the day-to-day activities and practices that most of the population take for granted illustrates how those in poverty experience and have to live with citizenship exclusion (Lister, 2004; Dwyer, 2010).

The work of 'getting by'

Importantly, while the dominant narrative typically characterises those on out-of-work benefits as inactive, Ruth's research instead illustrated the very hard work that 'getting by' involves. This work was often time-intensive, including activities such as hand washing clothes, collecting and selling scrap to make a few pounds, and going to several shops to try to make sure you paid the lowest price possible for your day-to-day essentials. Much has been written about the time expended by people living in poverty to search out bargains and low-cost items (cf Burchardt, 2008; Ridge, 2009; Pemberton et al, 2014), and this was certainly a common activity among those Ruth interviewed. Cath spoke about going to a number of shops in her effort to get the best deal, as well as shopping almost daily in order to take advantage of supermarkets' reduced shelves of food fast approaching its use-by date. As well as being time-intensive, 'getting by' often required considerable ingenuity in trying to find creative solutions to making limited financial resources last as long as possible. Examples included parents asking friends to have their children for tea when the money had run out, and participants using electric blankets rather than properly heating their bedroom(s).

Sue's account (see Box 11.3) of her 'life on benefits' powerfully illustrates the work that dealing with the benefits system itself entails, work that has often become more burdensome and emotionally draining during a time of benefit changes and repeat reassessments of eligibility for state support. The active work involved in 'getting by' on benefits is a pertinent challenge to notions of the passive, inactive out-of-work benefits claimant, a clear example of the mismatch between lived experiences of welfare and the dominant narrative.

Box 11.3: My life on benefits – Sue

Having worked for over 30 years I was devastated when I was diagnosed with severe rheumatoid arthritis (RA) in 2008. It is fair to say that at that point my life was turned upside down.

RA is a systemic autoimmune disease that can attack any organ in the body. It is a progressive, chronic disease for which there is currently no cure. Typical symptoms I face every day include joint stiffness and inflammation, extreme pain and fatigue, which affects my ability to carry out simple tasks.

At first, I used my salary and savings to pay the bills, but knew I would need to eventually turn to the social security system for financial support. Thus began my experience of benefits. Initially, I was not accepted for Disability Living Allowance (DLA) because I hadn't provided enough medical evidence to support my claim. But it was difficult to understand the computer-generated letters and at first I thought that there had been a mistake and that the letter I received should have been sent to someone else, such were the discrepancies and incorrect assumptions. A further application was made and this time I was given an 'indefinite' award. I was very relieved and grateful to receive this outcome. However, DLA is now being replaced by Personal Independence Payments and I am becoming increasingly anxious and fearful about this. I worry that I might not qualify for the same support even though my health has deteriorated and other, secondary, medical conditions have now been diagnosed. This only adds to the stress of waiting for a 'brown envelope' from the government to drop through the letter box.

My experience of moving from Incapacity Benefit to Employment and Support Allowance (ESA) was even worse. I was initially placed in the Work-Related Activity Group for one year. This meant I had to attend appointments at the job centre. The adviser that I saw there was very pleasant, but it became obvious that she could not help me, and that my medical condition was such that getting back to work was almost impossible. Our conversations revolved around her holidays and not much else. At the end of the year, I applied again for ESA and was rejected, even though my health situation had deteriorated. I applied for a mandatory reconsideration and was rejected for reasons I still do not understand. After getting nowhere with the Department for Work and

Pensions (DWP), I contacted my MP. Within a few days of my MP getting in touch with the DWP, I received a call from a Senior Decision-Maker. He went through my medical condition with me and confirmed that, in his opinion, I had been placed in the wrong group and that he was going to place me in the Support Group for three years. While I am grateful to my MP for helping me with the situation, I am very annoyed that I had to revert to this. It is quite appalling that he got an immediate response from DWP, whereas they just ignored me.

While I understand the necessity for completing disability benefit questionnaires when making a claim, the actual filling out of them can take me between two to three weeks as they centre on what I can't now do. It is very depressing and upsetting to continually focus on how my disability negatively affects my life.

Although I can no longer be in paid work, I help out on a voluntary basis at my GP's surgery where we have a community room used for various groups. I help with the craft group that meets once a week. I am also involved in a couple of local hospital public and patient involvement groups. This means I can use my experience as a patient to be involved in changing systems and speaking up for patients. I do this voluntary work only when I feel well enough, but it is really important for my mental wellbeing. Doing these things makes me feel like I'm making a contribution, albeit only a small one.

I did not choose to stop work or be diagnosed with a chronic health condition where I have to rely on the state for financial assistance, but such is life. If it can happen to me it can happen to anyone, and perhaps those who denigrate the out-of-work should consider the maxim 'those in glass houses...'.

Debt and informal borrowing

In their efforts to 'get by', individuals commonly got into debt and were often reliant on family for both emotional and financial support. Borrowing money from family and friends was particularly common, and this was often a source of strain and problems, something also highlighted in research by Daly and Kelly (2015).

Several spoke of borrowing money from their family very frequently (some daily, many weekly or fortnightly):

> 'It's "dad, can you lend me, can you lend me, can you lend me?" [laughs] all the time.' (Chloe)

While these sources of financial support were commonly appreciated, they were a source of embarrassment and shame, reinforcing the findings of other research (Lister et al, 2014; Fitzpatrick et al, 2016). Hall and Perry (2013) describe the 'relationship premium' of necessary borrowing from friends and family, which centres on the additional relational strain that these chains of borrowing and lending can cause. Sharon experienced this 'relationship premium':

> 'I were [borrowing] … money off people and stuff like that and it just got really degrading. One time I had to ask my little brother and … I was so embarrassed to ask him. I had no other way….'

Borrowing money from her ex-partner left Karen feeling worse about her own parenting abilities, suggesting that the relationship premium can extend both to those one has to borrow from but also those one is caring for:

> 'It feels like I'm not a good mum 'cause I can't provide for him.'

In this way, borrowing from family – although often appearing an essential mechanism for 'getting by' on a very low income – impacted negatively both on familial relations and individuals' self-esteem.

Contributions made by those 'getting by'

Another significant counter to the popular image of 'welfare dependency' lies in evidence – from Ruth's research and elsewhere (cf Daly and Kelly, 2015; Garthwaite, 2016) – that while those on out-of-work benefits may not currently be in paid employment, they are engaged in other forms of socially valuable contributions. Individuals were often active and busy as carers, parents and volunteers, forms of contribution that are undervalued in the depiction of paid employment as the primary responsibility of the dutiful citizen (Patrick, 2013).

Throughout the five years of the study, jobseeker Adrian volunteered at a local homeless persons' hostel:

> 'I proper love it [volunteering]. You feel satisfaction as well if someone's coming in really hungry. Give them some food, at least they've eaten for the night.'

Jim, who himself had serious mental health challenges, spoke about caring for his partner and brother, who both also had mental health issues:

> 'That's [caring's] all I do. I don't get any time apart from it, you know.'

Beckie described the daily work that caring for her adult daughter involved:

> 'I keep in touch with her on a daily basis; make sure that she's all right. Make sure she's had a bath and eaten....'

As well as caring for family members, there was also frequent evidence of informal support being given to friends, family and neighbours, with this often reported as simply part of everyday life. Examples of the provision of informal support included helping decorate friends' homes, raising money to support local foodbanks and informal assistance with childcare. Sophie helped out with childcare for friends:

> If they [friends] need help, then obviously I'm there. So like my friend up the road, she's been poorly so I've been watching her son....'

These informal chains and networks of support, with participants both givers and recipients of 'mutual aid' (Oxfam, 2010), were indicative of the 'bonding social capital' of families and friends (Forrest and Kearns, 2001, cited in Shildrick and MacDonald, 2013) on which participants could draw. Such activities help to form and bind communities and are a critical resource in efforts to 'get by'. Research has shown that there is more mutual aid work carried out in low-income communities than in more affluent communities (Williams, 2005), and Ruth's study certainly found a relative abundance of these forms of unpaid and yet critically important exchanges. The socially valuable forms of contribution in which those on out-of-work benefits are often engaged contradicts the popular characterisation of claimants as passive and inactive, and represent a form of citizenship engagement frequently neglected in accounts that narrowly equate paid employment with citizenship duty (Patrick, 2013).

Choice and agency

Another central element of the popular narrative on 'welfare' is the argument that, for too many, benefits have become a 'lifestyle choice', with individuals 'choosing' to stay on benefits rather than engaging in paid employment (Garthwaite, 2016; Patrick, 2017). This analysis individualises the 'problem' of 'welfare dependency', putting emphasis on individual rather than structural causes of poverty and benefits receipt (Newman, 2011). For example, it is argued that more needs to be done to improve individuals' work-readiness and employability to enable transitions from 'welfare' into 'work' (see, for example, DWP, 2010). This focus on the individual (and the changes *they* need to make) can be contrasted with an approach that foregrounds broader structural barriers (for example, the lack of decent work that can be effectively combined with parenting and caring responsibilities).

Further, the choices that individuals on benefits do make are subject to close censure and critique, with particular judgements meted out where individuals living in poverty are seen to be spending their limited income on the 'wrong' things (for example, on cigarettes or alcohol). A close monitoring of claimants' spending choices has been used to explain a reliance on emergency food provision, with the critical lens focusing in on claimants' (deficit) behaviour rather than on the inadequacies with the benefits system itself (Garthwaite, 2016).

As Wright (2016) has argued, the dominant model implies that benefit claimants require interventions to engineer behavioural change if they are to become 'active' and encouraged to make the right choices. Underlying this is the assumption that individuals have previously made the 'wrong choices', and that this can explain their present hardship. The agency of claimants is thus judged to be impaired.

In fact, it is quite rare to find that 'wrong choices' are the reasons behind individuals' receipt of out-of-work benefits. This comes through very clearly in Ruth's study, in Wright's own research (2016; Wright et al, 2016), and also from the wider evidence base of qualitative studies of out-of-work benefits receipt (see, for example, Shildrick et al, 2012; MacDonald et al, 2014; Garthwaite, 2016). The individuals in Ruth's study challenged the idea of benefits as a 'lifestyle choice', instead employing negative language to describe their life on benefits:

> 'People don't choose to live on benefits – it's not our choice. It's just the way that things have happened. We didn't choose to live on benefits, we don't want to live on benefits.' (Sophie)

> 'It [benefits] ain't a life choice, you don't want to be living like that. It's like a pigeon, innit, you're just there pick, pick, pick, and that's it really. You're just existing.' (Dan)

The triggers for benefits receipt among those Ruth interviewed included a sudden onset of ill health (as in Sue's case, see Box 11.3), relationship breakdown (as in Margaret's case, see Box 11.4), the loss of a job, and the difficulty of finding employment despite active efforts to do so. While the individuals Ruth spoke to often experienced a powerlessness in relation to their own situation, they were still able to exercise agency and make choices, albeit that these were heavily constrained. In understanding the agency of those living in poverty, Lister's (2004) work is invaluable, illustrating the forms of everyday and strategic agency in which those living in poverty engage. These include the work of 'getting by' (discussed earlier in this chapter), efforts to 'get off' benefits and more political expressions of agency tied to efforts to 'get organised' and 'get (back) at' what some claimants regard as the injustices within the benefits system.

In their efforts to secure employment and 'get off' benefits, the people Ruth interviewed sought to make choices, although these were often undermined by the structures of the benefits system, the interventions of street-level advisers and the constraints that their financial situation placed on them. For example, when Ruth first met jobseeker James, he was keen to retrain as a support worker to help those who had experienced homelessness and alcohol misuse. However, James was informed that he was not allowed to undertake full-time training while on Jobseeker's Allowance, and so was mandated to seek different forms of employment. He did so and – at the time of his fourth interview in 2016 – was about to start working 'picking and packing' in a warehouse. He was pleased to have secured this job, but disappointed that his longer-term aspirations to find work that he found rewarding could not be realised. James reflected on his experiences:

> 'It annoys you, because you're trying to better yourself, not to sort of do nothing and they say "No, you can't do that". So you can't go nowhere, can you?'

James' journey over time illustrates the ways in which his capacity to make 'choices' was mediated by the social security system and its associated bureaucracy, as well as by his necessary reliance on out-of-work benefits. The ways in which the structures of the benefits system, and the hardship that poverty creates, constrain individuals' choices is a recurring theme of research into lived experiences of poverty (Millar and Ridge, 2013; Daly and Kelly, 2015).

Benefits stigma

Claimants' capacity to make choices, and exercise agency, can also be undermined by the endemic and pervasive reach of benefits stigma (Walker, 2014; Baumberg, 2016). The process of claiming benefits is itself tied up in stigma and shame, and this is only reinforced by a benefits system that often seems to treat individuals with neither dignity nor respect. Margaret's account details how she felt 'worthless' while on benefits, with her appointments with job centre and Work Programme advisers reminding her of being a child sent to be told off by the headteacher (see Box 11.4).

In Ruth's study, individuals often described a personal stigma of benefits receipt – their own feeling that being on benefits is shameful. This was closely linked to – and sometimes hard to disentangle from – processes of stigmatisation: the experience of being treated differently by others because of being on benefits (Baumberg, 2016).

Disability benefits claimant Kane described how he felt about his receipt of benefits:

> 'It knocks your self-esteem [being on benefits], yeah, like, not contributing to society, taking from it, kind of thing. Yeah.'

Box 11.4: My life on benefits – Margaret

I am a single parent with a teenage daughter. I am now in work as a teaching assistant, but spent several years on first Income Support and then Jobseeker's Allowance. I was moved onto Jobseeker's Allowance when my daughter was only eight years old. Claiming Jobseeker's Allowance was really hard and stressful as I would start worrying about going to the job centre two or three days before my appointment. It was all the uncertainty of what would happen when I went in, whether I would be sanctioned, told off because I had not done enough job searching or failed at an interview. It made me stop feeling like an adult. It made me feel worthless and I became scared of my fellow human beings. There was only one lady that I felt was helpful and understanding and that was because she had just started that job after being unemployed for a while. She told me she used to cry every time she had to go to the job centre.

There was no help whatsoever from the job centre advisers regarding looking for work. I never felt supported but instead only criticised and looked down upon. The fact that I had responsibilities as a single parent with no support (having no friends or family close by) seemed to make no difference to them.

I was sent on the Work Programme. The first adviser I saw there was helpful. At that time, I was training to be a teaching assistant and my adviser was supportive and understood that I needed to complete the course and then look for work. I was then sent to another Work Programme office where I was told that I had to get a job, any job. By this point, I had finished my current level of teaching assistant training and my tutor wanted me to do the next level as I was doing really well. My Work Programme adviser told me that I had to stop wasting time with training and I had to look for other work because teaching assistant jobs were too competitive. This made me wonder why I could not compete with others, was I not good enough? I started to doubt myself and my own ambitions. Twice I had job interviews and I didn't get the job. I always compare that time to when I was little, in school and had to go to the headmaster's office because I had been naughty. That's how it felt when I went to the Work Programme and had to tell them I had not found work.

I finally did get a job as a teaching assistant, but this was not thanks to the Work Programme. Being in work feels so empowering and I wake up every morning feeling proud of myself. I may not be able to get everything I want because money is still a struggle, but at least I now have some choices. Life on benefits was a lonely and isolated one as I had no friends and couldn't afford to go out, let alone have a takeaway on a Friday night. Now, I have an army of friends and we go out at least once a month. I feel respected and valued, unlike when I was on benefits and felt worthless.

I have always said that I know there are a few people out there who abuse the benefit system but most people really need that help and should not be looked down upon or labelled. Most people on benefits want to work and should get support instead of criticism and punishment. People who work in job centres should be trained to be empathic to claimants as it is a time when people feel really low and in need of support.

James reflected again on the stigma he associated with being on benefits:

'I think it's stigma that comes with [being on benefits]. Do you know? You're seen going into the job centre or you're seen being about every day through the day and it's a stigma that sticks with you, like "get a job" sort of thing, but you do, you try. A lot of people are trying to get that job but it's just the stigma. It does make you feel shit, definitely.'

Navigating the stigma of benefits receipt adds to the hardship and emotional strain associated with receipt of 'welfare' and can ironically undermine efforts to move into work, given its negative impact on individuals' self-esteem and self-confidence.

Conclusion

This chapter has foregrounded everyday realities for those in receipt of out-of-work benefits. There is a stark contrast between these lived experiences and the popular and (so often seemingly persuasive) narrative promoted by politicians and in the media. While this chapter has focused on empirical data from Ruth's study, and the accounts of Sue and Margaret, there are strong parallels between the findings detailed here and the wider evidence base on contemporary experiences of poverty, social security receipt and welfare reform in the UK (see, for example, Shildrick et al, 2012; Millar and Ridge, 2013; Garthwaite, 2016). Key conclusions from these – and other – studies are that social security receipt is associated with significant financial hardship, pervasive stigma and enduring hard work. Further, studies repeatedly find that claimants, rather than choosing benefits receipt, are most often strongly orientated towards securing paid work, where this is a realistic option for them at that time.

The gap between popular narratives and lived experiences of 'welfare' is problematic, particularly given the extent to which policy responses are rooted in the dominant narrative. For example, the continued reliance on welfare conditionality rests on the assumption that individuals require behavioural change (and a system of incentives and sanctions) if they are to be activated from 'welfare' and into 'work' (Watts et al, 2014). But the research evidence challenges this assumption, and instead shows the extent to which benefits receipt is most often not chosen and claimants themselves already active (Wright, 2016). Working with a counter model (Wright, 2016), in which the agency and aspirations of claimants themselves are better recognised, would suggest a different policy approach. A closer and more finely grained engagement with lived experiences of out-of-work benefits receipt is a vital pre-requisite for better policy-making on social security. Further, all of us with an interest in 'understanding social security' need to take time to listen to experts by experience on poverty, welfare reform and social security receipt. It is only by so doing that we can begin to better comprehend social security policies and their impact.

Overview

This chapter has provided an overview of what 'getting by' on benefits entails, drawing on research and the first-person accounts of Sue and Margaret. Taken together, this shows the extent of the mismatch between the dominant narrative on 'welfare' and everyday realities for those in receipt of out-of-work benefits. The central arguments of this chapter are that:

- 'Getting by' on benefits entails 'hard work' and is time-intensive
- Out-of-work benefit claimants often make socially valuable contributions as volunteers, carers and parents
- Individuals in receipt of out-of-work benefits exercise agency, and make choices, but these are constrained by their poverty and the structure of the benefits system itself
- There is a pervasive stigma attached to benefits receipt.

Questions for discussion

1. In what ways does the political narrative on 'welfare' clash with lived experiences of benefits receipt?
2. What are the consequences of the mismatch between the popular narrative of 'welfare' and lived experiences?
3. How can ideas of 'agency' and 'choice' help us understand experiences of benefits receipt?

Key reading

Lister, R. (2004) *Poverty*, Cambridge: Polity Press.

Patrick, R. (2017) *For whose benefit? The everyday realities of welfare reform*, Bristol: Policy Press.

Wright, S. (2016) 'Conceptualising the active welfare subject: Welfare reform in discourse, policy and lived experience', *Policy & Politics*, vol 44, pp 235-52.

Website resources

www.atd-uk.org
ATD Fourth World

www.doleanimators.org
Dole Animators

www.thrive-teesside.org.uk
Thrive Teesside

www.povertyalliance.org.uk
Poverty Alliance

www.welfareconditionality.ac.uk
Welfare Conditionality Research Project

References

Age UK (2015) *Care and support*, London: Age UK (www.ageuk.org.uk/professional-resources-home/services-and-practice/care-and-support/experts-by-experience/).

Baumberg, B. (2016) 'The stigma of claiming benefits: A quantitative study', *Journal of Social Policy*, vol 45, pp 181-99.

Beatty, C. (2015) 'Unintended consequences? The impact of welfare reform on spatial inequalities', Paper presented to People, Place, Policy Conference, 10 September, Sheffield Hallam University.

Beresford, P., Green, D., Lister, R. and Woodard, K. (1999) *Poverty first hand: Poor people speak for themselves*, London: Child Poverty Action Group.

Briant, E., Watson, N. and Philo, G. (2013) 'Reporting disability in the age of austerity: The changing face of media representation of disability and disabled people in the United Kingdom and the creation of new "folk devils"', *Disability & Society*, vol 28, pp 874-89.

Burchardt, T. (2008) *Time and income poverty*, CASEReport 57, London: Centre for Analysis of Social Exclusion, London School of Economics.

Centre for Research in Social Policy (2017) 'What is MIS?', Loughborough: Loughborough University (www.lboro.ac.uk/research/crsp/mis/whatismis/).

CPAG (Child Poverty Action Group) (2001) *Poverty, the facts* (4th edn), London: CPAG.

Daly, M. and Kelly, G. (2015) *Families and poverty: Everyday life on a low income*, Bristol: Policy Press.

Dean, H. and Taylor-Gooby, P. (1992) *Dependency culture: The explosion of a myth*, Hemel Hempstead: Harvester Wheatsheaf.

Dole Animators (2013) *Dole Animators* (www.doleanimators.org).

Duffy, B., Hall, S., O'Leary, D. and Pope, S. (2013) *Generation strains: A Demos and Ipsos MORI report on changing attitudes to welfare*, London: Demos.

DWP (Department for Work and Pensions) (2010) *21st century welfare*, Green Paper, Cm 7913, London: The Stationery Office.

Dwyer, P. (2010) *Understanding social citizenship: Themes and perspectives for policy and practice* (2nd edn), Bristol: Policy Press.

Dwyer, P. and Bright, J. (2016) *Welfare conditionality: Sanctions, support and behaviour change: First wave findings: Overview*, May, York: University of York.

Fitzpatrick, S., Bramley, G., Sosenko, F., Blenkinsopp, J., Johnsen, S., Little, M., et al (2016) *Destitution in the UK*, York: Joseph Rowntree Foundation.

Garthwaite, K. (2011) '"The language of shirkers and scroungers?" Talking about illness, disability and coalition welfare reform', *Disability and Society*, vol 26, pp 369-72.

Garthwaite, K. (2016) *Hunger pains: Life inside foodbank Britain*, Bristol: Policy Press.

Gentleman, A. (2015) 'Labour vows to reduce reliance on food banks if it comes to power', London: *The Guardian*, 17 March (www.theguardian.com/society/2015/mar/17/labour-vows-to-reduce-reliance-on-food-banks-if-it-comes-to-power).

Golding, P. and Middleton, S. (1982) *Images of welfare: Press and public attitudes to poverty*, Oxford: Blackwell.

Hall, S. and Perry, C. (2013) *Family matters: Understanding families in an age of austerity*, London: Ipsos MORI.

Hickman, P., Batty, E., Dayson, C. and Muir, J. (2014) *'Getting-by', coping and resilience in difficult times: Initial findings*, Sheffield: Centre for Regional Economic and Social Research, Sheffield Hallam University.

Hills, J. (2015) *Good times, bad times: The welfare myth of them and us*, Bristol: Policy Press.

Hood, A. and Oakley, L. (2014) *The social security system: Long-term trends and recent changes*, IFS Briefing Note (BN156), London: Institute for Fiscal Studies.

Hudson, J., Lunt, N., with Hamilton, C., Mackinder, S., Meers, J. and Swift, C. (2016) 'Nostalgia narratives? Pejorative attitudes to welfare in historical perspective: Survey evidence from Beveridge to the British Social Attitudes Survey', *Journal of Poverty and Social Justice*, vol 50, no 5, pp 691-711.

Jensen, T. (2014) 'Welfare commonsense, poverty porn and doxosophy', *Sociological Research Online*, vol 19.

Jensen, T. (2015) 'Ignorance in the "golden age of television"', *Sociological Imagination* (http://sociologicalimagination.org/archives/16786).

Jensen, T. and Tyler, L. (2015) '"Benefits broods": The cultural and political crafting of anti-welfare commonsense', *Critical Social Policy*, vol 35, pp 1-22.

Land, E. and Patrick, R. (2014) *The process of using participatory research methods with film-making to disseminate research: Challenges and potential*, Sage Research Methods Cases, London: Sage.

Lister, B., Graham, H., Egdell, V., Mcquaid, R. and Raeside, R. (2014) *The impact of welfare reform in Scotland – Tracking study; Interim report to the Scottish Government on 1st sweep of interviews*, Edinburgh: Scottish Government Social Research.

Lister, R. (2004) *Poverty*, Cambridge: Polity Press.

Lister, R. (2015) '"To count for nothing": Poverty beyond the statistics', British Academy Lecture, 5 February, London: British Academy (www.britac.ac.uk/events/2015/To_count_for_nothing.cfm).

Macdonald, R., Shildrick, T. and Furlong, A. (2014) 'In search of "intergenerational cultures of worklessness": Hunting the Yeti and shooting zombies', *Critical Social Policy*, vol 34, pp 199-220.

Macinnes, T., Tinson, A., Hughes, C., Born, T.B. and Aldridge, H. (2015) *Monitoring poverty and social exclusion 2015*, York: Joseph Rowntree Foundation.

Millar, J. and Ridge, T. (2013) 'Lone mothers and paid work: The "family-work project"', *International Review of Sociology*, vol 23, pp 564-77.

Newman, I. (2011) 'Work as a route out of poverty: A critical evaluation of the UK welfare to work policy', *Policy Studies*, vol 32, pp 91-108.

Oxfam (2010) *Something for nothing: Challenging negative attitudes to people living in poverty*, Briefing paper, Oxford: Oxfam.

Padly, M. and Hirsch, D. (2017) *A Minimum Income Standard for the UK in 2017*, York: Joseph Rowntree Foundation.

Patrick, R. (2013) 'Work as the primary "duty" of the responsible citizens: A critique of this work-centric approach', *People, Place & Policy Online*, vol 6, pp 5-15.

Patrick, R. (2017) *For whose benefit? The everyday realities of welfare reform*, Bristol: Policy Press.

Pemberton, S., Sutton, E., Fahmy, E. and Bell, K. (2014) *Life on a low income in austere times*, Bristol: Poverty and Social Exclusion in the UK (PSEUK).

Plunkett, J. (2015) 'Benefits Street series two to feature scenes of drug-dealing', London: *The Guardian*, 29 April (www.theguardian.com/media/2015/apr/29/channel-4-benefits-street-drug-dealing-series-two).

Ridge, T. (2009) *Living with poverty: A review of the literature on children's and families' experiences of poverty*, Research Report No 594, London: Department for Work and Pensions.

Shildrick, T. and Macdonald, R. (2013) 'Poverty talk: How people experiencing poverty deny their poverty and why they blame "the poor"', *The Sociological Review*, vol 61, pp 285-303.

Shildrick, T., Macdonald, R., Webster, C. and Garthwaite, K. (2012) *Poverty and insecurity: Life in low-pay, no-pay Britain*, Bristol: Policy Press.

Snowden, C. (2014) 'The Minimum Income Standard: The wisdom of crowds?', London: Institute for Economic Affairs (https://iea.org.uk/blog/the-minimum-income-standard-the-wisdom-of-crowds).

Taylor-Gooby, P. (2015) 'Benefits and welfare', in R. Ormston and J. Curtice (eds) *British Social Attitudes 32*, London: National Centre for Social Research Methods, pp 74-101.

Trussell Trust, The (2017) 'End of year stats' (www.trusselltrust.org/news-and-blog/latest-stats/end-year-stats/).

Tyler, I. (2014) *'Being poor is not entertainment': Class struggles against poverty porn*, Manchester: Social Action and Research Foundation (http://mediapovertywelfare.wordpress.com/2014/10/30/being-poor-is-not-entertainment/).

Walker, R. (2014) *The shame of poverty*, Oxford: Oxford University Press.

Watts, B., Fitzpatrick, S., Bramley, G. and Watkins, D. (2014) *Welfare sanctions and conditionality in the UK*, York: Joseph Rowntree Foundation.

Williams, C. (2005) 'A critical evaluation of hierarchical representations of community involvement', *Community Development Journal*, vol 40, no 1, pp 30-8.

Wright, S. (2016) 'Conceptualising the active welfare subject: Welfare reform in discourse, policy and lived experience', *Policy & Politics*, vol 44, pp 235-52.

Wright, S., Dwyer, P., McNeill, J. and Stewart, A.B.R. (2016) *First wave findings: Universal Credit, Welfare conditionality: Sanctions, support and behaviour change*, York: University of York.

12

Jobcentres and the delivery of employment services and benefits

Dan Finn

Summary

This chapter discusses the role of Jobcentres and contracted providers in the delivery of employment services. It considers:

- the changing objectives and organisation of Jobcentres and the tension between their role in providing employment assistance while imposing benefit conditionality and sanctions;
- how the Department for Work and Pensions contracts with private and third sector providers to deliver employment services;
- how Jobcentre services are being reconfigured to deliver Universal Credit, including an increased role for local government;
- how Jobcentre performance targets and provider contract incentives shape service delivery and constrain their ability to work with other local providers.

Introduction

The Jobcentre network is part of the Department for Work and Pensions (DWP) and is responsible for the delivery of employment services and the administration of working-age benefits. Jobcentres provide a free job matching service to unemployed people and employers, and more intensive services for people who have greater difficulty in getting jobs. This includes a variety of programmes such as assistance with job search; basic skills training; work experience and job creation; and assistance with self-employment. Some services are contracted out and delivered through a diverse group of non-profit and for-profit providers.

Recent governments have shared a common aim to create a 'welfare to work' system combining a benefit regime that requires most claimants to prepare for or actively seek employment with minimum wage and tax credit policies that 'make work pay'. The rights and responsibilities of working-age claimants have been redefined, and work–related conditionality and sanctions have been extended to cover a more diverse group of claimants, including lone parents, partners/spouses, people with disabilities and/or health–related problems, and people in low paid employment (see Chapter 3, this volume). The objective is to reinforce individual work incentives and, through increasing self-sufficiency from employment, help reduce benefit dependency and the cost of working-age benefits. In this process, the activity of front-line Jobcentres and their staff has been transformed, and they are expected to simultaneously deliver services that 'activate' claimants and reduce poverty, unemployment and welfare dependency.

Welfare to work policies have been coupled with institutional and organisational reforms. The first phase of reform culminated in the Labour government's creation of the DWP in 2001 and Jobcentre Plus in 2002. A second reform phase commenced from 2010, and has since been driven by the imperative to reduce the costs of working-age benefits and to implement a 'digital by default' delivery system for Universal Credit. Over this period there have also been reforms in how the DWP designs and purchases complementary employment services for the most disadvantaged claimants where it now contracts mostly with a small number of large 'prime providers'. These organisations are paid according to their results, and are responsible for service delivery and for managing supply chains made up of smaller and more specialised providers.

This chapter considers the impact that high levels of benefit receipt have had on the public sector agencies and services that work most closely with unemployed people. It reviews different phases of organisational reform with a focus on the changing purpose of Jobcentres. It describes the role of the DWP and Jobcentre Plus and how they organise services to pay benefits, enforce job search obligations and assist claimants with job search. It assesses how the DWP and Jobcentres interact with local government and other partners, including those contracted to deliver employment services. It also considers the ways in which digital technologies are reshaping the welfare to work delivery system.

Delivery of employment and related services

In comparative terms, the governance of the British welfare to work system is highly centralised. UK ministers and senior civil servants in London control the main levers of the welfare to work policy and the design and delivery of cash benefits and employment services. The main government department with responsibility for the welfare to work policy is the DWP, which delivers employment services through a network of directly managed Jobcentres. In Northern Ireland, the functions of the DWP are delivered through a network of Jobs and Benefits Offices accountable to the Department of Community Services.

Over a long period, the DWP has complemented the work of Jobcentres by commissioning a diverse network of non-profit and for-profit organisations to deliver complementary employment services. These contractual quasi-market arrangements give the Department important advantages. External providers give access to specialist services that may be too expensive for the DWP to provide. Such providers may also act as a source of innovation and can provide a benchmark against which to measure the cost and effectiveness of Jobcentre provision. Most importantly, the scale of contracted-out services can be quickly adapted in response to rising or falling levels of unemployment and changing government priorities. There are risks, however, especially where strong financial incentives mean that providers may concentrate efforts on service users more easily placed in jobs ('creaming') while harder-to-place participants receive only minimal services ('parking'). The Department counters such risks through contract design, monitoring and regular performance management (Finn, 2012).

In contrast with other OECD countries, local government in the UK has played a limited role in the design, commissioning and delivery of employment services. Many UK local authorities play a leading role, however, in economic development programmes, especially in areas of high unemployment, and have developed separately funded skills and employment services to facilitate residents' access to the opportunities created through local economic growth. Local authorities also have responsibility for social services, which are important in supporting needy residents to obtain cash benefits and employment, including childcare services, welfare rights advice and specialised social inclusion programmes working with highly disadvantaged communities. Since 2010 the government has embarked on a programme of devolution that is giving many local authorities, especially those that formally combine their economic development competences, incentives to influence and shape local employment and skills provision, including greater coordination of their efforts with those of the DWP.

There has, however, been a long-standing tension between the DWP's highly centralised control of the welfare to work system and its capacity to work effectively with other local agencies. The primary criticism has been that the Department's national targets and centrally designed and standardised services and contracts restrict the capacity of Jobcentres and contracted providers to tailor service delivery to local circumstances and to work in partnership, especially with local government (Finn, 2015).

From Labour Exchanges to Jobcentres

The origin of Jobcentres is found in a national network of Labour Exchanges established after 1909. These facilitated vacancy matching between employers and jobseekers and administered the national Unemployment Insurance system introduced in 1911. These new services were part of reforms intended to decasualise the labour market and to free important groups of workers from recourse to the traditional Poor Law. This system of poor relief was underpinned by the principle of 'less eligibility', where the conditions for receiving support were so stigmatised and onerous that people were presumed to have taken all steps to support themselves before seeking assistance. Labour Exchanges, by contrast, introduced a more humane and efficient principle that, in the words of William Beveridge, the architect of the system, made 'the finding of work easy instead of making relief hard' (1909, p 216).

The unemployment benefit system was, however, underpinned by a legal conditionality system requiring claimants to show that they were genuinely unemployed (see Box 12.1).

Box 12.1: Jobcentres, benefit conditionality and sanctions

In the earliest period, unemployed claimants had to 'sign on' twice a day at their local office to show they were available for work, but now must usually attend fortnightly, and give evidence of the active steps they are taking to seek work. Failure to 'sign on' or to meet other 'reasonable' work-related conditions results in either disqualification from eligibility or financial penalties. Conditionality is designed to ensure that the availability of cash payments does not undermine a claimant's willingness to work, and sanctions penalise claimants for not meeting their responsibilities. Conditionality creates, however, a critical tension between the employment assistance objectives of front-line staff and their responsibility to 'police' the behaviour of jobseekers. The system of conditionality and its related sanctions has varied over time, but has often been controversial, especially in periods of high unemployment (Price, 2000).

In the 1940s, Unemployment Benefit Offices replaced Labour Exchanges. Coverage of unemployment insurance was extended, and 'poor relief' replaced by a system of means–tested benefits. Unemployed claimants had to register for work with the Unemployment Benefit Office before being referred to their local social security office. By the 1960s, Unemployment Benefit Offices were associated with unskilled claimants, had a poor reputation with employers and were not well placed to meet the 'manpower needs' of a full employment economy (Price, 2000). There was institutional change and a new agency, which combined employment and skills services, became responsible for finding and filling vacancies.

The Manpower Services Commission had a remit to coordinate publicly funded employment and skills provision, and its services were delivered through a new national network of Jobcentres often located in city centres. These new offices displayed vacancies openly, and were designed to be attractive to all jobseekers, including those in work, and to provide more comprehensive services to employers.

Unemployed claimants who 'signed on' at their local Unemployment Benefit Office were required to register with a Jobcentre where they could be matched with vacancies. The registration requirement was not rigorously enforced and, in the early 1980s, was further relaxed to ease administrative pressure when unemployment increased steeply.

Critics argued that the weak connection between Unemployment Benefit Offices and Jobcentres made the system passive because local managers gave too little attention to job placement work with unemployed people. This passivity contributed to increased long-term unemployment that had been 'ratcheting' upwards in the economic cycles of the 1970s and 1980s. Consequently, Conservative governments embarked on so-called activation reforms that included more explicit mandatory requirements for unemployed people. Claimants had to attend Jobcentre interviews, discuss their job goals, agree job search activities, accept a wider range of job opportunities, participate in mandatory programmes and agree and sign a regularly updated back-to-work plan. The emphasis changed to a 'work first' approach, influenced by welfare reforms introduced in the US. The new front-line approach placed greater emphasis on sanctions and aimed to move claimants into unsubsidised jobs as quickly as possible.

The new approach was accompanied by institutional change and by 1989, a national Employment Service had been created. Jobcentres were merged with Unemployment Benefit Offices and made responsible for employment assistance, monitoring conditionality and for the sanctions regime. Jobcentres thereafter provided few services for unemployed people who did not claim benefits or for those who claimed other working-age benefits. It administered Unemployment Benefit and encouraged those taking low-paid jobs to claim in-work benefits, but all means-tested social security benefits were administered by a separate Benefits Agency. Ministerial and departmental concerns about any weakening of the link between employment services, job search requirements and benefit administration have since been a major factor limiting collaborative work with local initiatives perceived to risk weakening the national 'work first' benefit regime.

Ministers and senior civil servants controlled the Employment Service through performance targets, with priority given to reducing the numbers claiming unemployment benefits (Considine, 2001). Delivery systems were restructured, making greater use of computerisation, and the Employment Service developed standardised service interactions with claimants, the results from which were monitored and managed closely. Critics suggest these changes induced a 'target mentality' in the Employment Service that drove greater use of sanctions and the increased transfer of unemployed claimants to other, especially health and disability-related, benefits, where claimants were no longer included in the published and politically sensitive monthly unemployment count. The lack of flexibility in delivering 'top-down' national programmes and procedures hampered efforts by Employment Service district managers to work with local government and other local partnerships (Finn, 2015).

Evaluations suggest that the activation strategy was successful in reducing long-term unemployment and more swiftly moving claimants off benefits (OECD, 2014). The reduction in claimant unemployment masked, however, a *major increase in the number of working-age people claiming social security benefits who did not have work-related requirements*. By 1997 this included nearly a million lone parents and over 2.5 million people who were claiming health and disability-related benefits. Multiple factors were driving increased reliance on welfare benefits, especially concerning changes in local labour demand and family composition, but the inactive design of these benefits appeared to contribute to long-term dependency. Because they faced no work-related requirements, these claimants had little contact with Jobcentres, and few returned to or entered employment.

An 'employment first' welfare state and Jobcentre Plus

In 1998 the Labour government announced ambitious plans to create what it called an 'employment first' welfare state (DSS, 1998). This saw the gradual extension of work-related requirements and Jobcentre services to lone parents and people on disability benefits. Initially, this took the form of voluntary employment programmes and requirements to attend 'work-focused interviews'. By the end of the following decade, however, job search requirements and mandatory programmes were extended to cover lone parents with children aged over five. Access to disability benefits was tightened up, and in 2008, a new Employment and Support Allowance was introduced. This replaced earlier income replacement disability benefits and, through a more rigorous and controversial assessment process, divided claimants into a 'work-related activity group', who could be required to prepare for work, and a 'support group', who were not subject to work-related requirements (see Chapter 3, this volume).

The 'employment first' welfare state was delivered through new institutional arrangements and a transformation in front-line delivery. This commenced with the creation of the DWP and Jobcentre Plus, which, between 2002 and 2006, were responsible for integrating the employment services and social security delivery systems (see Box 12.2).

Jobcentre Plus had its own chief executive and a board with seven full-time directors and three non-executive directors. The organisation was divided into nine English regions plus offices for Wales and Scotland, with the network subdivided into 50 districts. Jobcentre Plus worked with a complex array of strategic and operational partnerships. Local partnership arrangements were largely the responsibility of district and partnership managers who worked in strategic forums with local authorities, employers and other stakeholders. Operational partnerships involved liaison with contracted providers, contract management and the organisation of referral arrangements.

Box 12.2: Jobcentre Plus service delivery system

By 2006 front-line employment services were delivered through a national network of some 800 Jobcentres. The layout and organisation of these offices was modernised and a reception point, open-plan format and appointment system (which reduced queues) was designed to emulate practices in the commercial services sector. The new offices introduced touch-screen computer terminals known as Jobpoints through which service users could find and select vacancies. Benefit claims and payments were mostly administered through telephone contacts and specialised delivery centres, with cash entitlements paid directly into each recipient's bank account.

Jobcentre Plus enjoyed some operational autonomy but was accountable to DWP ministers through 'performance and resource agreement' targets. Jobcentre Plus's primary task was to place unemployed claimants, especially the hardest-to-help, into employment as swiftly as possible. Other responsibilities included reducing fraud and error and the efficient administration of benefit payments. Despite some local flexibility, national performance targets continued to shape delivery, and centrally designed service standards hampered the capacity of Jobcentres to work with other agencies.

A distinctive feature of the new Jobcentres involved the role of front-line 'personal advisers' tasked with tailoring support to the needs of individual claimants, enforcing obligations and making referrals to more specialised provision. This was known as a 'case management' approach that had become a leading paradigm for delivering welfare to work services in the US and Australia. Studies found that the ways in which advisers implement services within local offices had an important influence on outcomes. Unemployed claimants were more likely to cease claiming benefits and/or obtain employment in those offices that placed a strong emphasis on 'work first' practices and the use of sanctions (White, 2004).

There are mixed views on the contribution Jobcentre Plus made in reducing unemployment and benefit dependency. A post-implementation impact evaluation concluded that the introduction of Jobcentre Plus helped reduce the number of people on all the main working-age benefits (by an estimated 40,000), increased the effective labour supply, and the investment was judged to have been more than self-financing (Riley et al, 2011). The agency also played a major role in enabling the Department to respond effectively to changing government priorities and to local and national economic shocks. Between 2008 and 2010 Jobcentres coped with a sharp increase in benefit claims from those who lost their jobs following the recession, swiftly implemented new labour market programmes, and maintained their job entry performance (NAO, 2013). In combination with the government's wider economic stimulus package, this meant that the 2008/09 fall in employment and increase in unemployment was less severe than that which followed the recessions of the early 1980s and 1990s, even though the fall in economic output was swifter and greater (OECD, 2014; Coulter, 2016).

Jobcentres and the Universal Credit delivery system

The Jobcentre network and its front-line advisers entered a further phase of organisational transformation to deliver Universal Credit, public expenditure savings and the welfare reforms introduced by governments elected after 2010.

The most important driver of change concerns Universal Credit, which merged six working-age benefits and in-work tax credits, into a single, monthly household payment (see Chapter 3, this volume). Another factor has been a marked fall in the numbers of unemployed claimants following a long period of employment growth that commenced in 2012. The reduction in demand for Jobcentre services has, however, been offset by the extension of job search requirements to a wider group of Universal Credit claimants. Jobcentres will also play a key role in delivering services intended to contribute to meeting the Conservative government's commitment of getting an additional 1 million disabled people into work over a 10-year period (Conservative Party, 2017). Jobcentres may also play a key role in increasing labour supply and meeting employer demand as the existing UK workforce ages and 'Brexit' impacts on the supply of younger migrant labour.

Universal Credit is being implemented through new 'digital by default' administrative, communications and delivery systems (see Box 12.3).

There are various other service delivery implications arising from the design of Universal Credit. Digital delivery and the monthly payment system are intended to prepare households for mainstream employment and to encourage self-reliance. But DWP accepts that some claimants may experience transitional or longer-term difficulties. These groups are catered for by a new local service – Universal Support – which relies on collaboration between Jobcentres, local authorities, social housing providers and other agencies (Learning and Work Institute et al, 2016).

Various models of local support have been tested, but essentially, Jobcentre staff identify people with barriers to making Universal Credit claims, or who have more complex needs, and refer them to specialist online, telephone or in-person support. Services available include digital training to enable people to make and manage online claims; personal budgeting support, to help claimants better manage monthly payments; and employment assistance and other complementary advice and support services provided by local agencies. In future, these services are expected to align with new locally designed and integrated health and employment services being developed to support more people with disabilities enter employment (DWP and DH, 2016).

Box 12.3: 'Digital-by-default' Universal Credit

The Universal Credit claiming process is designed to be 'digital by default', with over 80 per cent of claimants eventually managing all benefit-related aspects of their claim online. Under the full digital service, Universal Credit claimants are expected to manage their interactions with the DWP through an online account and journal through which they report their income, changes in circumstances and work search activity. This account is integrated with Universal Jobmatch – a digital vacancy database and recruitment website on which most claimants must register and upload their CV. A digital advisory function allows Jobcentre staff to monitor individual job search commitments and activity; analyse CVs; identify skills or training gaps; and search, save and send targeted vacancies directly to claimants.

The introduction of Universal Credit has been hampered by technical problems, but implementation of the digital delivery system has accelerated, and from 2018, new applicants have to claim Universal Credit rather than the benefits and tax credits it replaced. Existing claimants of these so-called 'legacy' benefits will be migrated into the new system between 2019 and 2022.

Digital Jobcentres, work coaches and delivery flexbilities

Universal Credit implementation is being undertaken by the DWP and Jobcentre network that have been restructured following cuts in their administration and service budgets. In 2011 Jobcentre Plus's agency status was abolished with management of the network brought into the core Department. The regional tier of management was removed, and 34 large districts created. The Jobcentre network was reduced with the number of stand-alone Jobcentres planned to fall to just over 600 by 2020. Smaller Jobcentres have been closed but others have or will be co-located, mostly with local government services (House of Commons Library, 2017).

Between 2014 and 2015 Jobcentres were physically redesigned and Jobpoints and free phone facilities removed. In the new 'Digital Jobcentres', claimants use on-site computer facilities or their own Wi-Fi or Web Access Devices to make benefit claims, set up a Universal Credit account and search for employment. Unemployed claimants also 'sign on' using electronic pads that verify signature authenticity. The changes have been designed to facilitate claimant self-service and self-reliance, freeing up Jobcentre resources for advisory work, especially with those claimants who face most difficulty in securing employment.

The roll-out of Universal Credit and the extension of work-related requirements to additional claimants was accompanied by the introduction of 'work coaches', replacing the previous role of personal advisers. In 2016 there were about 11,000 work coaches, each of whom was responsible for a caseload of around 100 claimants, conducting 10 to 20 claimant interviews per day. The work coaches have mixed caseloads and their primary role is to support claimants into work by 'challenging, motivating, providing personalised advice, and using knowledge of local labour markets' (House of Commons Work and Pensions Committee, 2016). They are also expected to act as a gateway and provide referrals to a wider range of support and services, especially for claimants with health problems and disabilities. This includes delivery of early intervention mandatory 'work and health conversations', undertaken within a month, for any person who claims Universal Credit who indicates they are incapable of work (DWP and DH, 2016). Some 500 specialist disability employment advisers and work psychologists advise and support work coaches (as well as having their own caseloads of more complex cases).

The DWP further sought to improve efficiency and local coordination through the introduction of greater managerial flexibilities. District managers and work coaches have some discretion in setting the frequency of interviews required and the employment support made available. This discretionary activity is supported by a Flexible Support Fund. DWP managers use the budget to fund local partnership working and to procure small-scale programmes for specific target groups. Working within local guidelines and priorities, work coaches may also use the Fund to provide individual support, such as travel expenses or clothing for interviews. These flexibilities continue, however, to be exercised within the context of meeting the DWP's national targets.

Jobcentre performance targets and sanctions

There was a major change and simplification of the target regime in 2011. Previously Jobcentre Plus performance was measured against a range of indicators including the proportion of claimants entering employment and the number of adviser interviews. In the new approach, measures of activity were dropped and Jobcentres were primarily expected to move people off benefit and into employment as quickly as possible, and to reduce money lost to fraud and error. The key change concerned the methodology by which outcomes were assessed that measured off-benefit flows at 13, 26, 39 and 52 weeks from the start of a claim. This change was in part a response to criticisms of the cost and poor accuracy of earlier administrative methods used to validate actual job entries.

One significant problem is that, as in the 1980s, 'off-flow' simply means that an individual has ended their benefit claim – it does not necessarily mean that a claimant has found work. In 2011, for example, a cohort analysis of benefit leavers found that only some 68 per cent of benefit leavers got work, 41 per cent of whom were employed full-time, 18 per cent part-time and 9 per cent were self-employed. Another 14 per cent had claimed another out-of-work benefit and 18 per cent were neither working nor claiming (Adams et al, 2012).

The National Audit Office (NAO) also highlighted the risk that focusing on off-benefit flows could lead to perverse behaviour that might cause Jobcentre staff or contracted providers to falsely inflate their outcomes, impose sanctions or otherwise pressurise people to drop their benefit claims. Two NAO reports (2016a, b) found no evidence that pressure to meet targets led to falsified reporting. The sanction rate, however, did increase markedly after 2010, provoking controversy about the hardship caused, especially after the severity of sanctions was increased in 2012. Sanction rates declined after administrative reforms, but their imposition continues to be controversial, and in many high unemployment areas weakens the willingness of partner organisations (such as health services) to engage too closely with DWP provision.

A further criticism of the target-driven 'work first' approach of Jobcentres has been that it induces 'benefit recycling' where claimants are pressured to take casual and short-term jobs with many then returning to claim benefits. In this respect, the introduction of Universal Credit and contracts that pay providers for longer-term job outcomes may create a new dynamic in UK welfare to work services. Ministers have indicated that there will be an employment sustainability measure for those who are working and claiming Universal Credit. This may induce Jobcentres to behave more like contracted providers that now focus on maintaining continuity of employment and provide rapid reemployment assistance where job loss occurs (DWP and DH, 2016).

Changes in the welfare to work market and the Work Programme

In 2004/05 the DWP was purchasing employment services from an estimated network of 2,000 for-profit and non-profit organisations. Contracts typically lasted for three years and together were worth about £1 billion per year (equivalent to about a third of the cost of Jobcentre services). Jobcentre Plus was largely responsible for contract design and management.

By 2007 there was dissatisfaction with Jobcentre Plus control of the contracting process and poor provider performance. An independent review concluded that contracting arrangements were inadequate, and discouraged providers from investing in their service delivery capacity. The review culminated in the development of a 'commissioning strategy', the principles of which have since shaped the 'welfare to work' market (DWP, 2014) (see Box 12.4).

The payment-by-results contracting approach was first fully implemented in the coalition government's large-scale Work Programme that operated between 2012 and 2017. The Work Programme was delivered by 18 mostly for-profit prime contractors, and payments to providers were mostly made when a participant had been in employment for six months or three months for some 'harder-to-help' groups. Some 2 million claimants were referred to the programme, most of whom had been unemployed for more than a year or were in receipt of Employment and Support Allowance subject to work activity requirements.

Box 12.4: Payment-by-results, prime providers and flexible service standards

Core principles of the DWP approach to contracts include:

Payment-by-results: The DWP payment system mostly rewards longer-term employment outcomes differentiated in relation to the severity of the barriers faced by participants. Because outcome payments are paid in arrears, providers cannot recover the money they invest in services without getting participants into employment. The value of these sustained outcome measures is that they directly reflect the government's priorities, are relatively simple to check and are easy for those delivering welfare to work services to understand and relate to their day-to-day practices.

Prime providers and supply chains: Contract durations (usually five years) and large 'contract package areas' (which guarantee a large volume of participants) are designed to attract well-capitalised prime providers who can manage the risk associated with payment-by-results. This model excludes smaller, often non-profit organisations, but prime providers, who may deliver some services in-house, are also responsible for marshalling and managing an appropriate blend of subcontractors to deliver services for a wide variety of participants. The DWP directly manages prime providers, but smaller subcontractors no longer have a direct contractual relationship with the Department.

Service standards and flexibility: In return for accepting more risk, prime providers are given greater flexibility to design their service delivery system, albeit contracts specify varying levels of minimum service standards. This gives providers freedom to use their expertise and to innovate, but may make poor service delivery and 'creaming' and 'parking' harder to detect.

Implementation of the Work Programme attracted criticism and was punctuated by negative media coverage about weak performance, poor quality services, the reduced role of non-profit and specialist subcontractors and the interaction with the Department's sanctions regime (House of Commons Work and Pensions Committee, 2013). Much criticism concerned the failure of providers to meet early performance targets, but subsequent assessments concluded that the programme improved value for money by generating sustained employment outcomes equivalent to the schemes it replaced at half the cost. Two-thirds of unemployed participants were not placed in employment, however, and Work Programme providers struggled to assist those on disability benefits. There was evidence that the payment-by-results funding model induced 'parking' because it failed to provide sufficient incentives for providers to invest in more than job search support, with few services for participants who required more complex or costly interventions.

By 2017 long-term unemployment had fallen dramatically, and contracts for the Work Programme, and a smaller specialised disability-related programme, were not renewed. A smaller five-year Work and Health Programme was introduced to cater for up to 40,000 referrals a year (with a budget worth 80 per cent less than that of the programmes it replaced). The new programme delivers specialist *voluntary* support for claimants with health conditions or a disability and *mandatory* support for some of those unemployed for over two years. Delivery is the responsibility of a small number of prime providers, each covering large geographical areas, with 70 per cent of their funding tied to securing sustained employment and 30 per cent paid as monthly service fees. A major consequence of scaling down contracted provision is that Jobcentres increasingly cater directly for more of the long-term unemployed and for higher numbers of individuals with health conditions and disabilities who do not qualify for the Work and Health Programme.

Changing relationship between Jobcentres and local government

The implementation of welfare reform, Universal Credit and the wider devolution agenda are having a major impact on the ways in which Jobcentres, local government and other providers coordinate and align their services. The combined local authorities have also been given new powers that may enable them to integrate aspects of employment and skills provision. In Scotland, Manchester and London, the Work and Health Programme budget was devolved, allowing each area to design and commission their own programmes, and in some other areas, councils were empowered to help shape this contracted provision.

Partnership working and service coordination has always been largely voluntary, however, and local government, and even the combined local authorities, have only a limited influence in the design or commissioning of Jobcentre support and on how resources are deployed to meet local needs. The DWP approach to localism has been shaped by the requirement to meet centrally defined national objectives designed to reduce the number and duration of unemployment benefit claims. This target-driven approach is changing, however, where the DWP and Jobcentres help deliver services for, and work with, groups not well served by mainstream employment services, including 'troubled families', disadvantaged young people and other jobseekers not claiming benefits. The pressure to work more collaboratively has further increased as Jobcentres and work coaches become a gateway to complementary services for low-paid workers, claimants with limited work capacity, lone parents with younger children and the unemployed domestic partners of benefit claimants. This need to provide for a more diverse and challenging caseload of working-age claimants requires the DWP and Jobcentres to work more flexibly and collaboratively.

In many areas, more networked systems of local employment assistance and benefit services are emerging. These networks build on existing practices where, in varied localities, councils, Jobcentres and other service providers have agreed strategic objectives on poverty reduction and increasing local employment including cross-referral arrangements to coordinate service delivery. In some areas this had already resulted in more aligned, and sometimes co-located, services where, for example, skills, careers, health and money advice services, and DWP employment support are delivered alongside each other on a part- or full-time basis (Learning and Work Institute et al, 2016). Such local delivery networks may further develop to deliver locally designed and coordinated employment and health services (DWP and DH, 2016).

Conclusion

This chapter has assessed the changing role of Jobcentres and contracted providers in the delivery of employment services. This national network of provision has played a central role in enabling UK governments to facilitate job matching, ease problems of labour demand and manage the challenges posed by periods of high unemployment. Over the past two decades there has, however, been a major shift in the culture of Jobcentres as they have been required to deliver a stricter work first benefit regime and extend services to previously inactive benefit claimants. This has included changes in the actual structure of offices, in new job descriptions, in referral and attendance procedures for claimants, and the development of new digital services to help secure employment and monitor job search activity. Jobcentres are not simply a point of access to services. Their daily bureaucratic routines are designed to maximise employment-related outcomes and reduce the cost of working-age benefits by ensuring that most claimants prepare for and become more active and flexible in their search for work and increased earnings.

The increased strictness and severity of the benefit regime, eligibility rules and related sanctions has been associated with a marked increase in the gap between the number of unemployed benefit claimants registered with Jobcentres and the number of people who report in the national Labour Force Survey that they are unemployed and looking for work. This divergent trend emerged in the 1980s, but has since grown, and by 2016, the claimant unemployment count was less than half that of the Labour Force Survey count. Many of these unemployed people are not eligible to claim benefits and others, especially young people, choose not to claim or are deterred from doing so. The consequence is that a significant group of people who could benefit from access to Jobcentre employment services no longer do so.

Overview

The DWP and Jobcentres administer working-age benefits and provide services that both assist jobseekers and employers to fill vacancies while ensuring that claimants meet their work-related obligations. Jobcentres originally provided services for all jobseekers, but now work primarily with benefit claimants.

The DWP commissions complementary employment services, mainly for the hardest-to-help claimants, from a small number of for-profit and non-profit prime providers who are mostly paid for their results in getting service users into sustained employment.

The DWP has been successful in reducing the number of unemployed benefit claimants, but critics argue that the design of Jobcentre performance targets and provider contract incentives has negative effects, with claimants pressured into poor quality jobs or into dropping their benefit claims.

The implementation of welfare reforms and Universal Credit is transforming the work of Jobcentres and extending work-related conditionality to new groups of claimants. This is accelerating the emergence of local networks that seek to coordinate and align employment, skills, health and other related services.

Questions for discussion

1. How and why has the role of Jobcentres changed in the delivery of welfare to work services?
2. What are the advantages and disadvantages of using performance targets and payment-by-results in the delivery of welfare to work services?
3. What are the barriers to securing better cooperation between Jobcentres and other local service providers?

Key reading

DWP (Department for Work and Pensions) and DH (Department of Health) (2016) *Improving lives: The work, health and disability Green Paper*, Cm 9342, London: The Stationery Office.

Finn, D. (2015) *Welfare to work devolution in England*, York: Joseph Rowntree Foundation.

House of Commons Work and Pensions Committee (2016) *The future of Jobcentre Plus*, House of Commons, HC 57, London: The Stationery Office.

Website resources

www.nao.gov.uk
  National Audit Office

www.parliament.uk/business/committees/committees-a-z/commons-select/work-and-pensions-committee/
  House of Commons Work and Pensions Select Committee

https://policyexchange.org.uk/
  Policy Exchange

www.resolutionfoundation.org
  Resolution Foundation

References

Adams, L., Oldfield, K., Riley, C. and Skone James, A. (2012) *Destinations of Jobseeker's Allowance, Income Support and Employment and Support Allowance leavers 2011*, Research Report No 791, London: Department for Work and Pensions.

Beveridge, W.H. (1909) *Unemployment: A problem of industry*, London: Longmans, Green & Co.

Conservative Party (2017) *Forward together: The Conservative and Unionist Party manifesto*, London.

Considine, M. (2001) *Enterprising states: The public management of welfare-to-work*, Cambridge: Cambridge University Press.

Coulter, S. (2016) 'The UK labour market and the "great recession"', in M. Myant, S. Theodoropoulou and A. Piasna (eds) *Unemployment, internal devaluation and labour market deregulation in Europe*, Brussels: European Trade Union Institute, pp 197-227.

DSS (Department of Social Security) (1998) *A new contract for welfare: Principles into practice*, Cm 4101, London: The Stationery Office.

DWP (2014) *Commissioning Strategy*, London: Department for Work and Pensions.

DWP (Department for Work and Pensions) and DH (Department of Health) (2016) *Improving lives: The work, health and disability Green Paper*, Cm 9342, London: The Stationery Office.

Finn, D. (2012) *The design of the Work Programme in international context*, London: National Audit Office.

Finn, D. (2015) *Welfare to work devolution in England*, York: Joseph Rowntree Foundation.

House of Commons Library (2017) *Jobcentre Plus office closures*, Debate Pack No CDP-2017-0089, 10 March, London.

House of Commons Work and Pensions Committee (2013) *Can the Work Programme work for all user groups?*, House of Commons, HC 162, London: The Stationery Office.

House of Commons Work and Pensions Committee (2016) *The future of Jobcentre Plus*, House of Commons, HC 57, London: The Stationery Office.

Learning and Work Institute, BMG Research and Policy in Practice (2016) *Evaluation of the Universal Support delivered locally trials*, Ad hoc Research Report No 33, London: Department for Work and Pensions.

NAO (National Audit Office) (2013) *Responding to change in jobcentres*, London: NAO.

NAO (2016a) *Investigation into misuse of the Flexible Support Fund in Plaistow*, London: NAO.

NAO (2016b) *Benefit sanctions*, London: NAO.

OECD (Organisation for Economic Co-operation and Development) (2014) *Connecting people with jobs: Activation policies in the United Kingdom*, Paris: OECD.

Price, D. (2000) *Office of hope: A history of the Employment Service*, Policy Studies Institute, London: University of Westminster.

Riley, R., Bewley, H., Kirby, S., Rincon-Aznar, A. and George, A. (2011) *The introduction of Jobcentre Plus: An evaluation of labour market impacts*, Research Report No 781, London: Department for Work and Pensions.

White, M. (2004) *Effective job search practice in the UK's mandatory welfare-to-work programme for youth*, London: Policy Studies Institute.

13

Making it simple?
Universal basic income

Luke Martinelli

Summary

Following the standard definition, universal basic income (also referred to simply as 'basic income') denotes a regular financial transfer that is paid to everyone on an individual basis, regardless of past work history, free of labour market or other behavioural conditions, and paid irrespective of other income or wealth.

Universal basic income has the potential to dramatically simplify existing systems of social security and give rise to wide-ranging advantages for society. However, it is deeply contested on both normative and positive grounds, a situation exacerbated by a lack of direct empirical evidence, as well as the fact that basic income is best understood as a diverse family of proposals with varied labour market, fiscal and distributional consequences.

This chapter starts by defining universal basic income and the reasons for the current interest, across political boundaries and in a diverse range of countries. The main sections discuss:

- problems with the current system that basic income addresses;
- its potential for re-shaping wider society;
- arguments against basic income;
- the different forms it could take;
- experimental and microsimulation evidence on basic income's effects.

Introduction

Universal basic income would provide everyone with a regular cash payment and is, as van Parijs (1992, p 1) observes, a 'beautifully, disarmingly simple idea' – as well as one with potentially profound implications. Under conventional social security policies, the groups of people to which transfers are made are restricted on the basis of conditions of category, circumstance and conduct (or behaviour) (Clasen and Clegg, 2007). Basic income sweeps all that away. Box 13.1 summarises the main features and advantages of universal basic income that arise from its simple and unconditional nature.

Box 13.1: Universal basic income: what and why?

The idea of universal basic income is to provide all citizens with a periodic cash payment. As well as being paid to all, it is unconditional in four additional and important ways:

- No means testing on income from other sources (that is, payments are uniform and non-withdrawable).
- No prior employment or contributions histories (that is, payments are non-contributory).
- No behavioural requirements (that is, recipients are not inclined to participate in labour market or other authorised activities).
- No tests of living/partnering arrangements (that is, payments are individualised).

These characteristics give rise to the core strengths of basic income:

- It minimises costly, intrusive and stigmatising bureaucratic rules and conditions.
- Work is not discouraged by withdrawal of benefits or the risk of income disruption.
- There are no gaps in coverage – that is, universal basic income provides income security to all as a matter of *right*.
- It permits individuals freedom to organise their lives as they choose, in unpaid activities (for example, care work, education, entrepreneurship, volunteering, civic engagement) and in household living arrangements.

Universal basic income's appeal traverses a range of political perspectives (Torry, 2016a), giving rise to the common portrayal of basic income as 'neither right nor left but forward'. At basic income's heart is a compromise between 'justice' and 'efficiency' (van Parijs, 1990); proponents argue it is uniquely capable of fulfilling the protective functions of social security while minimising harmful labour market distortions (Martinelli, 2017a). Left-wing inclinations towards equality, solidarity and redistribution are coupled with libertarian ideals of freedom and efficiency. The juxtaposition of political philosophical values enshrined in basic income has a long pedigree; the modern concept can be traced back to Thomas Paine in the 18th century, where it was justified as compensation for infringement of inalienable common property rights through land enclosure (van Parijs, 1992). Since that time, interest in the idea has waxed and waned. However, in the past decade – and especially since 2013 – interest has soared.

A number of developments illustrate this shift: a Swiss decision (in 2013) to have a referendum (held in 2016) on whether to grant every citizen an unconditional payment; recent experiments in Namibia and India, and a host of experiments ongoing or planned in Finland, Kenya, the Netherlands, Canada and California; a general flurry of media and public scrutiny; and the growing membership – and sheer number – of organisations supportive of (or at least interested in) the idea of basic income. For example, in the UK, the idea has attracted support from the Trades Union Congress (TUC), the left-leaning Royal Society for the Arts (RSA) and Compass think tanks, and the free market Adam Smith Institute endorses a form of basic income. In terms of mainstream political actors, the Labour Party, Select Committee on Work and Pensions and the Scottish Parliament's Social Security Committee have all held consultations on basic income. Universal basic income is promoted in the UK by the Citizen's Basic Income Trust (http:// citizensincome.org/) and globally by the Basic Income Earth Network (http:// basicincome.org), which covers a large and growing number of national and regional affiliate organisations.

As discussed in Martinelli (2017a), the precise causes of increased interest and support are uncertain, but probably relate to (perceptions of) fundamental structural and technological changes that concentrate wealth in the hands of an ever-decreasing number, render swathes of jobs obsolete or wholly devalued, and push workers into more and more precarious positions (Goos and Manning, 2007; Standing, 2011; Srnicek and Williams, 2015). Other likely causes are more prosaic, and relate to widespread perceptions that existing welfare provisions are unfit for purpose.

Problems with the existing system

Universal basic income is intended to address some deep-seated and perennial problems with current social security systems. These include costly, intrusive and stigmatising rules, perverse incentives and gaps in coverage.

Costly, intrusive and stigmatising rules

The UK social security system is extremely complex, with entitlements based on a myriad of overlapping criteria, for example, relating to income and wealth holdings, living arrangements, previous insurance contributions and capacity for and willingness to work. The bureaucratic requirements of the system impose a burden on claimants as well as a financial cost to the state. Complex entitlement rules increase the prospects for error, fraud and 'gaming the system' (Goodin, 1992). Some costs to claimants are psychological in nature: as van Oorschot (2002) argues, means testing leads to the stigmatisation of benefit recipients and cultivates social division.

In the context of 'conditionality', claimants are also subjected to burdensome and intrusive labour market requirements, which now extend to previously exempt groups including lone parents and people with disabilities (JRF, 2014). Disability rights and poverty advocacy groups have documented the profound anxiety and material deprivation faced by individuals whose claims are delayed due to administrative factors, or erroneously rejected on the grounds that they are able to work or have not made sufficient effort to find work (DRUK, 2016; JRF, 2016).

Perverse incentives

Perverse incentives arise when criteria and conditions provide claimants with incentives to prolong the circumstances that give rise to benefit entitlement in the first place.

- *Poverty and unemployment traps* describe situations in which people face little if any financial incentive to enter employment, or to progress in work or increase their work effort, respectively. These occur when benefits are withdrawn sharply as claimants enter employment or increase their earnings, meaning that individuals would only gain very marginally or not at all.
- *Bureaucracy traps* occur when individuals fail to engage in desirable behaviour that risks disrupting their income. This problem is particularly pertinent in the context of an offer of short-term employment; even when the change of circumstance should result in a financial improvement, the claimant risks losing their benefits or facing delays in payment moving between claims. Another example is the way in which the UK disability benefit system provides 'a monetary incentive for claimants to "fail" the work capability assessment' and perversely discourages disabled claimants from taking work *even if they are willing and able to do so,* fearing that if a job 'does not work out they may then be moved onto a lower rate benefit' (Pickles et al, 2016, p 10).
- *Isolation traps* (van Parijs, 2004) can occur when couples retain separate homes to avoid being treated as 'partnered' (to avoid the so-called 'couples penalty' in benefit rates but also, perhaps more significantly, to maintain independent incomes and rights to tenure).

Gaps in coverage

One of the features of basic income is that it provides income security to everyone as a matter of right. In contrast, conditional systems will inevitably exclude a proportion of individuals whose circumstances do not meet the administrative criteria. One circumstance for which conventional social security systems are ill equipped is the precarious nature of employment for many people (Standing, 2011). When periods of employment are intermittent, claimants may need but not qualify for support. Furthermore, in the context of precarity, social security systems based on the contributory principle (such as in France and Germany) have become increasingly 'dualistic' as the gap between well-protected labour market 'insiders' and 'outsiders' continues to grow (Palier, 2012). Gaps in coverage also arise as a result of the complex criteria and conditions depicted above. Goodin (1992) describes the ways in which 'target efficiency' – how effectively transfers actually reach the poor – is limited in means-tested systems as a result of low take-up and invalid proxies for 'need'. Furthermore, increasingly stringent and punitive sanctions attached to conditions – even when 'correctly' applied – exacerbate the inadequacy of the system to meet the basic needs of the poor (JRF, 2016).

Reshaping society

These arguments relate to problems with the current social security system that universal basic income could potentially address. But for some, basic income is more than social security reform; rather, it is seen as wide-ranging in its potential to reshape standards of economic and social justice. In contrast to justifications that emphasise the policy's capacity to expand labour supply, some proponents suggest that basic income has the potential to emancipate people from the exploitation and domination that arises when they are compelled to perform labour in order to survive. Only with the availability of an 'exit option' are people truly free to engage in the activities and forms of work that really matter to them – including those that are highly worthwhile to society but to which no value is attached by 'the market' (Standing, 2013). Because labour would only be undertaken when freely chosen, the provision of a substantial basic income would tend to 'spread bargaining power so as to enable (as much as is sustainable) the less advantaged to discriminate between attractive or promising and lousy jobs' (van Parijs, 2004, p 17).

In a related argument, basic income is seen to have the potential to distribute existing employment opportunities more equitably between working and workless households. This results from what Groot and van der Veen (2000, p 24) call 'the reshuffle effect': 'more full-time workers will choose to work part-time, freeing up jobs for the unemployed.' The simple and intuitive idea is that some people do not have enough paid work while others would like to do less; basic income helps both groups to achieve more optimal outcomes. Van der Veen and Groot (2006) go further, arguing that basic income may be seen as the basis of an emergent 'post-productivist' welfare regime. 'Productivism' refers to a value system that prioritises economic growth over other values (for example, personal autonomy, community cohesion, equality or environmental sustainability). By explicitly enabling people to reduce their work effort, basic income permits a settlement to be forged that affords greater priority to 'individual autonomy in ... welfare and labour market arrangements' (van der Veen and Groot, 2006, p 595). By the same token, a number of 'green' activists promote basic income as a way to encourage production and consumption to be scaled back while also mitigating against any adverse distributional effects that arise from falling aggregate incomes (Andersson, 2009).

Last, but not least, it is argued that basic income should have important and wide-reaching gender equality impacts. With less compulsion to work full time, men would be able to more equally participate in unpaid care. At the same time, a basic income would go some way to recognising the importance and value of unpaid care work (by providing those so engaged with an independent income), would compensate dual-earner families for their use of formal childcare services, and would improve women's position in the labour market to a greater degree than that of men (given the feminisation of low-paid and part-time work) (Robeyns, 2000). It would also compensate for gaps in contributory pensions systems that predominantly affect women (Parker, 1993). However, the gender equality credentials of basic income are disputed by other feminist scholars (see, for example, Gheaus, 2008), who argue that given the existing gender norms around the division of paid and unpaid work – and women's relatively weaker attachment to the labour market – basic income would reinforce gender roles and exacerbate women's dependence and labour market disadvantage (see also Chapter 6, this volume).

Against universal basic income: the counter-arguments

So far, this chapter has focused on basic income's purported advantages. But there are, of course, a number of counter-arguments and objections, both normative and practical.

First, there are a number of fundamental ethical or normative objections to basic income. As Bowles and Gintis (2000, p 33) demonstrate, people 'support the welfare state because it conforms to deeply-held norms of reciprocity and conditional obligations to others.' Universal basic income explicitly contradicts such norms by surrendering conditionality, and permitting – in principle – the idle to freeload. This would appear to challenge visions of social justice featuring notions of 'deservingness' (Anderson, 1999). Against these objections, Offe (2008, p 14) argues that 'the "positive" injustice from which nonworking recipients would benefit is partly offset by an abolition of the "negative" injustice from which many non-receiving "workers" suffer today.' Nevertheless, the fact is that public attitudes to welfare have hardened in recent years (Park et al, 2013), generating serious political barriers to unconditional payments.

Universal basic income also appears to conflict with visions of equality informed by the concept of 'need' that imply that entitlement to state transfers (and their level) should be dependent on individuals' gross income levels and specific needs. The basis of this argument is that means testing enhances target efficiency by disqualifying the non-poor, leading to financial savings, as well as serving to flatten the income distribution in a progressive manner. However, as noted above, such systems may perform badly in terms of reaching all poor people, as well as stigmatising them and subjecting them to poverty and unemployment traps; in contrast, as van Parijs (2004) puts it, basic income gives to the rich to benefit the poor. Nevertheless – and irrespective of whether specific groups are materially disadvantaged in an absolute or relative sense – some basic income opponents have serious ethical objections to welfare based on uniform payments to rich and poor alike.

Second, there are concerns about basic income's *labour market, fiscal* and *distributional* effects. The corollary to the moral case against basic income as 'something for nothing' is the more practical argument that, unless compelled by fear of destitution, many people would simply choose not to work. Basic income would be unsustainable: widespread labour market withdrawal would lead to falling tax revenue and the incapacity of the state to maintain payment levels.

As discussed above, the elimination of poverty and unemployment traps has been presented as a key feature of basic income proposals. In fact, basic income's effects on labour market participation are fundamentally ambiguous. Against a reduction in marginal withdrawal rates for individuals currently entangled in the means-tested system, it is important to weigh two potentially countervailing tendencies: a more generalised increase in marginal tax rates that characterises most concrete basic income proposals, and the effects of the removal of conditionality on the realisation of an 'exit option' from paid work (Martinelli, 2017b). The net outcome of these effects on labour supply are expected to vary at the level of the individual (for example, in relation to preferences, earning potential and income, and interaction with means-tested benefits) and with the level of payment; as Gray (2017) observes, 'the higher the BI in relation to the individual's hourly wage, the greater would be the likely reduction in labour supply from people already in paid work.' The (limited) evidence on these effects is discussed below.

The corollary to the ethical concerns that it is preferable to target payments to those most in need are practical concerns that basic income will have adverse fiscal or distributional effects, or both. In a nutshell, these concerns can be stated as follows: *an affordable basic income is inadequate, and an adequate basic income is unaffordable.* Groups previously attracting high levels of support would be disadvantaged by such proposals in which basic income payments reflect a more modest level of support, and would fall deeper into poverty. On the other hand, if payments were set at a uniform level that assured that 'high support' groups faced no disadvantage under basic income compared to the prevailing system, the fiscal cost would be huge. As a form of compromise, it may be possible to balance the goals of adequacy and affordability more effectively by retaining targeted payments for those in greater need *alongside* universal payments. The downside here is that such a system necessarily sacrifices the administrative simplicity that motivates interest in basic income in the first place.

Universal basic income in practice

Although basic income has a number of core definitional attributes (as described above), it is best seen as a family of schemes, varying in a number of core features. (See also Box 13.2 for a discussion of cognate schemes, which share some of the characteristics of universal basic income.)

Arguably, the most crucial of these variable features is the level at which payments are made and the interaction with the wider tax and benefit system. As regards payment level, 'basic' does not imply 'a link with so-called basic needs … a basic income can in principle fall short of as well as exceed whatever level of income is deemed sufficient to cover a person's basic needs' (van Parijs, 1992, p 4). BIEN distinguishes 'full' and 'partial' basic income schemes, with the former 'high enough to be … part of a policy strategy to eliminate material poverty and enable the social and cultural participation of every individual' and the latter implying a more modest payment. Some advocates endorse a generous basic income, while others suggest that it should be more residual.

As regards interaction with the wider social security system, the key issue concerns which existing benefits, if any, would be replaced. It might appear that the higher the level of basic income payment, the stronger the rationale that this would replace, rather than supplement, other benefits. However, many proponents of very generous basic income schemes (see, for example, van Parijs, 1995) acknowledge that payments should be supplemented with extensive additional transfers. By the same token, some advocates of residual schemes – covering the costs of subsistence but sufficiently modest to maximise incentives for self-provision (see, for example, Murray, 2006) – only countenance basic income as a complete replacement for existing programmes of support. Between these polarised positions, there are an almost infinite number of schemes.

Another possible source of variation relates to coverage. Basic income schemes may be restricted on the basis of citizenship or residency criteria; prison inmates are another contested category. Beyond this, age criteria may be applied to delimit entitlement or vary the level of payments. Some more residual basic income proposals (see, for example, Murray, 2006) only apply to the working-age population; arguably, such schemes are still 'universal' within a more narrowly defined population. Other proposals cover all ages, but involve more generous payments for pensioners and less generous ones for children (Torry, 2016a; Martinelli, 2017c).

Box 13.2: 'Cognates' of universal basic income

Universal basic income has a number of close relatives that do not meet all of the definitional requirements but that share some core characteristics (van Parijs et al, 2000).

Negative Income Tax (NIT) schemes ensure a minimum level of net income by 'topping up' any shortfall between gross income and a specified threshold. Like basic income, there are no labour market conditions, so as well as having potentially equivalent distributional effects, NIT schemes retain a number of the benefits described above. The important distinction, following van Parijs (1992, p 4), is that a NIT retains a means-testing function. NITs are sometimes seen as more politically and psychologically feasible than basic income; the public favour restricting payments to 'the needy' despite the fact that 'the difference in these two scenarios is only nominal and that the real flows of money' are identical (Honkanen, 2014, p 132); as Torry (2016a) notes, the *framing* of a policy is crucially important in determining the level of public support.

Participation income schemes (Atkinson, 1996) differ from basic income in that they are not strictly unconditional. Instead, recipients are subject to a version of conditionality in which a broad range of non-labour market activities are permitted. The basis of Atkinson's proposal is that a requirement to engage in socially valuable behaviour should eliminate any incentives for idleness and thus curtail political opposition among those in favour of 'reciprocity' (discussed below), while retaining the core advantages of basic income. However, de Wispelaere and Stirton (2007) suggest that such a scheme would face huge administrative hurdles.

In-work benefits or work subsidies – like Working Tax Credit and Universal Credit in the UK and Earned Income Tax Credit in the US – top up the incomes of low-paid workers. In common with one of basic income's main objectives, their aim is to strike a balance between the alleviation of poverty and the removal of poverty and unemployment traps; they cover a larger proportion of the poor than out-of-work benefits alone, and reduce the overall rate at which benefits are withdrawn. In-work benefits schemes retain shortcomings that arise from means testing, and are more likely than basic income schemes to suppress wages (Martinelli, 2017b), but are also less costly. Universal Credit also serves to harmonise a large number of separate in- and out-of-work benefits within a single structure – reducing bureaucratic traps involved with labour market movements and other changes of circumstance, and thus relating to another of basic income's core goals – although payments remain attached to stringent conditions and sanctions.

Finally, there is the important issue of how basic income should be funded. Most proposals are based on tax revenue. Considering that most concrete proposals require additional revenue compared to existing systems of social security, basic income usually implies a combination of tax rate increases and the elimination of personal tax exemptions and allowances, as well as the removal of other benefits. Most commonly – perhaps partly due to the practicalities of simulating fiscal impacts – it is assumed that expenditure would be funded through Income Tax. But taxes on wealth (for example, land value), consumption goods (for example, VAT), environmental pollution (for example, a carbon tax) and financial transactions have also been considered. Another alternative is to fund basic income through dividends on publically owned assets, as in schemes implemented in Alaska, the US and Iran (de Wispelaere, 2016a), discussed below.

Generally, how basic income is conceptualised in terms of specific design features depends on the precise goals that are being pursued (or prioritised, assuming they are all pursued to some degree). In turn, these goals and priorities are shaped by political–philosophical considerations. For example, advocates on the libertarian right tend to prioritise arguments in favour of labour market activation, and the elimination of bureaucratic intrusion; accordingly they favour modest schemes that replace most benefits on the condition that they imply only negligible tax increases. In contrast, basic income proponents on the progressive left are more likely to favour generous payments bolstered by a range of targeted benefits; they tend to be more sanguine about people withdrawing from the labour market (indeed, they see the provision of an 'exit option' as a strength), and prioritise poverty alleviation and redistribution over issues of economic efficiency.

In this way, basic income has features that appeal across a broad political spectrum. While this is often seen as a strength, it also poses difficulties in terms of political strategy. Design features are actualised and objectives prioritised in specific schemes. Basic income's multifaceted character enables detractors to criticise their least favourite version of the family of schemes, ensuring that it has strong opposition across the political spectrum. Furthermore, although they are both sold on basic income's abstract qualities, there may be very little agreement between (for example) libertarians, egalitarians and Greens when it comes to policy design – the problem of *persistent political division* among supporters (de Wispelaere, 2016b).

Evidence on desirability and feasibility

Empirical evidence on how basic income might work in practice is limited. The only policies that conform to the definition of universal basic income that have entered into legislation and been implemented are the Alaska Permanent Fund Dividend and Iran's price subsidy reform (de Wispelaere, 2016a). However, these programmes differ in several crucial respects from proposals of most basic income advocates – namely, in their low and fluctuating value of payments and in their funding mechanisms – so can only make a small contribution to attempts to evaluate basic income as a fundamental social security reform. However, there are two additional and important sources of evidence: experiments and microsimulations.

Experiments

Existing evidence is mainly drawn from two sources: a series of NIT experiments across the US and Canada between 1968 and 1980, and, more recently, basic income trials in Namibia (2008–10) and India (2011–13). In addition to these past studies, a number of experiments are being carried out or entering advanced planning stages in a number of mature welfare state. The most prominent of these (and most advanced in implementation) is in Finland, where the government launched an experiment in January 2017, paying 2,000 unemployed recipients of means-tested benefits a basic income of equivalent value (€560 per month) instead (Kela, 2016).

The US and Canadian experiments point to small but significant contractions in labour market effects (Widerquist, 2005). Evidence suggests that such effects are especially pronounced for married women, perhaps vindicating the concerns of feminists that a basic income would tend to reinforce pre-existing gender roles. However, the data are not unambiguously 'against' basic income. For one, the effects were hardly the labour market exodus predicted by basic income's fiercest critics; and second, it is not clear that labour market withdrawal is necessarily bad. Indeed, it could be desirable from a societal perspective, if basic income permits people – especially women overburdened by a combination of domestic and paid work – to balance (or 'reshuffle') their work and home lives more effectively. Looking beyond the labour market effects, Forget (2011) has uncovered evidence of positive health effects – including significant drops in hospital admissions and mental health complaints – which further support advocates' position. Turning to the more recent experiments in developing countries, Haarmann et al (2008) and Davala et al (2015) report a host of positive findings in Namibia and India respectively; these included a fall in poverty levels plus positive effects across a range of social indicators (including health, education, crime, entrepreneurial activity and gender inequality).

Nevertheless, it is essential to recognise a number of unavoidable limitations when considering the implications of these types of study. One is the extent to which the findings have validity beyond the specific contexts in which the experiments took place and the specific details of the policies being trialled. In this regard, the Namibian and Indian experiments are obviously limited in their applicability to the prospects for basic income as a reform to the social security systems of high-income welfare states. The US and Canadian experiments were household-level NIT schemes – not basic income 'proper' – and payments were not truly universal. In addition, being several decades old, outcomes may not be generalisable to contemporary labour markets. A more fundamental problem with experimental evidence is that the behavioural response to a trial of limited duration is likely to differ from the response to a policy that provides income security for a lifetime. Furthermore, there are likely to be macroeconomic and demand–side effects not captured by experiments of limited scale, and issues involved with upscaling and ensuring the fiscal viability of the policy. In this regard, the Finnish experiment is limited because researchers are not able to implement and evaluate the effects of simultaneous tax changes (Kela, 2016).

These limitations are applicable, to a greater or lesser degree, to planned experiments in the Netherlands and Canada as well as those in Kenya (run by the non-governmental organisation [NGO] Give Directly) and California (organised by the tech start-up company Y-Combinator). Although they might still generate important data on the effects of the removal of conditions and high withdrawal rates on employment transitions, these types of experiment do not test for the crucial effects of accompanying tax changes, nor do they examine how changes in income and behavioural responses would be distributed across different demographic groups in the case of a truly universal payment. For this, evidence from microsimulation studies may be instructive.

Microsimulation

Microsimulation is an important technique for evaluating the fiscal and distributional consequences of tax and benefit reform, prior to implementation. One of its great strengths is that the technique permits the researcher to compare large numbers of proposals; another is that it avoids the practical, political and ethical issues of designing and implementing a pilot or trial. Microsimulation is therefore a useful part of the policy design phase, and contributes to debates about the specific details of the basic income schemes that advocates should pursue.

Most, if not all, of basic income's detractors – from a range of political perspectives – argue that it is too expensive to implement. In fact, this depends on the specifics of the scheme – in particular, the level of payment and the magnitude of compensatory cutbacks to other benefits – as well as how 'affordability' is defined. Unless pitched at a very low level, the cost of a basic income would exceed current social security expenditure by some distance (Martinelli, 2017c). However, it is possible to incorporate changes to the tax system and remove some existing benefits in order to reduce net costs.

A series of microsimulation studies have modelled various universal basic income schemes in the UK context. Torry (2016b) and Reed and Lansley (2016) both arrive at what they describe as immediately implementable schemes in which modest basic incomes are paid alongside the full complement of existing benefits, payments of which are adjusted to take the universal payment into account. These studies show that if personal Income Tax allowance and National Insurance upper and lower earnings thresholds are eliminated, a basic income of around £60 per week for adults would imply a 3 per cent increase in Income Tax rates across all tax bands. Both authors report significant reductions in poverty levels, with very minimal numbers of households actually losing income compared to the existing system.

Martinelli (2017b, c) takes a different approach, modelling a large number of alternative schemes with various levels of adequacy, in combination with the elimination (rather than recalculation) of most income replacement benefits. For schemes with similar fiscal implications to Torry (2016b) and Reed and Lansley (2016) there were less favourable distributional consequences, including a significant number of poor households becoming poorer. Modelling more generous rates of payment – including supplements for individuals classified as disabled – resulted in more acceptable distributional effects, but at considerable cost. And even then, unacceptably high proportions of households – including those at the bottom of the income distribution – were found to face significant income losses.

In combination, these studies offer important insights into the trade-offs between the objectives and probable impacts of alternative schemes. The design of basic income schemes is subject to a three-way trade-off between the goals of controlling cost, meeting need and retaining simplicity/work incentives, as shown in Table 13.1. The ticks indicate which of the three goals can be achieved by different types of basic income scheme, with the crosses denoting which objective must remain unsatisfied.

It appears impossible to design a scheme that retains all of basic income's purported advantages over complex means-tested systems, and is at the same time affordable and adequate to ensure that poverty and inequality do not increase. This trade-off has important implications for questions of political feasibility,

Table 13.1: Stylised illustration of trade-offs in universal basic income goals and policy design

	Modest payment alongside retention of existing benefit structure	Modest payment alongside elimination of large proportion of existing benefits	High payment alongside elimination of large proportion of existing benefits
Controlling cost	✓	✓	✘
Meeting need	✓	✘	✓
Retaining simplicity/ work incentives	✘	✓	✓

Source: Martinelli (2017c)

since much interest in basic income is motivated by the way in which it would drastically simplify the existing system (Martinelli, 2017a).

Conclusion

The existing empirical evidence base on basic income is highly partial. Perhaps the most significant limitation of the aforementioned microsimulation studies is that they are 'static', meaning that they assume no behavioural (that is, labour market) change in response to policy. Clearly, given that the nature of labour market effects is perhaps basic income's most contested attribute, this severely limits the insights permitted from such studies, and does nothing to assuage fears that basic income would lead to a large decline in labour supply. In this regard, forthcoming experimental evidence will be crucially important, notwithstanding limits to the external validity of insights pertaining to specific forms of basic income implemented in idiosyncratic policy and institutional contexts.

In any case, arguments about basic income's desirability do not turn solely on the nature of the empirical evidence. Advocates will also have to overcome ethical objections to basic income's departure from the principles of reciprocal obligation and need.

In this context, the prospects for basic income are thus unclear. On the one hand, socioeconomic and labour market changes and tensions in existing welfare provision appear to lead inexorably towards basic income. On the other, there are a number of seemingly intractable trade-offs in policy design, considerable uncertainties around basic income's behavioural effects and significant levels of normative opposition, all of which give rise to critical political difficulties in implementation.

Overview

Universal basic income has been moving up the policy agenda due to shortcomings of existing social security with respect to socioeconomic and labour market change.

As well as a number of theoretical advantages of basic income, there are important normative and practical objections, including crucial questions around likely labour market effects.

Theoretical and microsimulation evidence suggests that policy-makers face significant trade-offs between the goals of controlling cost, meeting need and retaining simplicity. These make it harder to actualise all of basic income's purported advantages in a single scheme.

These trade-offs, coupled with political barriers, render the prospects for universal basic income's implementation in the UK – and the form it should take if implemented – highly uncertain.

Questions for discussion

1. To what extent do you agree with basic income's proponents that it could help to overcome endemic failings in conventional social security systems? Who do you think would stand to benefit from moves towards basic income, and who would stand to lose?
2. Do you think that basic income would damage people's incentives to work? What level of basic income would you need before you considered not working at all?
3. Do you think it is feasible to replace all or most social security provisions with a single universal payment, or would other payments have to continue in parallel? What are the advantages and disadvantages of each approach?

Key reading

Kela (2016) *From idea to experiment: Report on universal basic income experiment in Finland*, Kela Working Paper 106/2016, Helsinki: Kela.

Martinelli, L. (2017) *Assessing the case for universal basic income in the UK*, IPR Policy Brief, Bath: Institute for Policy Research, University of Bath.

van Parijs, P. (2004) 'Basic income: A simple and powerful idea for the twenty-first century', *Politics & Society*, vol 32, no 1, pp 7-39.

Website resources

http://basicincome.org
  Basic Income Earth Network (BIEN)

http://citizensincome.org
  Citizen's Basic Income Trust

www.kela.fi/web/en/experimental-study-on-a-universal-basic-income
  Finnish Basic Income Experiment (Kela website)

www.givedirectly.org/basic-income
  Give Directly Basic Income Experiment (Kenya)

www.bath.ac.uk/projects/examining-the-case-for-a-basic-income/
  Institute for Policy Research Basic Income Project

References

Anderson, E. (1999) 'What is the point of equality?', *Ethics*, vol 109, no 2, pp 287-337.

Andersson, J. (2009) 'Basic income from an ecological perspective', *Basic Income Studies*, vol 4, no 2, pp 1-8.

Atkinson, A. (1996) 'The case for a participation income', *The Political Quarterly*, vol 67, no 1, pp 67-70.

Bowles, S. and Gintis, H. (2000) 'Reciprocity, self-interest, and the welfare state', *Nordic Journal of Political Economy*, vol 26, no 1, pp 33-53.

Clasen, J. and Clegg, D. (2007) 'Levels and levers of conditionality: Measuring change within welfare states', in J. Clasen and N.A. Siegel (eds) *Investigating welfare state change: The 'dependent variable problem' in comparative analysis*, Cheltenham: Edward Elgar, pp 166-97.

Davala, S., Jhabvala, R., Standing, G. and Mehta, S.K. (2015) *Basic Income: A transformative policy for India*, London: Bloomsbury Publishing.

de Wispelaere, J. (2016a) 'Basic Income in our time: Improving political prospects through policy learning?', *Journal of Social Policy*, vol 45, no 4, pp 617-34.

de Wispelaere, J. (2016b) 'The struggle for strategy: On the politics of the basic income proposal', *Politics*, vol 36, no 2, pp 131-41.

de Wispelaere, J. and Stirton, L. (2007) 'The public administration case against Participation Income', *Social Service Review*, vol 81, no 3, pp 523-49.

DRUK (Disability Rights UK) (2016) *Submission to National Audit Office study on benefit sanctions* (www.disabilityrightsuk.org/news/2016/april/our-submission-nao-sanctions-study).

Forget, E. (2011) 'The town with no poverty: The health effects of a Canadian guaranteed annual income field experiment', *Canadian Public Policy/Analyse de Politiques*, vol 37, no 3, pp 283-305.

Gheaus, A. (2008) 'Basic income, gender justice and the costs of gender symmetrical lifestyles', *Basic Income Studies*, vol 3, no 3, pp 1-8.

Goodin, R. (1992) 'Towards a minimally presumptuous social welfare policy', in van Parijs (ed) *Arguing for Basic Income: Ethical foundations for a radical reform*, London: Verso, pp 195-214.

Goos, M. and Manning, A. (2007) 'Lousy and lovely jobs: The rising polarization of work in Britain', *The Review of Economics and Statistics*, vol 89, no 1, pp 118-33.

Gray, A. (2017) *Behavioural effects of a Citizen's Income on wages, job security and labour supply*, Citizen's Basic Income Trust (http://citizensincome.org/research-analysis/behavioural-effects-of-a-citizens-income-on-wages-job-security-and-labour-supply/).

Groot, L. and van der Veen, R. (2000) 'How attractive is a basic income for European welfare states?', in R. van der Veen and L. Groot (eds) *Basic income on the agenda: Policy objectives and political chances*, Amsterdam: Amsterdam University Press, pp 13-38.

Haarmann, C., Haarmann, D., Jauch, H., Shindondola-Mote, H., Nattrass, N., van Niekerk, I. and Samson, M. (2009) *Making the difference! The basic income grant in Namibia: Assessment report*, Windhoek: BIG Coalition.

Honkanen, P. (2014) 'Basic income and negative Income Tax: A comparison with a simulation model', *Basic Income Studies*, vol 9, no 1-2, pp 119-35.

JRF (Joseph Rowntree Foundation) (2014) *Welfare sanctions and conditionality in the UK*, York: JRF.

JRF (2016) *Destitution in the UK*, York: JRF.

Kela (2016) *From idea to experiment: Report on universal basic income experiment in Finland*, Kela Working Paper 106/2016, Helsinki: Kela (https://helda.helsinki.fi/handle/10138/167728).

Martinelli, L. (2017a) *Assessing the case for universal basic income in the UK*, IPR Policy Brief, September, Bath: Institute for Policy Research, University of Bath.

Martinelli, L. (2017b) *Exploring the distributional and work incentive effects of plausible illustrative basic income schemes*, IPR Working Paper, March, Bath: Institute for Policy Research, University of Bath.

Martinelli, L. (2017c) *The fiscal and distributional implications of alternative Universal Basic Income schemes in the UK*, IPR Working Paper, May, Bath: Institute for Policy Research, University of Bath.

Murray, C. (2006) *In our hands: A plan to replace the welfare state*, Washington, DC: American Enterprise Institute Press.

Offe, C. (2008) 'Basic income and the labor contract', *Basic Income Studies*, vol 3, no 1, pp 1-30.

Palier, B. (2012) 'Turning vice into vice: How Bismarckian welfare states have gone from unsustainability to dualization', in G. Bonoli and D. Natali (eds) *The politics of the new welfare state*, Oxford: Oxford University Press, pp 233-55.

Park, A., Bryson, C., Clery, E., Curtice, J. and Phillips, M. (eds) (2013) *British Social Attitudes: 30th report*, London: NatCen Social Research.

Parker, H. (1993) *Citizen's income and women, Basic Income Research Group Discussion Paper no 2*, London: Basic Income Research Group.

Pickles, C., Titley, H., Holmes, E. and Dobson, B. (2016) *Working welfare: A radically new approach to sickness and disability benefits*, London: Reform.

Reed, H. and Lansley, S. (2016) *Universal Basic Income: An idea whose time has come?*, London: Compass.

Robeyns, I. (2000) 'Hush money or emancipation fee? A gender analysis of basic income', in R. van der Veen and L. Groot (eds) *Basic Income on the agenda: Policy objectives and political chances*, Amsterdam: Amsterdam University Press., pp 121-36.

Srnicek, N. and Williams, A. (2015) *Inventing the future: Postcapitalism and a world without work*, London: Verso.

Standing, G. (2011) *The precariat: The dangerous new class*, London: Bloomsbury Academic.

Standing, G. (2013) 'Why a Basic Income is necessary for a right to work', *Basic Income Studies*, vol 7, no 2, pp 19–40.

Torry, M. (2016a) *The feasibility of Citizen's Income*, Basingstoke: Palgrave Macmillan.

Torry, M. (2016b) *An evaluation of a strictly revenue neutral Citizen's Income scheme*, Euromod Working Paper EM 5/16, Colchester: University of Essex.

van der Veen, R. and Groot, L. (eds) (2000) *Basic Income on the agenda: Policy objectives and political chances*, Amsterdam: Amsterdam University Press.

van Oorschot, W. (2002) 'Targeting welfare: on the functions and dysfunctions of means testing in social policy', in P. Townsend and D. Gordon (eds) *World poverty: New policies to defeat an old enemy*, Bristol: Policy Press, pp 171–93.

van Parijs, P. (1990) 'The second marriage of justice and efficiency', *Journal of Social Policy*, vol 19, no 1, pp 1–25.

van Parijs, P. (1992) 'Competing justifications of Basic Income', in P. van Parijs (ed) *Arguing for Basic Income: Ethical foundations for a radical reform*, London: Verso, pp 3–43.

van Parijs, P. (1995) *Real freedom for all: What (if anything) can justify capitalism?*, Oxford: Clarendon Press.

van Parijs, P. (2004) 'Basic Income: A simple and powerful idea for the twenty-first century', *Politics & Society*, vol 32, no 1, pp 7–39.

van Parijs, P., Jacquet, L. and Salinas, C. (2000) 'Basic Income and its cognates, in R. van der Veen and L. Groot (eds) *Basic Income on the agenda: Policy objectives and political chances*, Amsterdam: Amsterdam University Press, pp 53–84.

Widerquist, K. (2005) 'A failure to communicate: What (if anything) can we learn from the negative income tax experiments?', *The Journal of Socio-Economics*, vol 34, pp 49–81.

Conclusion

14

Facing the future: Where next for social security?

Roy Sainsbury and Jane Millar

We opened Chapter 1 by saying that the provision of social security is one of the most important functions of government in modern economies. The contributions to this book have amply shown this to be true. But writing any sort of book on social security is a risky undertaking. When we reflected earlier on the last edition of this book (published in 2009), we noted that it was rooted in the political and economic circumstances at the time. Successive Labour governments from 1997 had maintained consistent policy aims for over a decade – to reduce poverty, especially child poverty, and to promote paid employment – that it pursued through a variety of means, including, but not only, the social security system. But we were not to know as the book was being prepared in 2008 that the global economic and financial systems on which the generally prosperous first decade of this century was built were about to come crashing down. The 2nd edition did not have a chapter called 'Facing the future' but we are fairly certain we would not have foreseen Universal Credit, the Bedroom Tax, restricting Child Benefit, the retrenchment in disability-related benefits and the benefits cap as likely developments in the coming years. And we would not have predicted that universal basic income would have become a serious topic of policy debate in the UK and the subject of trials in Finland, the Netherlands and elsewhere (as explained in Chapter 13, by Luke Martinelli).

This chapter therefore makes no attempt to predict the future in any way (we would only get it wrong), but we consider in 2017 what the social security system of the UK (and of other countries too) is likely to face as challenges and opportunities in the future. As argued in Chapter 1, social security is a powerful instrument of social policy that can be used to meet a variety of contingencies and to promote a diverse range of social aims. So we offer no predictions about the scale, shape and substance of social security in the next 10 years. The only thing we might be sure of is that when we come to write the 4th edition of *Understanding social security*, these will be different, possibly very different, to the social security system of 2017. How the challenges of the future are met is a story that can be told only in retrospect, as we have done in this volume for the period since 2009.

In each of the preceding chapters the authors have concluded with a number of questions that readers and students might usefully reflect on. In this chapter we take a slightly different approach in that the entire chapter is intended to serve as stimulation to further thought and debate. We begin by looking at some of the more immediate economic and societal changes that will have an impact on the UK social security system and require a policy response. We go on to talk about the language of social security and discuss, as promised in Chapter 1, what is meant by 'welfare reform'. But 'welfare reform' is not something that is bounded in any way – it is effectively going on all the time. There may be more intensive spells of change and the nature of that change might vary in scale and scope, but social security never stands still. We end the chapter therefore with a look at some of the current thinking about how social security could, and some argue should, develop in the coming years.

The economy, society and social security

As we saw in Chapter 1, a substantial amount of money is spent on social security benefits and tax credits in the UK. As a proportion of GDP, the amount is not particularly high or low in comparison with other advanced industrial societies. Nevertheless, over £210 billion in 2015/16 is undeniably a lot of money, and takes by far the biggest slice of total national income. We prefer to talk about 'spending' on social security rather than the 'cost' of social security because social security is not something that has a natural, market-driven cost determined by the interaction of supply and demand. Spending is a matter of choice by governments. They can choose what benefits to pay, who is entitled to receive them, how much each benefit should be and how long they should last. There is no Adam Smith 'invisible hand' determining an optimal level of spending.

However, the choices about social security spending are also conditional on how existing commitments play out over time as well as by external changes in the economy and society. A clear example of this is demographic change and in particular, the increasing number of older people who are entitled to some form of pensions payment and who may also be entitled to other benefits as a result of health and disabling conditions and the need for care. As Stephen McKay explained in Chapter 5, successive governments' policies on pensions and other benefits for older people have all but eradicated the phenomenon of pensioner poverty. The current 'triple lock' policy maintained by the current Conservative government (itself a continuation of the policy of the 2010-15 coalition government) will ensure that pensioners' incomes continue to rise into the foreseeable future. Spending on pensions accounts for some 44 per cent of the total expenditure of the Department for Work and Pensions (DWP). Funding the inevitable rise in this amount will be one of the main and continuing challenges for governments in the future. Payments for long-term social care for elderly people are not currently part of the UK social security system, unlike some other countries such as Germany, where a long-term care insurance benefit is available. But the demand for long-term care is predicted to rise significantly and, as the Dilnot report showed, the current funding system is 'confusing, unfair and unsustainable' (Report of the Commission on Funding of Care and Support, 2011, p 5). This could become the focus of more attention within the social security, as well as healthcare, system.

A common pressure on social security budgets over many decades has been the number of unemployed people entitled to social insurance or social assistance out-of-work benefits. However, as we have seen in Chapter 1, expenditure on these benefits is extremely low by historical standards. Levels of employment in 2017 in the UK are at a 40-year high, and levels of unemployment at a 40-year low. However, increased levels of employment, and lower unemployment, are partly explained by the growth in insecure, low-paid work, which has led to a rise in in-work poverty and therefore in the demand for in-work benefits (that is, tax credits and Universal Credit). Changing labour market conditions and opportunities are an important factor in shaping the demand for social security provision. Forms of non-standard employment – including, for example, temporary jobs, agency work, part-time work, zero-hours contracts and various forms of self-employment – have become the experience of many more people (Eurofound, 2017). Up until recently, these sorts of work patterns were more typical for young people entering the labour market and for women with children combining work and care, but now are much more widespread.

One of the aims of Universal Credit is to help smooth labour market transitions, by providing a single system of support for people in and out of work, as discussed by Jane Millar in Chapter 3. Universal Credit received wide political support during its passage into law, but its implementation has been dogged by delays and technical problems that have led to severe hardship for thousands of claimants. Its original design has also been changed as part of the anti-austerity cuts such that it is less generous and has much weaker work incentives than when its roll-out began. Whether Universal Credit achieves its primary aim of contributing to more people entering and sustaining employment, and progressing in employment until they no longer need Universal Credit, remains to be seen. The challenge of providing social protection to people with precarious employment is a key issue in many of the future reform proposals, discussed further below.

The nature and level of social security for families with children is also an ongoing issue. The number of lone-parent families, mainly women bringing up children alone, has remained relatively steady over the past 20 or so years, from 2.3 million in 1996 to 2.7 million in 2017 (ONS, 2017). These lone-parent families have a higher than average risk of poverty, as do large families, families with no adults in work and families from some minority ethnic groups (Dermott and Main, 2017). As discussed in Chapter 1, the alleviation of poverty is just one of the goals of social security policy. But the issue of child poverty has been a central concern in recent years. From the introduction of Family Allowances by the postwar Labour government (following the Beveridge report of 1942), social security has been one of the main policy instruments used to alleviate child poverty. Arguably Child Benefit (the latest manifestation of Family Allowances) has at least partly served its intended purpose by contributing to the costs of raising children. There have, of course, been disputes over the years about the level, and (in)adequacy, of Child Benefit, but no government has ever claimed that it would cover the full costs of raising children. Nevertheless, its universal (that is, non-means-tested, non-contributory) nature has ensured that almost every family entitled to the benefit actually received it.

As Tess Ridge (in Chapter 2) explained, however, Tony Blair's Labour government went further than any previous government and committed itself and future governments (in the Child Poverty Act 2010) to *eradicate* child poverty by 2020 principally through the policy instruments of social security and tax credits. However, in 2017, it is safe to say that the eradication of child poverty will not happen; indeed, as Tess Ridge has noted, the Institute for Fiscal Studies has projected that the number of children in relative poverty (after housing costs) will rise to over 30 per cent of all children by 2021-22 (Hood and Waters, 2017). Furthermore, the David Cameron government of 2015-16 repealed the Child Poverty Act 2010 such that there is currently no government commitment, let alone a legal requirement, to end child poverty. How has this new increase in child poverty happened? Although changes in the labour market and the economy are part of the explanation by hugely increasing levels of low-paid work, it is also clear that reforms to the social security system have in themselves exacerbated a problem that social security was intended to alleviate. The freezing of Child Benefit, its restriction to the first two children only, the benefits cap and Bedroom Tax have together increased the number of families, and therefore the numbers of children, in poverty.

The austerity measures that have been so important in recent years have also led some commentators to conclude that the important 'safety net' function of social security has been deeply eroded (Bradshaw, 2017). The rise of 'destitution' in the UK, as documented by the Joseph Rowntree Foundation (Fitzpatrick et al, 2016), is one indicator that people are falling through gaps in provision. About 1.25 million people are estimated to be unable to afford the basic essentials required in order to eat, keep clean and stay warm and dry. And local government, as discussed in Chapter 1, is struggling to meet these needs and to maintain an adequate safety net (House of Commons Work and Pensions Committee, 2016). The private and voluntary sector is responding, most visibly through the rapid rise in foodbank provision, but such support is limited and not necessarily accessible to all who need it (Dowler and Lambie-Mumford, 2015). This leaves the family to provide much more material, practical and emotional support (Hall, 2016; O'Brien and Kyprianou, 2017). But family members cannot always provide such help, and people are often reluctant to rely too much on their families, especially if they are not in a position to reciprocate (Daly and Kelly, 2015).

How the UK system fits within the framework of international obligations and requirements is also an important driver for change. We know that other countries do things differently from very different basic approaches to welfare state provision (as, for example, discussed in the work of Esping-Andersen, mentioned in Chapter 1). Although this book has deliberately focused on the UK social security system, it is important to draw lessons from other countries, and to understand the international frameworks under which UK social security policy operates (as Nicola Yeates has done in Chapter 8). The context of international obligations will change as the UK withdraws from the European Union (EU), as discussed by Emma Carmel and Bożena Sojka in Chapter 7. But apart from European citizens having the right to some social security benefits in other countries, individual countries have wide powers to design and implement their own social security systems. Some form of convergence of social security has been a political aspiration of the EU for some years, but not something that it can enforce. Having said that, the full effect of Brexit on UK social security is far from clear in 2017.

Why increasing understanding of social security is a good idea

In Chapter 1 we argued that understanding social security is important for us all in order that debates about its future are informed and not based on ignorance and prejudice. People's attitudes to welfare are important, as John Hudson has shown in Chapter 10, and can influence the direction policy takes. A politician who wants to impose greater conditionality can mobilise public perceptions about work-shy and fraudulent claimants. And yet such perceptions can be far from what the evidence tells us. In his book *Good times, bad times* John Hills presents a powerful analysis of how the many 'myths' about the welfare state do not stand up to scrutiny. The main beneficiaries of the social security system are not unemployed people (as many people think); they are pensioners. The majority of people out of work are not feckless and lazy; on the contrary, most want paid employment. And fraud is not rife in the social security system; less than 1 per cent of the benefit bill is accounted for by fraud. Nevertheless, as John Hudson's chapter demonstrates, these myths persist and colour people's attitudes to social security. This is important because, as John Hills argues, people are unlikely to support policies that increase spending on social security 'if they misperceive what the system does and who benefits from it' (Hills, 2017, p 268).

People's understanding of social security is arguably tied up with the language and rhetoric used in public debates, announcements and policy documents. Somehow, over the past 20 years or so, we have lost the language of 'social security' in public discourse to have it replaced by 'welfare'. Step one in this process can be traced to 2001, when the former Department of Social Security mutated into the Department for Work and Pensions following its merger with parts of the Department for Education and Employment. The name change accompanied the introduction of a range of back-to-work programmes that included the New Deal for Lone Parents, the New Deal for Disabled People and the New Deal for Young People, to name a few. It was presumably intended to reflect a new commitment to use social security to support active labour market policies rather than remain a passive system of financial support only for people with no other form of income. Thus 'social security' was effectively lost to mainstream political vocabulary in favour of 'welfare'. Since then, welfare has become something of a pejorative term, echoing its use in the US where it is almost exclusively reserved to refer to out-of-work lone mothers receiving minimalist benefits that are time-limited. Ruth Lister (the former social policy academic who has sat in the House of Lords as a Labour peer since 2011) locates a change from a positive language of social security to a negative language of 'welfare' in the early years of the New Labour government elected in 1997. She identifies '… negative language and a tough stance' that contributed to an erosion of support towards 'welfare' even among its own political supporters (Lister, 2016, p 30).

Recognising this change in language, Lister and other some commentators argue that 'social security' needs to be reclaimed as a positive component of the UK welfare state. Lister, for example, poses the question, 'how would we develop an authentic story on social security … that might start to re-build public support?' (2016, p 29). And she issues a rallying cry to 'progressives' (that is, people on the political left): 'It's time that progressives stopped treating social security as a burden that "we" bear on behalf of "them", a "cost of economic failure", a problem, and instead started seeing it as a *key element in a good and fair society*' (2016, p 42; original emphasis).

Unpicking 'welfare reform'

Among all the changing vocabulary on social security in the last 20 years, one of the recurrent phrases in debates about social security has been 'welfare reform'. In Chapter 1 we said we would reflect further on this topic in light of the analyses of the various components of social security in the individual chapters of this volume. One conclusion we might justifiably reach is that 'welfare reform' is actually a fairly meaningless term, a piece of political rhetoric that can be turned in various directions to suit the purposes of whoever is using it. It has clearly been seen as useful to Labour, coalition and Conservative administrations since 1997, all of whom have passed a 'Welfare Reform' Act (in 2009, 2012 and 2016 respectively, although the 2016 Act had the longer title of the Welfare Reform and Work Act). The last Acts of Parliament actually to have 'social security' in the title appeared in 1998, 2000 and 2001 (Social Security Act, Child Support, Pensions and Social Security Act and Social Security Fraud Act, respectively).

Perhaps this now ubiquitous use of 'welfare reform' reflects what has become a shared political language that implies that 'welfare' is a bad thing, or at least a flawed idea, that is constantly in need of reform. What the future observer and student of social security policy should therefore probably bear in mind is that 'welfare reform' can mean all things to all people, and that what is claimed in its name should be carefully analysed and scrutinised, and certainly not taken to be synonymous with social progress.

Taking the temperature of contemporary debates

As mentioned earlier, social security policy is constantly subject to calls for reform and transformation, and that is as true now as it has ever been. Luke Martinelli discussed the universal basic income proposals in Chapter 13. Here, we point to some other recent proposals, to give readers a flavour of the range of ideas being promoted. No doubt many others will emerge over the coming years.

Royston (2017) offers a powerful up-to-date critique of the current social security system, arguing that there are many aspects that are 'broken – from its cost, and its failure to support working families, through the sense that it no longer rewards those who make a contribution, and that its administration is a mess' (2017, p 4). His remedy, which he says aims to avoid yet more 'radical' reform (p 9), is based on 'four key themes' – providing an effective safety net, responding to variations in household needs, supporting socially desirable behaviours, and creating a system that is simple from the claimant's perspective. The 'socially desirable behaviour' referred to is defined principally as preparing for and looking for work (rather than anything more sinister that might constitute some worrying form of social engineering), and a system that is simple from the claimant's perspective is defined as one that is easy to access and navigate. In fact, Royston dismisses the idea that a simpler social security system *per se* should be pursued as he sees it as unnecessary. In his view, complexity is inevitable, and as long as claimants are not exposed to this, it is not a problem. Hence, Royston proposes an incremental approach to further reform that fixes the 'broken benefits' rather than 'build a new benefits system' (2017, p 10).

Lister (2016) defines the core challenge as the failure of the current system to provide 'genuine security'. She offers a set of principles to guide reform, starting with the International Labour Organization (ILO) principles of 'universality of protection based on social solidarity', which means both pooling of risks and treating people with dignity and respect. She argues that people should be treated as individuals, with financial autonomy, and that this is particularly important for recognising the needs of women and thus, for gender equity. The system should recognise contributions beyond paid work, in particular, care work and community building. In these ways the social security system can help create 'a culture of human rights in which claimants are treated with dignity and respect, are supported as individuals, and are listened to as experts through experience' (p 35). She concludes that a means–tested system cannot meet these principles, and so reliance on means-testing should be reduced.

Bell and Gaffney (2012), for the Trades Union Congress (TUC), make the case for a return to a system based on the contributory principles that underpinned Beveridge, updated to manage current risks and contingencies, including (as with Lister) recognition of social contributions such as caring. They put forward two main arguments to support this direction of travel. The first is the *inclusion* argument, that this would generate wider public support and not be perceived as a system just for poor people. The second argument they make is that those countries that have maintained a *stronger contributory system* have been able to achieve much better labour market performance. By contrast, Harrop (2016), for the Fabian Society, argues for a mix of means testing, contributory benefits, private protection and universal provisions.

As a final example, Atkinson (2015) proposes wide-ranging reforms in order to address the growing (and multi-faceted) problem of inequality that has been documented by authors such as Wilkinson and Pickett (2009) over a number of years. Atkinson's proposals (which are further refined and modelled in Atkinson et al, 2017) encompass income and capital taxes, investment policy and savings policy as well as recommending a 'participation income' (a variant of universal basic income that includes an element of labour market conditionality) or a 'renewal of social insurance' to raise benefit levels and extend coverage.

Conclusion

When we think about one of the (more consistent and enduring) aims of social security – the alleviation of poverty – we are faced with something of a contradiction in the evidence. This suggests that while spending on social security has generally increased across many countries, poverty not only continues to exist, but is also on the increase. Does this mean that social security, as an instrument of social policy, is a failure? Throughout this volume we have drawn attention to the *potential* of social security, but also its limits. David Piachaud (2015, p 3) sums up the situation well: '… poverty depends on levels of employment and rates of pay, on economic activity rates, on costs of childcare, on housing costs and the price of food. Without the growth of social protection, poverty would in almost all cases have been worse but social protection relieves rather than prevents poverty.'

Piachaud is useful here in providing a warning to us not to expect too much of the social security system. To paraphrase him, we should not attempt a 'social service' solution (that is, the social security system) to solve an economic problem. Social security cannot address structural flaws in the economy or labour market. It can deal, perhaps, with the symptoms of problems, but not the causes. We should not over-stretch social security beyond its capabilities.

As a final word, in a book called *Understanding social security* we should, in the year of its 75th anniversary, acknowledge the Beveridge report (Beveridge, 1942) and its seminal role in placing social security at the heart of social policy and the welfare state, not only in the immediate postwar years, but to this day. The social security system of 2017 bears the traces of Beveridge, but in many ways would be unrecognisable to him. Beveridge understood the potential and promise of social security, but his overall plan for social progress encompassed big ideas for the health service, education, housing and work, and therefore demonstrates that he also understood its limits. Understanding social security in the 21st century is clearly a different enterprise from understanding social security 75 years ago, but, to allow ourselves a final emphasis, it is important that we do if we are to have a chance to achieve its potential as an effective instrument of social progress, as Beveridge envisaged.

References

Atkinson, A. (2015) *Inequality – What can be done?*, Cambridge, MA: Harvard University Press.

Atkinson, A., Leventi, C., Nolan, B., Sutherland, H. and Tasseva, I. (2017) *Reducing poverty and inequality through tax-benefit reform and the Minimum Wage: The UK as a case study*, Working Paper 2017-04, Oxford: Institute for New Economic Thinking.

Bell, K. and Gaffney, D. (2012) *Making a contribution: Social security for the future*, London: Trades Union Congress (www.tuc.org.uk/sites/default/files/contributory_benefits.pdf).

Beveridge, W.H. (1942) *Social insurance and allied services*, Cmd 6404, London, HMSO.

Bradshaw, J. (2015) 'The erosion of the UK safety net', *Discover Society* (https://discoversociety.org/2015/01/03/the-erosion-of-the-uk-safety-net/).

Daly, M. and Kelly, G. (2015) *Families and poverty: Everyday life on a low income*, Bristol: Policy Press.

Dermott, E. and Main, G. (2017) *Poverty and social exclusion in the UK Volume 1 – The nature and extent of the problem*, Bristol: Policy Press.

Dowler, E. and Lambie-Mumford, H. (2015) 'Introduction. Hunger, food and social policy in austerity', *Social Policy & Society*, vol 14, no 3, pp 411-15.

Eurofound (2017) *Aspects of nonstandard employment in Europe*, Dublin: Eurofound.

Fitzpatrick, S., Bramley, G., Sosenko, F., Blenkinsopp, J., Johnsen, S., Little, M., et al (2016) *Destitution in the UK*, York: Joseph Rowntree Foundation.

Hall, S. (2016) 'Everyday family experiences of the financial crisis: Getting by in the recent economic recession', *Journal of Economic Geography*, vol 16, issue 2, pp 305-30.

Harrop, A. (2016) *For us all: Redesigning social security, for the 2020s*, London: Fabian Society (www.fabians.org.uk/wp-content/uploads/2016/08/FAB_J4556_For_Us_All_Social_Security_Report_V5_08-2016_WEB-002.pdf).

Hills, J. (2017) *Good times, bad times* (revised edn), Bristol: Policy Press.

House of Commons Work and Pensions Committee (2016) *The local welfare safety net*, HC 373 (www.parliament.uk/business/committees/committees-a-z/commons-select/work-and-pensions-committee/inquiries/parliament-2015/welfare-safety-net-15-16/).

Hood, A. and Waters, T. (2017) *Living standards, poverty and inequality in the UK: 2016-17 to 2021-22*, Report (R127), London: Institute for Fiscal Studies.

Lister, R. (2016) 'Putting the security back into social security', in L. Nandy, C. Lucas and C. Bowers (eds) *The alternative: Towards a new progressive politics*, London: Biteback Publishing, pp 28-43.

O'Brien, M. and Kyprianou, P. (2017) *Just managing? What it means for the families of austerity Britain*, OpenBook Publishers.

ONS (Office for National Statistics) (2017) *Families and households 2017* (www.ons.gov.uk/peoplepopulationandcommunity/birthsdeathsandmarriages/families/bulletins/familiesandhouseholds/2017).

Piachaud, D. (2015) 'The future of social policy – Changing the paradigm', *Asia & the Pacific Policy Studies*, vol 2, no 1, pp 1-7.

Report of the Commission on Funding of Care and Support (2011) *Fairer care funding*, London: HM Government Licence.

Royston, S. (2017) *Broken benefits: What's wrong with welfare reform*, Bristol: Policy Press.

Wilkinson, R. and Pickett, K. (2009) *The spirit level*, London: Penguin.

Index